A
Place
for
Everything

A Place for Everything

My mother, autism and Me

Anna Wilson

ONE PLACE. MANY STORIES

HQ
An imprint of HarperCollins*Publishers* Ltd
1 London Bridge Street
London SE1 9GF

This edition 2020

1

First published in Great Britain by
HQ, an imprint of HarperCollins*Publishers* Ltd 2020

A catalogue record for this book is
available from the British Library.

HB ISBN: 978-0-00-834253-1
TPB ISBN: 978-0-00-839519-3

Typeset in Simoncini Garamond by
Palimpsest Book Production Ltd, Falkirk, Stirlingshire

Printed and bound in Great Britain by
CPI Group (UK) Ltd, Croydon CR0 4YY

To Dad and Mum – *ad astra cinis*

Omnia vincit amor, et nos cedamus amori
Love conquers all; let us, too, yield to love

Virgil, *Eclogues* 10:69

Terminology

Is it Asperger's or autism or . . . what is it?

When it was initially put to us that Mum might have autism, the psychologist used the term 'Asperger's', which had been in common usage for a while. When writing this book, I came across many different terms for people with autism and quickly realised that, whatever the accepted clinical terminology at any given time, individuals will have their own preferences. I have tried to stick to the terms used in quoted text; for this reason there may seem to the reader to be certain discrepancies throughout.

Many people with autism who would be described as 'high-functioning' (in that they have a high intelligence and can, in the main, function well in society) prefer to be referred to as someone 'with Asperger syndrome' or 'with Asperger's', as they say that this easily identifies them at that particular end of the autistic spectrum. One friend said, 'The minute you say "autism", people have this set of assumptions, like "Oh dear – does she sit in the corner of the room rocking back and forth and not speaking?" That's why I say I have Asperger's.' Others prefer the more blanket term 'autism' as they feel this acknowledges that there is a spectrum within the syndrome.

The DSM-5 (*Diagnostic and Statistical Manual of Mental Disorders*, fifth edition) uses the term 'autistic spectrum disorder' or ASD. There is some controversy surrounding this term among people with autism. The DSM was updated as recently as 2013, so if you had been given a diagnosis before that date and had been referred to as someone with Asperger's, you might well prefer to continue using that terminology. Also, I have met many people with autism who dislike the use of the word 'disorder' attached to them. Some therefore use ASC instead – autism spectrum condition. One friend said, 'I consider my autism to be a syndrome, not a disorder. I feel that the word "disorder" is attached to people who are not coping. I am coping very well, so I don't like this word applied to me. My autism means I see the world differently from you, that's all.'

I have met people too who resent the fact that autism is included in the DSM as they feel that it is not a mental illness per se – mental illness may be a result of undiagnosed or unsupported autism, but it is not the cause or the general characteristic of the syndrome.

In conclusion, I have learnt that while diagnosis is extremely important in being able to access support and in helping neurotypicals (i.e. people without autism) to understand the autistic brain, it is most helpful to see the human first and to realise that a label on its own, with no support, is not going to help anyone. Hence my preference for the generic term 'a person with autism'.

Capacity

This was another minefield into which I walked the minute I entered the bewildering world of mental health terminology. The first time someone mentioned the phrase 'your mother has capacity', I assumed they meant that she was 'capable'. In other words, I thought they were referring to the fact that she could do things. It took someone in the know to explain that 'a person has or does not have capacity' is mental-health shorthand for 'this person has or does not have capacity under the terms of the Mental Capacity Act 2005 to make decisions for themselves.' In other words, quoting directly from the Act:

People who lack capacity
1. For the purposes of this Act, a person lacks capacity in relation to a matter if at the material time he is unable to make a decision for himself in relation to the matter because of an impairment of, or a disturbance in the functioning of, the mind or brain.
2. It does not matter whether the impairment or disturbance is permanent or temporary.
3. A lack of capacity cannot be established merely by reference to—
(a) a person's age or appearance, or
(b) a condition of his, or an aspect of his behaviour, which might lead others to make unjustified assumptions about his capacity.

In my opinion, the unexplained shorthand use of such terms is extremely disempowering to patients and families who are trying to care for loved ones. I have therefore tried to unpick such terminology in the writing of this book in the hope that it will be helpful to people going through a similar situation.

Prologue

'Bloody kids, bloody kids, bloody, bloody, bloody kids!'

Mum is standing in front of the mirror in the hall. Her teeth are bared. Her eyes are wide. Her face is stretched and red. Her hair is wild. She's staring at herself and chanting those horrible words, over and over and over again. Her fists are clenched and she's shaking them. Can she see us in the mirror too? I don't want her to.

Carrie and I are hiding by the cupboard under the stairs. We have to make ourselves as small as possible, then Mum won't see. I keep an eye on Mum through the banisters. She is still saying those words. Her voice is high and breathless. It's not her normal, Kind Mum voice. She doesn't look like our normal mum at all. Even her hair is wrong. It's as though Kind Mum has disappeared completely and been replaced by a monster. She's holding her fists up by her face now and shaking them and shaking them. Her face is getting redder and redder. It looks as though she might explode. I can't remember what we did to make her be like this. I know it was our fault – my fault. It must have been my fault because Carrie is too small to have done anything bad. Carrie never does anything bad, anyway. I know that because Mum says, 'Why can't you be like your sister?' So it must be my fault that Mum is like this. I need Kind Mum to come back. I hold my breath and start counting. Can I bring her back if I hold my breath and count for long enough?

I also need to stay brave for Carrie. She's crying. I want to reach out and put my arm around her, but I mustn't move. We mustn't move. Mum might hear us. We have to let her chant and shake her fists until she feels better.

What did I do to make her angry this time? If I knew, I could make sure I don't do it again. But, try as I might, I can't remember. All I know is, I wish the anger-storm would pass so that we can have our lovely mum back again.

One

'People with autism have been described as having an inability to communicate feelings of emotional disturbance, anxiety or distress, which can make it very difficult to diagnose depressive or anxiety states and can lead to challenging behaviour.'[1]

'There's nothing to eat!' Mum says. 'I need to go shopping.'

It is January 2015. Mum's in a bad way. She paces from the kitchen to the hallway, grabbing a coat, going back to the kitchen to take a shopping bag from the peg on the back of the door. Her hands are shaking and her face is sweaty. She's moving fast and I have to jog to catch up with her.

'Mum – Mum, wait!' I try to block her way as she reaches for the car keys.

'I have to go to the shops!' Her voice rises to a shout.

'Mum, the fridge is full. You don't need to go out.' I am trying to sound calm. I don't feel calm. 'And I don't think you should drive.'

The idea of my manic mother getting into a car and navigating her way out of the drive is frightening enough. There's no way she can make it to the other end of the High Street safely in the state she's in.

'There's nothing to eat!' she says again. 'Get out of my way!' Her eyes are wide and her breathing is fast and furious.

'OK, OK. I'll drive you,' I say, taking the car keys out of her hands.

I am expecting a fight, but I don't get one. 'Thank you,' she says, suddenly meek.

I don't wait for her to change her mind. I bundle her out of the house, going through a quick checklist as though taking a small child on a trip to town: bags, coats, umbrellas, bottle of water. Should I ask her if she needs a pee? I decide not to as this will only upset her train of thought and make her panic again. Her panicking makes me as frightened as her anger did when I was small.

We shouldn't be going out. We definitely don't need to go shopping. The fridge is full to bursting, with packets of ham and smoked salmon and lettuce – some of them already starting to decompose. I've tried to sort through the mess and throw out the rotting food, but Mum caught me in the act. I am not allowed to throw food away; it's wasteful.

Mum is quiet as we drive down the High Street. The sight of familiar landmarks acts as a sedative. As we approach the supermarket, however, she starts to pant and give a high-pitched cry, her lips pursed into a small 'o': 'Whoop! Whoop!' It sounds desperate. Child-like. It tears at my chest.

I have to contain this behaviour before it becomes a full-on panic. I think of asking Mum to stay in the car while I go and pick up some food, but then I think I'd have to lock her in. I can't do that. What if she banged on the window, begging to be let out? What would people think?

'Come on!' Mum says, opening the door before I have put the handbrake on. 'We need to hurry.'

We don't need to hurry. There is nothing happening today. Nothing other than me watching Mum like a hawk as she paces around the house, obsessing about food and clothes and cracks in the wall.

No wonder Dad is happy to be back in hospital, I think. *No wonder he told me he needed a rest.*

Mum is already halfway across the car park when she steps out in front of a van. The driver brakes abruptly and scowls as I run after Mum and grab her arm.

'Slow down, Mum,' I say. 'We've got loads of time.'

I keep my head low as we enter the supermarket, my arm linked through Mum's as she pulls me along. I pray we won't bump into any friends or neighbours. I know what Mum looks like. She looks as alarmed as she feels. Her hair, once so regularly and obsessively coiffed, is woolly and white. Her eyes, once bright green and flashing with passion and life, are glassy and staring. Her jaw hangs slack and she is shuffling, panting and whooping in between repeating, in panicked gasps, that she must buy 'ham and smoked salmon and lettuce'.

I try talking to Mum in a low voice, which I am hoping sounds soothing. I suggest that she buy something else.

'What about some chicken? And some fruit and veg? I could make you a couple of things to put in the freezer for when Dad comes home?'

'No, no, no!' she says.

Her voice is loud. I know people are staring. I take deep breaths and hold on to her firmly as she tries to pull away. I'm good at this, at least; I've had years of practice with my own children when they were small. I find myself calling her 'love' and 'darling' as I did with my kids too. In the past she might have laughed at this. Today she doesn't notice.

'Salmon,' she says. 'Salmon and lettuce and ham.'

I grit my teeth. I want to scream. I want to shout, *Your fridge is full of rotting lettuce! Can't you see that? Why can't you see that?*

People are definitely staring now. Some are less obvious and are merely flicking glances in our direction – some curious, some concerned, some just bloody rude. I also want to scream at them. Yes, my mother is a weirdo. She is odd, she is slow, she is whatever else you want to bloody call it. She is round the fucking bend. What do you expect me to do?

I want to take them all on. To stand up on the check-out conveyor belt and tell them: this is my mum. She has a degree in Latin and Greek, she speaks French and Italian and knows more about Ancient Rome than most of you probably know about the back streets of this very town. She brought me and my sister up to be independent adults. She loved us and cared for us and supported my dad while he commuted every day to London. She was stunningly beautiful as a young woman. Men fell at her feet. Yes, she is anxious. Yes, she has problems. But she has lived a life. There is more to her than this.

We get to the checkout, our basket laden with packets and packets of the same things. I tried to slip in other items while Mum wasn't looking, but she has seen them and already thrown them out. I start to load the shopping onto the conveyor belt, seeing the end in sight, looking forward to packing the bags and getting the hell out of here.

Suddenly Mum lets out an especially loud 'WHOOP!'

'What?' I'm so close to shouting at her. This is worse than the worst supermarket trip with an angry two-year-old. Worse than the time my son stood up in the trolley and ripped open a packet of bread, sending the slices cascading onto the floor.

'I can't find my purse!' She starts trotting on the spot, as though she is treading water.

'OK, slow down.'

'I can't find it! Can't find it!' She begins scrabbling in her handbag and shopping bags. The panting and the whooping and trotting get worse as her panic rises. 'I can't! I can't!'

'It doesn't matter. Really, Mum. I'll pay.' I lower my voice in opposition to hers. 'We'll look for it when we get home.'

'No, no, nooo!' Mum's face is etched with fear.

People are shuffling away from us now. Mum is scrabbling ever more fiercely through her bags. The man at the checkout shoots me a look that is probably one of compassion but in that moment feels more like one of judgement. *What are you doing, taking your mother out when she is in this state?* he seems to be saying.

I don't know, I want to tell him. I don't know what I'm supposed to do any more.

∽

When we eventually get home, the purse still unfound, I am wrung out, my reserves of nervous energy worn away to a shred. It's all I can do not to reach for a drink. I wish Mum were a toddler. Then I might be able to give her a cuddle and put her down for a nap or stick on a video to soothe her, not to mention myself. But there is nothing I can do to calm this highly anxious seventy-one year-old, who once used to soothe and cuddle me.

'My purse! My purse!' She has not let up since she left the shop.

All thoughts of soothing evaporate, and I snap. 'I'll look for your bloody purse in a minute.'

I storm out of the sitting room and go to make myself a coffee. I can allow myself that at least.

Mum isn't going to let me be, though, until that purse is

found. 'Anna! Anna! I can't find my purse!' She's rushing from room to room, sweating and breathing like a racehorse after winning the Grand National, whooping and moaning and catastrophising.

'It has all my cards in it – where can it be? – I am stupid, stupid, stupid.' She beats out the rhythm of the words with smacks against her forehead. 'I've lost it! – Where is it? – It has all my cards in it—'

As I wait for the kettle to boil I glance around the kitchen. I see a Boots bag on the breakfast bar and pick it up. The purse is inside. I take it to Mum.

'There,' I say. 'It's all right.' I hear my voice: a scant approximation of patience. 'I've found it.'

If I am hoping for thanks, or even relief, on Mum's part, I am to be disappointed. There is a change in her manner: a change so abrupt it's as though a spell has been cast. A black cloud enters the room, stilling the air. Mum's expression has changed from one of pure terror and high panic to one of a silent, sullen child. 'Bolshie' is the word she would have used, back in the day.

She snatches the purse from me. 'I knew it was here somewhere,' she says, and turns to leave the room.

I feel winded. I clutch the edge of the kitchen surface. I bite down on the words I want to hurl at her. I swallow back the torrent of accusations. I push the memory of her panic attack in the supermarket out of my mind.

I walk to the kettle, fetch down the coffee from the cupboard above, fill a coffee pot with grounds and hot water. I follow Mum into the sitting room, where she's already settled serenely in the green wing-backed chair that's become her fortress in recent months. I perch on the pink sofa on which my children were never allowed to sit in case they flattened the cushions or made it dirty.

Mum's breathing has stilled. She stares at me. 'Talk to me,' she says.

I can't. My mind is a seething hot pool of anger, fear and resentment. I escaped all this. I ran away from the source of own anxieties. I ran from the unbearable boiling spring of Mum's tantrums and her controlling behaviour. I bolted from this small trickle of a town with its gossips and its limitations. I have followed my own course, cut my own way through the valleys and hills. I have made my own life with my husband and my children and my dog, all of whom are having to cope without me as I sit here in a darkened room staring at the wall while my mother sits in a chair and stares at me. A weirdo. A raving lunatic. Mental.

Two

'Some Aspies, particularly females, do very much want to fit in and they can learn to do so, or at least seem to do so, by copying what they see around them. This makes them less likely to draw attention to themselves, so it would seem to be more likely that females rather than males will go undiagnosed.'[2]

Friends of the family are baffled by what they see as Mum's sudden decline. Their foreheads crinkle as they take in this gibbering, shrunken figure before them. 'How did she get like this?' they ask. 'How did it happen?' As though just one thing happened – a fall or a push or a bang on the head – which sent Mum spinning out of control. One friend even asks, 'What has she got to be depressed about?', as though all she needs is a pat on the back and an encouragement to 'cheer up'. I can't blame them. The way they see it, one day, Mum was their intelligent, confident, outspoken, beautiful friend. The next, she was . . . this.

But what 'this' is, none of us can explain. Her friends wouldn't go as far as to call Mum 'mental', but they don't have to. I can tell it's what they're thinking. They can't bring themselves to talk openly about her mental health. It's discussed, if at all, carefully, cautiously. Under their breath, with sidelong glances. After all, it might be contagious, who knows? Who's to say where 'this' starts – the transition from sane to insane?

When I try to explain, I find it's too hard to go back, to catalogue the events that might have led to Mum's startling behaviour. In any case, I'm pretty much in the dark myself. Instead I tell people that 'this' started on Sunday 12 May 2013.

That was the day my uncle called me. He rarely does, so that in itself unnerved me; and to call early in the morning, on a Sunday, was enough to set my bones jangling. My immediate thought was that someone had died. The last time John called so early was after his wife had dropped dead from an aneurism. No warning signs. Here one minute and gone the next.

No one had died this time. Not literally anyway.

'I've just spent a week in France with your parents,' John tells me.

I pick up on his tone before he says another word. He sounds calm. But this isn't lovely, gentle Uncle-John-calm; this is professional Dr-John-calm. He hasn't rung to tell me about his holiday; he's quiet, serious, taking his time, getting ready to deliver bad news in as caring a way as possible.

'I'm concerned about Gillian,' he says.

Not 'my sister'. Not even 'your mother'.

Cold fingers walk down my spine.

'Her behaviour has become manic,' he goes on. 'I'm worried that your father is exhausted.'

Concerned.

Manic.

Worried.

Exhausted.

I know what this means. I have known for months, if I'm honest. Months during which I have done my best to listen and offer support to Mum. Months during which I have become frustrated with Dad's refusal to discuss how bad things were getting. Months during which my frustration with both my parents has turned to anger and then panic, ending in me closing down, refusing further communication. This is why John is calling now – to force me back into the game.

I hold my breath and the edge of the kitchen sink.

Steady, now.

Steady.

'I came back from France feeling that Gillian should go into respite,' he is saying. 'Your dad wouldn't listen to me while I was with them, so I thought perhaps I should leave well alone. But Gemma's just phoned.' He pauses.

Gemma is my cousin, John's daughter. A capable, logical, clear-thinking medic, just like her father.

I hear John sigh – a funny sound, as though he too is trying to keep it all together. 'Gillian called Gemma first thing this morning to wish her a happy birthday,' he says. 'She apologised for missing it. Then she blurted out that the house was filthy. This set off a rant about having to clean the house all the time because it was too dirty. She added that she could see it was also falling apart.' He pauses again.

Mum would be upset for having forgotten Gemma's birthday, I think. But this isn't the point he's making. I don't say anything. I wait for John to continue.

'Gillian is convinced that there are huge cracks opening in the walls and ceiling of the house,' John goes on. 'She also told Gemma that she's given herself third-degree burns while cleaning the oven with her bare hands, using caustic soda. This was why she'd missed her birthday – because she had to go to A&E.'

This is it. This is the bad news. He's built up to it and he's not going to stop now. I let out a sob; I can't help it.

'I'm sorry, Anna. She's become dishevelled and unkempt and has developed a shuffling gait,' John says.

Each word he utters is an exploding firework. *Dishevelled. Unkempt. Shuffling.* Dr John again: detached, professional, telling me what I need to know. I don't want this diagnostic tone. I don't want this detachment. Where has my Uncle John gone? Where are all the grown-ups?

Shuffling gait . . . What he really means is—

No. Can't go there.

I've tried to push this out. I knew things were bad. I tried to say. So many times. The last time I saw Mum it was awful. She had looked 'dishevelled and unkempt' even then, if I am honest. I had taken the kids to London to meet up with my sister Carrie and her children. Mum had been on edge the whole time and had barely spoken to her grandchildren, whom she adores. She had obsessed over meal times and train times and wouldn't come into the exhibition at the museum because the rooms were 'too dark'. She had gulped the hot chocolate I had bought her and had scalded her mouth. Carrie had tried – I had tried – to talk to Dad, to say, 'Look! Look at her!' He had nodded and smiled and pushed our worries aside, and in the end we had done what we always do and taken his lead. Dad knows best. From then on we had decided to leave them to it.

'She's paranoid,' John says.

And there we have it. I know he's using the word in its medical sense, but I am the daughter of two classicists who always took pains to teach me the Greek and Latin source of words that we take for granted in English. I know where 'paranoid' comes from. Paranoia: from the Ancient Greek meaning 'beyond the mind'. Panic. Pandemonium. Chaos. Paranoia. All from the Ancient Greeks. Didn't they have a hell of a lot of good words for occasions such as this?

Because Mum is 'beyond her mind'. Out of it.

Mad.

I stare at some water marks next to the kitchen taps. I try to focus, to hear what Dr John is advising.

Those water marks, though. Mum hates water marks. I fight the urge to grab a cloth and wipe the spots away.

Cracks in the wall. Caustic soda.

Water marks. Wipe them up! They'll leave a stain!

John is still talking. He still sounds calm, but there is something off-key; a dislocation, a gap between the words he's using and his measured, professional tone; she might be my mum, but she's his sister too.

'Your father is hiding his head in the sand, Anna. He is burying himself in an ever-expanding list of jobs that he feels need doing around the house – presumably to try to appease your mother. He is continuing with his canoeing and his singing, and he is ratcheting up their social life. These are distractions, but they are not working. Your mother is exhausted. She is entering a phase which I would say is border-line delusional. This isn't depression, Anna,' he says with emphasis. 'She needs to go to hospital where she can be properly monitored and possibly even have electro-convulsive treatment.'

I hear myself whisper, 'Electric shocks?'

'It can be highly effective,' John says.

I have seen the scenes played out in television dramas. Tied to a bed. Biting down on rubber. The sharp pain as a bolt of lightning surges through the body. I have read Sylvia Plath's

The Bell Jar. I don't want Mum to feel as though she's been shaken 'like the end of the world'. I don't want her to see the air 'crackling with blue light', to feel 'a great jolt drub through' her till she thinks her bones might break.

What kind of a daughter am I?

How have I let my own mother get to this point?

What have I been *thinking*?

Back in February it felt as though I had to take a stand. It felt as though things had reached crisis-point – for me. I wrote to Dad and told him I couldn't be involved any more, that Mum was sucking all the air out of me with her constant crying 'Wolf' – phoning me at all hours every day, sometimes multiple times a day, telling me how miserable she was, asking me to fix her, and then, when she didn't like what I had to say – about her being depressed – turning the tables on me: telling me *I* was the one who was depressed. I told him I was having panic attacks and sleepless nights, worrying about Mum, but that everything I had tried to do to help was being ignored. And so I was cutting off contact for a while. To focus on me and my own family. To give myself space. For the sake of my own survival.

How self-centred and self-righteous my behaviour looks now. Now, I am so far away, so distanced, that when Mum really needs help (and Dad, poor Dad!), I am too removed to grasp how bad things have become.

Still, I can't think of the right questions to ask. I am terrified in case John answers me with the very words I don't want to hear.

He says them anyway.

'I'm afraid you're going to have to step in and take control. I've tried talking to your father, but he's not listening.' John pauses, then says it again: 'You are going to have to step in.'

I want to say something sensible, to show that I understand, even though I don't. Not really. Because I can't. I can't do this. Not me. This is my mum. She is the one who looks after me. I am the child here; don't ask me. There must be someone else who can step in.

'I've already tried to help!' I say. I sound like an eight-year-old. 'I've tried talking to Dad. I've suggested . . . everything! CBT, counselling, therapy. Yoga, even!'

And look how all that turned out. What was it she called it? 'Namby-pamby nonsense'.

John's voice takes on a quieter, warmer tone. 'I know. I'm sorry.' My uncle is back. He's not going to let me off the hook, though. 'Ring me if you need me. Let me know what happens.'

And that is that. End of conversation. No more discussion. Over to me.

I put down the phone and feel the walls close in.

Three

'There are several coping mechanisms [for a child whose parent is a person with AS]. [One] mechanism is to escape the situation . . . leaving home as soon as possible.'[3]

I am not ready for this.
I have my own life.
I have two children who are still at school.
One is doing her GCSEs soon, for goodness' sake.
My husband works abroad.
I see him only at weekends.
I am trying to develop my career.
In between looking after the kids and running the house.
I can't take on my mother as well.
I can't.
I have my own life and I have fought hard for it.
I moved away from all this.
I don't know how to cope with madness.
I feel as though I'm going mad myself.
I am not going back.
I am not.

❧

I talk to myself as I pound the towpath.

I run and I run and I run.

I run down to the river.

May is the best month of the year to be here. And here is where I want to be, with the cow parsley and the kingcups and the herons and the moorhens and the ducklings and the cormorants and the kingfishers.

Not there. In my neat and tidy childhood home. With my mother.

Mum had been livid when we'd moved here.

'What on earth are you moving to the bloody West Country for? It's too far!'

Too far from her, was what she meant. But that was part of the allure by then. Not that we had a choice, as it was work that brought us here. But by 2007 I'd had enough of Mum demanding that I spend more time with her; complaining that I didn't live down the road, near my mother, as she had done; ranting that I didn't care about her feelings, that I seemed to care more about my friends than about her; that I was not a good daughter, that I should make more of an effort to let her see her grandchildren. Calling me every other day, sometimes twice a day, to catalogue my failings and list how I had let her down.

And now she really needs me. Now I can deny it no longer: this life was never really mine. What kind of a fool was I, thinking that I could move away, put some distance between us, save myself?

I can't break the bonds that tie me to my mother. I can run and run as fast and as far as I like, but I will never escape.

Four

'The real end, for most of us, would involve sedation, and being sectioned, and what happens next it's better not to speculate.'[4]

I call Dad later that Sunday.

'It's fine, love. Things are fine. You shouldn't worry.' His voice is quiet and over-patient. Kind, as always. 'Mum has hurt her hands, and been a bit pig-headed and stubborn, but otherwise everything is all right.'

I don't believe him. I want to, but John's words ricochet before my eyes. I am about to push Dad to tell me, honestly, how things are, when Mum gives me the answer. There is a clatter as she picks up the other phone. She breathes heavily into the receiver.

'The house is disgusting,' she blurts out. 'And insanitary and probably unhygienic.' Her voice is skittering, shaky, high-pitched.

Dad cuts across her, tries to mollify her. I listen to them talking to each other. They have forgotten about me. I am listening to two characters in a radio play.

These stereophonic conversations are not a new thing; Mum and Dad have been doing this for years, one answering the phone and the other picking up 'on the other end' to listen in. It always infuriated me, the way they ended up talking to one another, forgetting I was there.

Today is different. Today I am grateful for Dad's stage management. I listen as he distracts Mum, moves her on from her cyclical rant about the state of the house, gently tells her that I have phoned for a chat.

Not forgotten then.

'So, how are you, Mum?' I ask.

Stupid question.

There is a brief pause, and then Mum turns on herself, attacking herself, reprimanding herself for being stupid. For having done nothing with her university degree (not true), for being useless.

'Useless,' she chants. 'Useless, useless, useless, useless.'

Dad breaks in again. He soothes her with loving words. I can say nothing. I'm the one who is useless.

Mum goes quiet for a while. As Dad talks I'm reminded with a stab of panic of a friend of mine who was diagnosed with bipolar disorder. I went to visit her when she was being treated in a mental health unit during a frightening psychotic episode. She told me repeatedly, at high speed, how useless she was and how she could no longer study, how she would never get her degree, how the words were nonsense on the page; black, jumpy shapes that held no meaning.

'Mum's gone,' Dad says, breaking into my thoughts.

For a second I misunderstand. *Yes, she's gone all right.*

I take a breath. Now's my chance. I have to make Dad see. Things can't go on like this.

'I don't know how to say this, Dad, but the way Mum's talking reminds me of F when she was sectioned.' I'm referring to the friend I have just been thinking about; Dad knows it.

'Oh God,' he whispers.

All forced jollity gone. All pretence abandoned.

I hear heavy breathing coming down the line.

'Dad?'

'Oh shit and fuck, she's picked up the other phone again!' There is a clatter and I can hear Dad shouting, 'Gillian!' The swearing and the anger in his voice shake me. He never used to swear or shout. Even if I had wanted to be reassured by Dad's patient voice earlier, I can't ignore the facts now.

I hear hectic sounds, of Dad chasing Mum around the house, shouting then soothing and cajoling, trying to get the phone off her so that he and I can talk in private. He finally succeeds in grabbing it from her, then tells me – spitting the words at me – that he is spending too much money, that he is booking things to do, to take Mum out to 'distract her' and then she is insisting he cancel them.

'She doesn't want to go out, but she doesn't want to stay in either!' he cries.

The sudden change from soothing, comforting Dad to frightened, confused husband is too awful. I should pack a bag and go to him, right now. He has reached his limits. No more smiling and nodding. Everything is clearly not 'fine' any more.

Why don't I put down the phone and go?

I know that things are serious. John's right. It's not depression; it's more than that.

Yet, still, I don't go, because I'm not ready; I don't think I ever will be.

Five

'Myles and Southwick . . . described a Rage Cycle for adults and children with autism spectrum disorder (ASD) which includes high functioning autism. They describe what happens when the person with ASD fails to recognise or is unable or unwilling to prevent their build-up of anger. This Cycle of Rage has three parts: rumbling, rage and recovery.'5

Mum is gripping me around the wrists, shaking me. Her fingers are tight on my skin, like hot wires. Her eyes flash emerald poison; her teeth are bared like a wild dog.

⌒

It's 3.15 a.m., the next morning. I wake, gasping. Mum's face is burnt on to my retina: her teeth clenched, her face taut with fury. Her face as it used to be so often when I was younger. The familiar old questions nagging at me: What have I done? Or not done? How have I made her so cross?

Memories of the day before rush in. The phone call, the discussions with my husband and sister. The rising panic. The fear. I feel as though someone is standing on my chest.

I can't go back. I can't step in. Mum hasn't done anything violent for years, but memories of her past rages rush towards me every night now. Why? Why, when she is so meek and mild and frightened, when she needs love and understanding, why am I being reminded now of those darker times? They have haunted me recently: her anger at me being late, at making a mess, at 'answering back'. Her fury that often seemed well out of proportion to the sin at which it was directed, and yet felt, to a smaller, younger me, justly deserved. It was the look on her face that always frightened me more than anything. Those eyes; wild, glistening. Those teeth. The rage that used to come from her was worse than anything else she could throw at me. Yes, she sometimes hit us, but I knew so many children whose parents slapped them. It was the Seventies – no one thought to question physical punishment. The thing I feared most was the shaking. The last time she shook me I was no longer a child. I had children of my own. She had taken hold of my wrists and shaken me, spitting fury into my face, her expression as it had been so often in my childhood: stretched, red, out of control. And grown woman that I was, I had been terrified. I realise now that it wasn't actually violence or anger that I was frightened of. It was hatred. That was the look I saw on Mum's face. And that was the most unbearable thing – that my own mother could hate me, no matter how hard I tried to be a good girl.

It's getting to the stage that I'm dreading sleep. I don't know why I'm having these dreams when my mother is now incapable of any emotion other than fear. But then fear is what has always been at the root of all her behaviour. Anger was a defence mechanism. Now that all her defences have evaporated, the fear is exposed. And it is contagious.

Later that morning – Monday 13 May 2013 – I call Dad to try one last time to persuade him to take Mum to hospital as John suggested.

'John thinks that she really needs a rest.' I am aware that the time for such euphemisms is gone, but I also know that I haven't the strength to use raw, terrifying words such as 'mental health unit' or 'psychosis' – or to mention sectioning again.

There is a pause on the other end. I assume Dad is preparing himself to tell me, yet again, that I shouldn't worry and that 'everything is fine'. The silence lengthens.

'Would you like me to come and stay?' I ask, my voice high, overly patient, as though speaking to a young child.

Still I get no response.

Then he howls.

A huge, keening, animal howl from somewhere deep inside him.

It rips right through me. My hands start to shake. I stagger and thrust the phone at my husband so that he can hear.

'Go. Go now,' he tells me.

Six

'I understand that my autism makes me a difficult person to deal with: I don't know when to back off.'[6]

The drive from Wiltshire to Kent passes in a blur. At one point I realise I'm holding my breath, which is what Mum does when she's frightened. I force myself to breathe in slowly, deeply, to breathe out to a count of three. It doesn't work. I gulp and snatch at the air. I'm going to have a panic attack like the one I had in February when I was driving to see a friend. I drove the wrong way down a one-way street and arrived at my friend's gasping and sobbing. I turn on the radio, find some soothing music. I pull myself together, count down the motorway exits.

This leg of the journey is so familiar. In the past, on my visits back home after leaving it for the first time, this length of the A21 was where I would feel a warm rush of nostalgia. There is a bridge that crosses the A road shortly after you leave the M25. It is an arc of concrete – hardly a thing of beauty – but to me it has always said 'home'. As I passed beneath it I would exhale the word, feel my shoulders go down, knowing that I was going back to where I belonged.

Shortly after passing under this bridge, the Weald of Kent is laid out beneath you. A bowl of green and pleasant land which, in my childhood, was full of orchards, oast houses, farms and weather-boarded cottages. It represented to me the ideal of what home was: calm and comforting and familiar. Like Mum on her best days.

∽

Because Mum could be everything you ever wanted in a mother. She could cuddle you and stand up for you and help you with your homework and make cakes for you and cook delicious meals from scratch and sing along to your favourite songs in the car and smile when you picked her a bunch of daffodils. She could be the most beautiful mum at the school gate in her lovely dresses with her soft, fluffy dark hair combed into pretty styles. She could look at your drawings and your stories and smile and say she was proud of you. She could sit and listen to you play the piano and tell you how clever you were.

She could keep the house neat and tidy too, hoovering and dusting on the same day each week, changing the sheets and towels on the same day each week, polishing the parquet floor on her hands and knees on the same day once a month, ironing everything that could be ironed into crisp piles.

She was there for us, all the time. Even when she had a teaching job, she made sure that her hours fitted around us. She took us to school, she fetched us from school, she mended our clothes, she polished our shoes. She was constant and solid and she made us feel safe.

Most of the time.

Dad commuted to London. Unless he was travelling for work, he would come home at the same time every evening.

When we were small he would make it back in time to read bedtime stories. As we got older and stayed up later we would wait to eat our evening meal with him. When I visited as a young adult, the sound of his key in the lock still had me running to give him a hug.

Everything had a rhythm to it. As long as you didn't make Mum angry, as long as there were no unwelcome surprises, as long as you were good, then everything was ordered and quiet, comforting and safe.

When I was living in student accommodation or a dingy flat, going home to Kent was a welcome break. I knew I would be greeted with hugs and lovely food and fresh, clean linen. I looked forward to going back.

So when did I start to dread this journey? When did the sign for the A21 make me wish I hadn't agreed to come? Was it when I got engaged? Was it the leaving and cleaving that did it? Or was it when I ventured into motherhood and dared to go back to work when my daughter was six months old? Whenever it was, David became used to the way I would start to jitter as we approached the turn-off. My right leg would start to jiggle up and down. I would check my watch over and over to make sure we weren't going to be late, the cardinal sin that could wreck a visit before it had even begun.

It's hard to know when any relationship veers off course. What had become increasingly clear over the years between my marriage in the mid-Nineties, and now in 2013, was that Mum did not deal well with me and my sister growing up – and away from her.

Arguments started around the planning of my wedding. I had always been a pretty compliant child and teen, but suddenly I had strong opinions that I wasn't about to compromise. I didn't want to have the service in the same church that Mum and Dad had got married in. It was too big and didn't feel right for me and David. Then I 'insisted' on living in London rather than moving back to Kent. The fact that work kept us both in the capital was not a good enough reason – Dad worked in London, but he commuted from Kent. Why couldn't we do the same? Once grandchildren came on the scene, my geographical distance made things so much worse for Mum. No matter that I called and visited regularly. No matter that Mum saw my daughter once a week when I went back to work. Nothing was enough because I had not followed the pattern preordained for me by Mum.

The clashes escalated over the years. We still saw one another and spoke regularly on the phone. But when my grandmother died, I felt that Mum's dependency on me grew and grew until it became suffocating; I hadn't realised how much of a buffer Grandma was until she was gone.

Grandma died on 26 September 2008. Mum's mental health started to decline after this, but because it manifested in a series of worries about her physical health, nothing was put in place to help. Looking back in her medical notes now, I see that at various points health professionals had observed 'heightened levels of anxiety' and that Mum was assured that her physical complaints were not as serious as she believed them to be. And yet, apart from a seemingly rogue prescription for Prozac at one point around the time her father died, and some Valium to calm her the night before my wedding, nothing else was done to help.

By 2012 Mum had undergone surgery for uterine prolapse – something she had been advised against as she was becoming increasingly anxious and the consultant feared that the operation would be too much for her mental state. He was reluctant to operate, but Mum insisted. Sleeplessness was also becoming a huge problem for her, and she was calling me and Carrie daily, if not multiple times a day, to tell us that she couldn't sleep, was 'on edge' and didn't know what to do. It was at this point that Carrie and I were reading up obsessively in a bid to find a magic cure for Mum. We were convinced that Mum's insistence on her body 'falling apart' was an outward manifestation of the state of her mind. We looked up and sent her advice on the benefits of the CBT the GP wanted her to try. We sent her links and articles on aromatherapy, yoga, meditation apps, even Epsom salt baths. We both regularly sent her gifts of things we hoped might help; we met up with her, organising outings, following the example of our grandmother whose first response with Mum was always to take her out 'for a treat' or buy her something 'to cheer her up'.

By the end of 2012, Mum was seeing a psychiatrist privately. She had been to her GP on many occasions about her sleeplessness and had quickly given up on the CBT that had been recommended. Both Carrie and I were sceptical that anything was being achieved by the psychiatric appointments. The consultant had diagnosed depression and had started Mum on a series of drugs. When these had no effect on Mum's insomnia, he had told her, according to Mum, that she would 'probably always be miserable' and that there wasn't really much more he could do.

Mum relayed this conversation to me in February 2013. I will never forget it because it was half-term and I had taken the kids to London. I remember it was evening – dark and cold. I was walking across Brook Green in Hammersmith to pick my daughter up from a sleepover with a friend I had never met. Mum had already called me twice that day. I nearly didn't answer because by then the very sight of the word 'Mum' on the screen was enough to send me into a panic, and I didn't want to arrive at Lucy's friend's house in a state. However, I also knew that Mum would ring and ring if I didn't pick up. I continued walking as I answered.

'Hi, Mum? I can't talk now. I'm on my way to get Lucy.'

Mum answered with the sort of half-snort she gave when she wanted to convey maximum disapproval. 'I don't know why you couldn't come to *us* for half-term. I wanted to tell you: the psychiatrist says I will probably always be miserable. I don't know why you think I need to see this man anyway,' she added. 'It's a waste of money. There's nothing wrong with my mind – it's my body that's the problem. And I can't sleep. The psychiatrist says you and Carrie should be kinder to me and then I'll be fine.'

I remember stopping, the cold air catching in my throat. Kinder to her? *Kinder?* It was like a slap. Or a shake. I ended the call hastily and pulled myself together so that I could be the mum I needed to be for my daughter.

The next morning Mum called again. She said the same things and berated me for not helping her. I remember I was with both my children and my mother-in-law was there. I remember hurling my phone down and bursting into sobs. I remember my mother-in-law looking horrified before putting her arms around me. I remember saying, 'She won't leave me alone!' I remember feeling guilt and shame at the way I was talking about my mother to my mother-in-law. I remember feeling utter, utter despair.

It was shortly after that that I had a panic attack and wrote to Dad and said I couldn't cope any more. I needed to cut off contact for a while.

∽

I have passed that beautiful view of the Weald now. I have passed the village where my loving, gentle grandmother lived, where I would stop off on my way to seeing Mum and Dad. I have driven past the little church where David and I were married, in spite of Mum's protests. I have driven past my little primary school where I made my first relationships outside the family. I am approaching the house now. What on earth will I find when I get there? It's been over three months since I've been there, and after that phone call with Dad, I'm dreading what lies in wait.

Seven

'The child of a parent [with ASD] learns not to express emotions such as distress.'[7]

I don't know what I imagined I would find when I arrived, but it wasn't this. I pull in to the drive to see there are workmen painting the white weatherboard. A swarm of them, crawling over the flat roof above the study, scaling the walls outside the sitting room, brandishing paintbrushes, like the playing cards in *Alice's Adventures in Wonderland*.

Maybe I am the one who's become delusional. Am I seeing things? Am I making this up? Mum is out of her mind, Dad is howling down the phone – and there are workmen painting the house as though it's just a normal Monday morning.

I get out of the car to see my mother's face peering at me through the glass in the front door. Small, wide-eyed, white-haired and frightened. Not the upright, well-dressed, fiery-tempered woman of only a year ago. Not the mother who would bark, 'You're late!' even when I had phoned in advance to let her know I was stuck in traffic.

She opens the door a crack.

'Dad's out,' she says, her voice high and quavering.

'Where's he gone?' He can't have left her alone, surely?

'He's gone to do some shopping. We've got no food.' She is speaking too fast. 'The fridge is making a funny noise.' She gives a funny little gasp. Her hands are shaking.

I push the door open, put my bags down, take her into my arms. I hold her and kiss her head while she asks, 'Why did you come? I didn't want you to come. The walls are cracking up.'

I let her go and point to my bags. 'Dad didn't need to go out. I've brought lunch. And some flowers.' I sound like a nursery school teacher mollifying a crying child.

'I don't want flowers. I can't eat that food. I can't eat a thing,' she says. 'I'm losing weight. Look.' She grabs the waistband of her trousers and pulls it away.

It is alarmingly loose. She says she's lost half a stone. Looks more like a whole one to me. Mum has struggled with her weight since the menopause. She always wanted to lose that tricky last half stone. But not like this. Not like this.

She begins to pace up and down, wringing her hands and moaning.

'The house is in a state. Look at it! I'm in a state. I'm useless, useless, useless.'

She is a textbook picture of a madwoman. Unkempt, as John said, her hair sticking up on end, her eyes staring, she is constantly on the move, talking in a loop, moaning, gasping and whooping. Stick her in a long white nightie and dim the lights and she could be a nineteenth-century loony, straight out of the asylum.

Her ranting goes up a notch as she paces. Her sentences are short and breathlessly sharp. My heart begins to race in time with her galloping words.

'I *know* what the problem is. It's the house . . .

'. . . I have let it get out of control . . .

'. . . Everything's cracking up!

'Look at the weeds!

'Look at that bush!

'We've had decorators in and they've left dust everywhere . . .

'. . . We've got nothing to eat. There's no food in the house.

'You shouldn't have come . . .

'. . . What am I going to wear? I've got no clothes . . .

'. . . I have to do some washing . . .

'. . . I have to do the ironing . . .

'I need to get my hair done!

'Look at the state of everything . . .

'There's nothing wrong with *me*. I *know* what the problem is. It's the house.'

She is a river in spate; her words rushing, gushing, teeming, spilling over the banks and flooding the air around her. The word 'house' has acted like a trigger for her to list everything that is 'cracking up' or 'falling down' or 'getting out of control'. This panicky tour of the house and garden is punctuated by alarming exclamations about how she's 'tried and tried' and how she has 'behaved very badly', and she is 'useless', can't I see?

I occasionally manage to distract her for a few moments by asking her to sit and hold my hand. I tell her random, disjointed anecdotes about her grandchildren.

Within seconds she is up, pacing again, and the talking resumes. Round and round and round. On a loop. *Loopy.*

Dad comes home and quietly goes about unpacking shopping, barely acknowledging my presence.

I follow him into the kitchen, Mum hot on my heels. 'What are those men doing, Dad?'

'They're painting the drainpipes and fixing things up a bit,' Dad says calmly. 'Would you like a coffee?'

Fixing things up a bit? Papering over the cracks. Fiddling while Rome burns. It's what we've all been doing for years.

Mum comes up behind me.

'Listen to the fridge,' she insists.

I listen.

'I can't hear anything,' I say.

'It's not working,' Mum says, opening and closing the door.

'I mean – I can hear the normal noise a fridge makes,' I say hastily, trying to reassure her. 'And everything seems cold enough to me—'

'Why did you come? We haven't got any food. I didn't want you to come.'

Didn't want me to come?

She doesn't want me to be here? *Seriously?*

After years of begging me to come. To see her, to sit with her, to 'just talk' to her, to move back to Kent, to be there, just be there, be there for her, to not spend all my 'bloody time in the bloody West Country'? Now, when she's – what? Ill? Manic? Insane? – she doesn't *want* me? WHAT AM I SUPPOSED TO DO?

Dad keeps his head down. He doesn't look me in the eye.

I bite back frustration and fill the air with empty words instead. Witterings about the journey, about the work Dad's suddenly decided to do on the house, about the coffee. Dad joins in gratefully. *Move along now, nothing to look at here.*

I go to the loo, and after I have washed my hands I glance in the mirror and see that I look as 'unkempt' as Mum. Unwashed hair, scraped back because I had been about to go for a run when I called earlier. No make-up. Wild and wide-eyed and frightened. Mad as a hatter.

I shiver. The house is freezing. It's grey outside, yes, but it's May. I shouldn't be shivering. I realise I haven't brought a change of clothes, a jumper or a coat. I rushed out too fast.

I go and take a sleeveless Puffa of Dad's from the coat stand in the hall.

Dad has gone back into his study. I know he's hiding, that he needs a break. But I need *him*. I need him to tell me what to do, to take the lead. To be Dad. To step in. For once.

I hover in the doorway. 'Have you taken Mum to the doctor?'

'We're still seeing the psychiatrist,' he says carefully. He doesn't look up from his computer screen. The implication is, 'case dismissed'.

He knows I'm not buying it, though – that this is not the answer I'm looking for. He knows that this psychiatrist is next to useless as far as Mum's condition is concerned, that nothing has improved while she's been under his care. That everything has got immeasurably worse. And now this man is still taking my parents' money, still pacifying Mum with platitudes and pills, and still not putting in place any continuity of care for Mum at home.

I think about all these things as I stand in the door to my father's study while my mother runs through the house pointing out cracks in the wall and calling out in a high-pitched wail.

I think about everything that has led to me being here and I feel my fury rise up against this psychiatrist. Where is he now that Mum has lost her grip on reality? How can he say that a holiday in France and a bit of kindness will stop Mum's delusions? I would like to get hold of him and force march him round here and show him what his empty words and pills doled out like sweets have done.

But I mustn't take it out on Dad. I must breathe and stay calm and breathe and stay calm and breathe . . .

Dad is still typing at his computer and ignoring me.

'Dad.' I take a careful step towards him. 'I don't think this particular psychiatrist is getting to the bottom of things. I think Mum needs to be referred by the GP to an NHS psychiatrist so that she can have proper joined-up care. John thinks—'

'I'm sick of hearing what everyone *thinks*!' Dad snaps. He whips round in his chair to face me, his expression such a Molotov cocktail of anger and fear that I run from the room.

Dad never gets angry, Not with me, not with Mum, not with anyone. And yet today he has sworn down the phone, howled and now shouted at me. What is happening?

I retreat to my old bedroom, the place I always went to when things kicked off. My old bedroom, which has not felt like mine for over twenty years. I fling myself onto the bed. I wish I could scream and shout like Dad. I want to pound my fists against something. Break something. Preferably the psychiatrist. Instead I bite it all back. Like I did when I was a child and Mum had 'had enough' of me and Carrie and had gone to shake her fists in the mirror and yell.

I am still a child. Their child. But even as I think that, I know that the time has come for me to be the parent.

Eight

*'I hated having showers as a child and preferred baths. The
sensation of water splashing my face was unbearable.'*[8]

I sit and stroke Mum's hair.

'I want my mum!' she wails.

So do I.

I want my grandmother. The woman who mothered me when
Mum could not. The large, cuddly, soft, smiling grandma who
sat me on her lap and sang to me; who let me play with her
precious Singer sewing machine; who taught me how to make
pastry and didn't mind when I made a mess; who had me and
my sister to stay when things got 'too much' for Mum; who
tucked us in at night and kissed us three times, saying, *'Een,
tween, toi* – that's French, that is,' with a twinkle in her eye.

But Grandma is long gone; her ashes cast under a forgotten
tree by the river. She is dead. And with her passing, any real
understanding of how to cope with this woman, her daughter,
my real mother, has also died.

I try to persuade Mum to rest. She shouts back, 'No! I
need to wash my hair. It's disgusting.'

It's a relief to have her talk about something new, even if

I immediately recognise the signs of a new obsession. At least she's not talking about the house falling down or the lack of food. I say I will wash it for her.

'You can't,' she snaps.

'Mum, I can. You have burnt your hand with caustic soda. It's bandaged. You are not allowed to get it wet.' I'm being bossy. A bossy mother to my child-parent.

Mum jumps up from her chair, whooping and moaning, and begins the incessant walking in circles again, repeating that she needs to wash her hair. To do it herself, like the Little Red Hen.

I manage to lead her upstairs to the bathroom, talking calmly. (I hope I sound calm; I don't feel it.) I run water into the basin while I keep talking. I go over to the bathroom cabinet to fetch shampoo.

Mum watches me. 'I want you to use the red cup.'

'I know.'

'Not the shower.'

'I know.'

'The red cup. Up there.'

'Yes.'

'And don't drip water everywhere.'

'I won't.'

Mum has always hated marks, smudges, mess, things in the wrong place. Things not done her way. She does everything the way she always has. Washing her hair in the basin, not the shower. Using the red cup. Always the red cup. Only the red cup. She is attached to this red beaker, which we used to take on picnics. I remember the warm orange squash that was poured into it. It always made me gag, but I drank it anyway. Gagging for a few seconds was better than making Mum upset. I have always disliked orange squash. I have always hated washing my hair over a basin.

Nothing really changes. Even in her madness, Mum is not changed; she is just Mum with the volume turned up.

When we were children Mum used to wash our hair over the basin on the same day at the same time every week – no more and no less frequently. She would scrub our scalps hard, scratching at them with her fingernails. It was a brisk, rough affair. I quite liked the massage. I didn't like the shampoo trickling into my eyes, making me squirm. Mum didn't like it when as teenagers Carrie and I insisted on changing from baths and weekly hair washes to daily showers and washing (and dyeing) our own hair.

I look for the red cup in the bathroom cabinet. I keep talking to Mum, making sure my voice is even and calm. I don't know what I'm talking about. It doesn't matter so long as I can prevent her from leaving the room. I need to keep her away from Dad, who is in his study, pretending to do something on the computer. Taking a break. I can't allow Mum to upset him again. I can't have two crazy old people on my hands.

Bathrooms invite crises. I think of Carrie and hair-dyeing escapades gone badly wrong – her begging me to touch up her Monroe roots with peroxide that had already burnt her scalp, me wincing as I applied the bleach, trying to avoid the scabs on her skin. I remember, too, screaming arguments ending in running to this room. It was the only one in the house with a lock on the door.

I remember the evening before my wedding, locking myself in here with Carrie.

⌒‿⌒

I was staying here in Kent while David spent the night in London with his best man and the friends who were going to be his ushers. Mum had planned a big family get-together: uncles and aunts and cousins from both sides of the family. I didn't question whether this was what I wanted; at every stage of planning this wedding Mum had made it clear that it was she, not I, who was in charge. She was giving away her eldest daughter and she was going to do it the way tradition demanded. And tradition demanded that the bride did not see her groom the night before the wedding. So I was given a bed in my old bedroom, already stripped of anything that reminded me of childhood, and the whole family was invited round. And that was that – no arguments.

I knew Mum was on edge – she was jittery and irascible, which were warning signs that I needed to keep my head down. I didn't pay her too much attention, though. Why would I? I was too excited, too fixed on the next day and the rest of my life to come. It was only after the wedding that someone – Carrie, I think – told me that Mum was on Valium and that Grandma and Dad had had to keep her calm before I arrived. It was years later that I found out that the build-up to the wedding had made Mum so distraught that she had convinced herself that she had serious gastro-intestinal problems and had had a colonoscopy, which proved negative. Yet another occasion on which her levels of anxiety had not been considered to be the real medical problem.

I knew enough that night to instinctively keep my own nerves to myself. I knew I didn't want an explosion the night before my wedding. So when I got my cheap hairbrush tangled fast in my hair while blow-drying it, I certainly wasn't going to call for Mum. I called down the stairs to Carrie instead, keeping my voice careless and calm, asking if she could come to me. I had to keep any hint of panic from my tone, or Mum might have rushed in. She might have screamed and shouted.

She might have even tried to rip the brush from my head, or cut off my hair in chunks.

Carrie came, clocked the situation immediately, whispering that it would be fine. She gently locked the door before carefully teasing the hairbrush free. It took well over an hour. Mum shouted up to us more than once, wanting to know what we were 'up to'. We never told her what had happened.

$$\sim$$

I test the water for Mum now. The basin is full. The water is warm. I feel a surge of longing – to plunge my own head into it, to breathe in the water, to give myself to it, to be submerged, to stop the hammering in my chest, the whirring in my brain.

Instead I fetch a towel to put over Mum's shoulders. I ask her to bend over the basin and close her eyes, explaining what I am going to do.

She becomes meek, doing as I ask, dipping her head forward. I scoop some water into the red cup and then empty it over Mum's hair. A baptism. A cleansing. Her white roots flatten and the skin of her scalp is revealed. It is so pale, so pink, so pure. Baby-soft.

'Is that OK?' I ask.

'Hmmm.' Mum sounds content.

I look at Mum's fragile scalp and listen to the quiet trickle of the water running off her. The last time I did this was for my children, a good five years ago, when they too refused to use the shower. I would tip them back in the bath, holding their little bodies in the crook of my elbow, cradling their heads to make sure they didn't fall or get shampoo in their eyes. Then I would gently massage their soft pink scalps as they smiled up at me. It was always a pleasure, washing their hair. They would giggle and gasp when I poured the water using their own plastic cup.

Mum's head blurs under my massaging fingers. Mothering Mother.

I want my mum.

Nine

'Some adults report being "blinded by brightness" and avoid intense levels of illumination . . . There can also be an intense fascination with visual detail, noticing specks on a carpet.'[9]

I'm in a dark house with my son. We have been travelling all day and this is the only place we could find to stay the night. Now we can't find the way to our room. The light is fading rapidly and I can't see any light switches. Tom is holding on to me as I feel my way along the walls. Entrances open before us, then close as soon as we approach. Tom is chattering to me as he did when he was nine; telling me about bats and how many species there are in the UK. I am groping into narrower, darker corridors, my right hand before me, doing the best I can not to scream and frighten my son. I touch the walls again and feel that the wallpaper is moving. It bulges and writhes with living things. I grip Tom's hand tighter and we run. We find our room. It is wallpapered all over, from the floor beneath our feet to the ceiling above. Even the basin in the bathroom is wallpapered, as though wrapped up for Christmas.

∽

I wake. The nightmare is still in the room with me. I can't shake it off. It brings back memories of a book I read years ago – a short story, called *The Yellow Wallpaper* by Charlotte Perkins Gilman. I used to be morbidly fascinated by this story of a woman's descent into madness. She obsessed over patterns in the wallpaper in her room, believing them to be alive. At the time, I didn't think of the book's portrayal of insanity as anything other than fiction. Until now.

I reach above my head and run my fingers over the lumpy woodchip paper on my bedroom wall. A relic from my Seventies childhood. The bumps are not moving, thank goodness. Of course they're not. In any case, it's not the wallpaper in this room that haunts me. That is the role of the green carpet with its old indelible stain. Such a bad mistake. On both my part and on Mum's. But I can't go there now. That is one memory I have worked hard to erase – to fade, anyway. I sit up and swing my legs over the edge of the bed, pushing the nightmare away.

I look around this room. Its sparseness is nothing new. This was never a typical child's bedroom. Toys were always neatly packed away, nothing left lying around. As a teen, I was not allowed posters on the walls. Blu Tack made 'nasty marks', drawing pins were the devil's own work. I was allowed a small corkboard, but it was barely large enough for a couple of postcards. Carrie and I couldn't leave so much as a towel on the floor without being reprimanded.

'A place for everything and everything in its place!' The mantra of our childhood. Mum would chant it regularly as she tutted and sighed over dropped clothes, unwashed dishes, make-up stains – what I know now to be the normal flotsam and jetsam of adolescence. But Mum couldn't cope with it and she noticed every detail – you couldn't pull the wool over her eyes. You couldn't rumple the woollens in the airing cupboard either. Not without running the risk of her wrath.

'Who's been rootling in here?' she would cry, noticing if a sweater had been so much as brushed by our fiddling fingers. 'If you want something, ask me for it!'

Now an adult, I let my teenage daughter live 'in a pigsty'. It's her room, after all. In truth, I can't be bothered to spend the energy and time that Mum did over nagging her into submission. If Mum had been more relaxed about these things, perhaps she would not now be obsessing about a mess and a chaos that isn't there. Cracks in the wall, a broken fridge, 'filth' and chaos. Things she has always feared, always tried to prevent gaining a foothold.

As I pick up my clothes from where I threw them down last night, I think again of *The Yellow Wallpaper* and the narrator, losing her mind. I am going to have to press Dad to get a psychiatric assessment for Mum. Today.

I just wish I had the smallest idea of how to do this.

Ten

'Some A&E departments have a liaison psychiatry team (specialist help for mental health) that you can ask to see. If there isn't a liaison psychiatry team, A&E staff might contact other local services such as a crisis team (CRHT) to help assess you.'[10]

'You have to start somewhere,' as my English teacher used to say.

I start by spending the morning on the phone, trying to find someone who can help. I need advice. I need a professional to take control. It's all very well saying I must 'step in', but what can I do on my own?

I walk up and down the path in the back garden, as much to keep out of Mum's way as anything. The workmen are back. They watch me pacing outside. They watch Mum pacing inside. What must they be thinking?

When I finally get through the various switchboards, I am always put on hold. After holding I am immediately passed on to someone else who puts me on hold. I hold and I count. I count the red bricks beneath my feet. I count the tiles on the roof. I count and I walk and I talk and I listen.

I have had a habit of counting things for as long as I can remember. Lamp posts between my house and my best friend's down the road. Flowers on the curtains in my room. Tiles in the shower. Telegraph poles on the way to school. I count to distract myself; to calm myself. It's not working today. No one wants to be the one to offer help. With each call, feelings of panic increase. With each call I feel myself slipping further and further away from the shore. No one can help us. We are going to be left to drown.

'You've called the Tunbridge Wells number. You're in Tonbridge – you're under Sevenoaks, so you should call them.'

'Your mother's nearly seventy, in which case she'll be classed as a geriatric case. You'll need a different number.'

'You can't request a psychiatric assessment without a GP referral.'

I try butting in. I try making our case. I try to sound reasonable.

'She's seen a psychiatrist. She's had an assessment. That isn't what I'm asking for. I'm asking for help. Right now. She's raving!'

I repeat myself. Over and over.

No one is listening.

No one wants to help.

I am passed on and on and on.

I drift further and further out to sea.

Even when I say, 'This is an emergency!' The answer I receive is, 'I suggest you call 111.'

I do – and I'm given another list of numbers to try, some of which I've already called. I call the rest, 1 by 1 by 1.

Same thing.

Over and over.

I am passed on again

and again

and again.

'Your mother must be referred through her GP.'

'She has *seen* a GP. She can't wait weeks for a referral!' I decide to ramp things up. 'Mum is psychotic – she's seeing things that aren't there. She's talking nonsense and making whooping noises and pacing like a mad woman.' Actually, that is not ramping things up. That is the truth.

'Would you say that she is a danger to herself or others?'

'No, but—'

So much for the truth. It doesn't get you anywhere.

'I can only advise that you go back to the GP.'

Dead end. Back to the beginning. Square one.

I am going to have to exaggerate if I am ever going to get us out of this labyrinth.

When the next call is answered, I take a deep breath and blurt out the most shocking thing I can think about Mum's current state of mind.

'I am worried that my mother is going to do something stupid. She has already burnt her hands with caustic soda.'

A gasp. At last – a reaction. 'That's awful. I'm sorry. Let me take your details and I'll get someone to call you back as soon as possible.'

Call me back? I can feel a scream building. I can feel the urge to punch, to kick, to shout and swear. I can see now why Dad howled down the phone at me. It's tempting to hurl my mobile at the path. But then 'someone' would have no way of calling me back as soon as possible.

Why do I do as I'm told?

Why do I answer questions truthfully and wait and listen and hold and nod and do as I'm told?

Why don't I bundle Mum into the car and drive her to A&E and shout, 'Somebody do something! My mother's a lunatic!'?

Because that's not what we do in this family. We listen to the professionals. If the doctors are busy, you don't disturb them. If they tell you to wait, you do. I've been brought up not to bother doctors with trivial things and certainly not to go to A&E unless I have broken something or it is a life-or-death situation. Even in the turmoil of the past thirty-six hours, even as Mum jibbers beside me, I cannot, in all honesty, say that this is a life-or-death situation. Rules are rules. A place for everything.

I clutch my phone like a talisman. Now I am the one pacing. I'm not whooping, but I'm not breathing properly either. I'm holding my breath while I wait for calls from the mental health services, from the geriatric mental health team, from Mum's GP. *It can take a while. Don't hold your breath!*

⌒

It is afternoon before Mum's GP calls back. Dad and I have spent the hours following Mum around to make sure she doesn't do anything dangerous. We are exhausted, so when the call comes I almost sob with relief, thinking, 'Now. At last. The cavalry.'

But no.

'I'm afraid there's nothing I can do right now,' the GP says.

I can hear the weariness in her voice as she explains how hard it is to get an older patient assessed for psychiatric care.

'It's particularly difficult in your mother's case as the psychiatrist she has been seeing appears to have officially signed her off since yesterday,' she explains. 'He says there is nothing more he can do for her.'

Anger roars through my chest. That man! I have to grit my teeth and swallow to stop myself from shouting, *Signed her off? How can he do that? Does Dad know?*

Mum's words in February come back to me. *He says I will probably always be miserable.*

The bastard. He's given up.

The only consolation is that the GP now sounds as angry as I feel.

'I'm sorry,' she says. 'If all else fails, you'll have to take your mum to A&E. That's the only way to get her assessed quickly. Otherwise it could take months.'

Months!

'She needs a full medical screening to rule out the possibility of her having an infection, which might have precipitated this episode—' I make an incredulous noise but the doctor raises her voice to finish what she has to say. 'I know it's probably not the case with your mother, but some elderly people become delusional as a side-effect of a urinary tract infection.'

A fucking *what*? Nonononono. Mum does *not* have an infection. She is *insane*. This has been building for months and months, possibly *years*!

The thing is, even in the state I'm in, I know there's no point in saying this. This GP knows Mum. She knows what's wrong. She is the one who has counselled alternative therapies, relaxation techniques, CBT. None of this current situation has come as a surprise. It was a nightmare waiting to happen.

So I don't shout. I don't protest. I thank the GP and put the phone down. I tell Dad what to do and he tells Mum.

Any scrap of resistance that Dad had left has vanished. He has accepted it now: Mum needs urgent help. Damn it, *he* needs urgent help.

'Come on, Gilly,' he says. His face is drawn, determined, grim.

He bundles Mum into the car. 'No,' she says, her voice dangerously high, as though she might scream. 'No, I don't want to go.'

She holds on to the car, so that we have to prise her fingers away. We all but push her in. It's like putting one of my cats into the travel basket before going to the vet. I half expect her to snarl and spit and lash out. I hope to God no one passes by and sees this. It must look like kidnap. Or abuse. Thank goodness the workmen have gone.

She collapses into the seat and I reach across and strap her in while Dad starts up the engine. I rush around and get in the other side and Dad starts driving before Mum can try to get out.

Dad pulls out of the drive onto the road. Mum whoops, holds her breath, gasps, says over and over that she doesn't want to go. Dad ignores her. I ignore her. I stare out of the window at the park opposite our house where only a year ago Mum came for a walk with me and the children. I used to have tennis lessons in the corner of that park. Every Saturday with three of my friends. Mum used to play there too with her friends. I have a sudden image of her in pristine tennis whites, her long legs smooth and brown in an impossibly short skirt. She was very beautiful as a young woman. I wanted to look like her. Glamorous. Slim. Stunning.

I can't look at her now. I'll cry if I do. I reach out and hold her arm as she puffs and gasps and writhes in the seat. I meant the gesture to be calming, but it feels more as though I am restraining her.

Restraints.

Straitjackets.

Electric shock therapy.

What are we taking Mum to? Are we doing the right thing? What else can we do?

I can't think. I can only act. I must focus on Mum. On getting her out of the car and into the waiting room at the hospital.

Dad pulls in to the car park. He drops me and Mum at the entrance to A&E before going to find a space.

'I'll join you inside,' he says.

We both know Mum would never make it across the car park into the building without causing a huge scene. Better – for her or for us? – to bundle her in, just as we bundled her out of the house.

I hold on to Mum as we go inside. In case she slips from my grasp and skitters off. Like a cat. We wait in the lobby. I can't go up to the desk without Dad. I can't do this without Dad.

Mum is trotting on the spot again. 'I don't want to be here. I want to go home. I don't want to be in hospital. Let me go home.' She is very distressed now.

My stomach and chest are squeezed tight. A small part of my brain is saying, 'What am I doing to her? Poor Mum, poor Mum, poor Mum.' The rest of me is desperate to hand her over to someone who knows what to do with her.

Dad walks in. I can tell by his face that he has shut down. He's not looking at me and he's not speaking. I am coaxing, keeping my voice low, crooning almost.

'It's all right, Mum.'

Empty words. But I have to say something to reassure her, even if in truth I am as frightened as she is. Dad goes to the desk to explain why we are here while I take Mum to sit down. She sits for a second, then shoots up as though scalded, sits down again, whoops, stands up, lurches towards the door. I'm aware of people around us, convinced they are staring at her. At me. What do they see? A grim, badly dressed woman, her hair scraped severely from her face, holding on to an older woman and forcing her to sit. It looks bad, I know it does. Oh, let them think what the hell they like; I have to fix my attention on Mum. Her face is pale and sweaty. Her

forehead is crumpled with anxiety, her eyes wide, her mouth
pulled down.

I want to hold her – not to restrain her, to hug her. I want
to cuddle her, to smooth her hair.

I want her to shut up too.

Once, when my daughter Lucy was small, she had an asthma
attack that drained her face of colour and squeezed the air
from her lungs. It was just before Christmas. It was a dark,
dank evening. The moisture in the air made it harder for
Lucy to breathe. She was too weak to protest when I scooped
her up and put her in the car. I drove fifteen miles to our
nearest A&E, strapped her in to the buggy and told her even
smaller brother to hold tight to the buggy board behind her.
I ran with them from the car park through air white with
fog. A Salvation Army brass band was playing Christmas
carols. The warmth of brass tones from trombones, trumpets
and tubas washed over me, soothed me; carried me and my
children through the doors and on to the ward. A&E was
welcoming and the nurses were kind. We were seen quickly.
I felt cared for and reassured.

This time there is no comforting music; there is no calming
movie soundtrack to this drama.

We sit on plastic chairs as the waiting area fills with more
and more people. Dad goes to buy sandwiches. I realise we
haven't eaten since the porridge he made at breakfast. I didn't
eat that. I'm not hungry. I have a sharp pain in my stomach.
I'm thirsty, though. So thirsty. But Mum is very agitated, so
I can't leave her. I hope Dad gets some water.

'Martin? Where's Martin? Where's he gone?' Mum shouts,
looking around wildly.

'He's gone for sandwiches.'

'Martin!'

Dad comes back. He looks so tired I could cry. He hands

Mum a sandwich, murmuring softly. She rips the sandwich from the packet and bolts it so fast I'm afraid she'll be sick. I feel too sick to take one bite.

We sit.

We say nothing.

We wait.

Mum whoops and gets up and down and up and down.

Where has my real mum gone? Where is the woman who cared for me when I was sick, who sat by me and sang 'Golden slumbers kiss your eyes' when I was feverish and tearful? Where is the strong, opinionated woman whose bright-green eyes flashed with passion when discussing politics and history? Where is the mother who mopped up grazed knees and sewed on loose buttons and cuddled me?

She has gone. And, right now, I feel as though she will never come back.

Eleven

'A person with Asperger's syndrome "starts to suffer if they encounter unexpected change".'[11]

E ventually, two women come to find us.
'We're going to take your mother for a screening,' the first woman says. I glance at her blue uniform. I think she's a nurse. It's hard to tell. There are so many different coloured uniforms coming and going through this place. Blue, white, purple, red. 'We need to make sure she hasn't got an infection,' she's saying. 'Could you and your father follow my colleague, please?' She gestures to the second woman, who's wearing a white blouse and black trousers.

'I'm a mental health nurse,' the second woman says. 'You'll need to give me Mum's medical history. Then we'll go from there.'

Both women speak in a tone that is kind but brisk. Well rehearsed.

Dad and I ask no questions. We nod. We get up to follow. We do as we are told.

Mum is less compliant as she goes for her screening. She calls out, 'Martin! Martin, don't leave me! Martin! I need you, Martin!'

Dad and I turn away, heads bowed. We follow the mental health nurse as she leads us down a corridor and into a white room.

The nurse picks up a clipboard from the table next to her. 'Please.' She gestures to the chairs in front of her. 'Take a seat.' She doesn't smile. She settles herself and pulls a blue Bic out of a slot in the side of the clipboard. 'This will take some time,' she says, 'but don't worry. Gillian will be fine. She will be seen by a psychiatrist after the tests have been done. I'll take you to her when we've finished.'

I don't ask what tests Mum will have. I'm numb, waiting to be told what to do. Other people are in charge now.

The mental health nurse starts a long list of questions, most of which seem perfunctory and have very little to do with Mum's mental health. After asking a few things about how Mum is behaving, she goes on to ask when she last saw her GP, whether she has any allergies, whether she has had any problems passing urine, whether she smokes or drinks, what her living arrangements are, whether she has had any operations, whether there is any history of medical problems in her family . . .

I keep waiting for the important questions. I don't know what they will be, but I know I'll know them when I hear them. They will be the questions that will unlock the secret room: the one full of answers, full of diagnoses and relief and solutions. They will be the questions that will lead to fixing Mum. Because isn't that why we're here? To get my broken mum fixed?

Apparently not. The nurse continues to ask banal, pointless things. What does Mum eat? How does she sleep? Any recent physical ailments? The woman's quiet voice and her calm manner seem to act on Dad like a sedative. His responses are low, slow and deliberate. He stares at a point on the floor in front of him as he speaks. He answers each question as though he's taking an exam. As though it's essential that he choose his words carefully in order to give the correct answer and score the highest possible marks. He goes into great detail about what Mum has eaten recently and about how she can't take penicillin.

She doesn't need bloody antibiotics! She needs . . . she needs . . . I don't know what she needs! That's why we're here!

I don't feel we're getting any closer to the point. I should say something, butt in. But Dad is talking. He is the husband, and I am the daughter and I mustn't. Mustn't interrupt.

This room is too small. There is not enough air in it. My breath comes in short bursts, my stomach hurts so much, I'm still very thirsty, I have a headache. I want to stop this woman. There should be a sense of urgency, surely? Doctors running, stethoscopes, beeping noises, syringes. *Watch out, everyone! There's a mad woman on the loose!*

The dreary questions go on and on and on, as though we have all the time in the world. I grip the sides of my chair to stop myself from jumping up and shouting, 'I don't care about what she had for breakfast and nor should you! She is mad! SHE'S BONKERS!'

Dad continues to give long and involved answers. He has adopted his serious lawyer voice and is using complicated words to say simple things. This is what he does when he's embarrassed or stressed. He once came to my school to give a talk about his job. He was nervous and hid his nerves behind a speech that was so complicated, friends told me afterwards that they hadn't been able to understand a word. He's doing the same now.

'Gillian has been more than a little obdurate of late . . . she has not been very compliant with the medical advice we have sought . . .'

The nurse listens patiently, makes notes. Nods, murmurs to show she understands. Asks questions, questions, questions.

I am a coiled spring. I don't know how much longer I can contain myself.

Then the nurse seems suddenly to change tack. She says, 'So, it would seem that for years your wife has been showing patterns of behaviour that could be seen by some to be odd or even disturbing?'

No kidding! This is more like it.

'Oh. Do you think?' Dad seems astonished. As though he has never thought about Mum in this way before. In spite of everything John has said recently. In spite of everything Carrie and I have said in recent months. In spite of what has happened since I came down yesterday. In spite of him howling like a wounded dog.

He is silent. He looks paler. Frightened, even. He begins to speak, and the more he talks about what his life's been like with Mum since his retirement, the more he gathers momentum. The scales have begun to fall. He talks about how she won't go anywhere without him and how she didn't like him to go out alone.

'She just didn't like me doing things without her,' he says. 'She needed me with her all the time. It was exhausting.'

I bite my lip. I swallow and blink as tears threaten to spill. Dad had told me this, more than once. He had tried, I realise, to tell me how hard it was for him, looking after Mum 24/7. And what had I done about that? What had I done to help *him*? Nothing.

Nothing.

I had been too wrapped up in how Mum's increasingly control-ling and anxious behaviour was affecting *me*. I had wanted Dad to step in and sort things out for *me*. I hadn't allowed myself to think about how bad things were getting for *him*.

Two summers ago I had bought tickets for Dad and me to participate in a Big Sing at the Royal Albert Hall in London. A rare attempt at spending some time alone with Dad, without Mum at his elbow, haranguing me for not coming to see them more often. During a break in rehearsals we had gone to sit in the park opposite, near the memorial. We had been laughing and joking as we always did. Then, out of the blue – or that's how it seemed to me – Dad's face had crumpled; he had drawn his hand down over his eyes and said, 'She does nag me, you know. I don't know how much more of it I can take.'

How did I react? I know I was shocked. Embarrassed, probably. Struck dumb, at any rate. Dad never had anything negative to say about Mum. He would become defensive if anyone ever dared to point out that Mum's behaviour had been difficult or inappropriate. So where had this blurted confession come from? I was inadequate, brushing the comment away, as I would later accuse him of doing to me. Only now, now that things have reached crisis point, am I beginning to see just how much has been swept under our living room carpet. The elephant in the room, contained, caged. Out of the way, hidden from view, neat and tidy, like the linen on the shelves in the airing cupboard.

The nurse nods and writes. Nods and writes. She moves on to questions about Mum's levels of anxiety in childhood.

'Was she an anxious child?'

Dad hesitates. This is my chance. I jump straight in before I can stop to think whether I should or not. I recount the family anecdotes that have been passed down from Grandma and John about Mum's social anxiety, about her extreme stress over academic work, about huge crises of self-doubt, self-loathing.

'She would constantly berate herself for being stupid, then spend hours locked away, reading and ignoring everyone. And she was convinced she was fat, even when she was stick-thin and model-pretty. Grandma told me once that Mum would wash the skin off sausages before allowing them to be cooked. And when we were small she would go on diets of hard-boiled eggs and black coffee.'

Dad says nothing, either to elaborate or to contradict me. Now that I've started, I can't stop. The nurse writes everything down. I tell her about the time Mum threw herself into the sea as a child. It's a story that used to be repeated as though it were nothing, a snippet, a mere memory of something that couldn't be helped. Funny, even. But then one day I asked John what that day was really like, and he told me.

'Mum was about twelve,' I tell the nurse. 'Her mum – my grandmother – had taken her and her younger brother John to visit their aunt by the sea in north Kent. One afternoon they went for a walk along the pier. John says Mum was in one of her moods and that Grandma had thought some fresh air would help to calm her down.'

I glance at Dad, but he's still staring at the floor. Is he angry with me for saying all this? Too bad; I have to. It's not the funny story we had all been led to believe for so long. And it's urgent that everyone hears it now, knows it for what it is.

'John says that the three of them sat down on a bench,' I say, 'then suddenly, for no reason, Mum had an outburst about something and just ran off. John says the next thing he remembers was hearing her crying for help. Her voice was coming from over the edge of the pier. John was only eight, but he says he remembers that he was the one that got up and tried to find his sister. He can't remember what Grandma did. He says he could see there was a flight of stone steps to the beach and that Mum's voice was becoming more and more distressed. He ran to the top of the steps, looked down and saw his sister, by some rocks. He reckoned she must have fallen from these because she was struggling in the water, slipping and sliding, losing her footing, and grabbing helplessly at the rocks. John ran down the steps, and got close enough to hold out a hand. Grandma had followed him and she grabbed his other arm while John pulled at Mum. They hauled her out, crying. I remember John said to me that the weirdest thing was that Mum never seemed sorry for what she had put everyone through. When John asked her why she had done it, she said it wouldn't have happened if their mother had been nicer to her that day.'

As I tell the story I hear myself saying the words. This familiar story now reveals itself for what it really was. And it's because of the way the nurse is looking at me. She has stopped writing for a moment. She's doing her best to keep her face blank, but I've already clocked the shock in a flex of her shoulders, a tightening of her mouth.

It's nuts, isn't it? To do that? To throw yourself, wilfully, into a raging sea? In front of your kid brother?

Still Dad says nothing.

The nurse finishes writing it all down. Methodical. Solemn.

'What about postnatal depression?' she asks next.

Hell, yeah. I am on a roll now. Bring it on. Ask me more. I can do this. I can't stop Mum going mad, but I can do this. At last someone is listening. Someone is taking all this seriously. We're getting somewhere.

Yet, at the same time as I feel elated, I feel hollow. Where is this 'somewhere'? Where am I leading Mum to next? Will we have to leave her here? Will Dad ever forgive me for saying all this about Mum? To a stranger who is writing it all down?

'Yes, she did have postnatal depression,' I say.

Dad doesn't disagree, although he has never ever referred

to Mum's behaviour after I was born as 'postnatal depression'. It wasn't ever called that. Just another anecdote, that's all. Never examined or explained.

'Mum told me, "When you were born, I didn't know what to do with you." She told me she was terrified.'

She had told me this after Lucy was born. My first baby. She told me as though to reassure me, 'It's OK. We all feel scared witless after giving birth.' I know now that many of my friends didn't feel that at all. They felt ecstatic. Overjoyed.

I was none of these things. I was terrified, just as Mum had been. I had been in labour for thirty-six hours, was exhausted. All I wanted was for my mum to put her arms around me and tell me it would be all right. She didn't do anything of the sort. A few hours after Lucy was born, Mum rushed onto the ward and grabbed my baby and held her to her chest. She didn't look at me, didn't ask me how I was, didn't kiss me, hug me, say 'Congratulations'. She didn't say a word to me. Just clutched at Lucy and said, 'Thank God, she's all right!'

She had been convinced that I would die in childbirth or lose Lucy because the labour was so long and complicated and Lucy was already two weeks late. I know now that Mum's behaviour was about fear, but I realised that much too late to be able to empathise. At the time I took her aggressive phone calls when I was in labour as an unwanted intrusion. I told her to leave me alone. And when she wouldn't look at me when she came to the hospital – I hated her.

But seeing me, pale, worn out, fearful; I suppose it must have brought back all the horrors of what it had been like, giving birth to me.

'She was so terrified when she had me,' I tell the nurse, 'that the doctor had to sedate her and I was handed straight to my grandmother.'

The nurse flinches. Dad says nothing, stares at the floor. I have betrayed Mum, telling this story. I shiver. A small voice whispers: *She handed you over, the minute you were born. What does that mean?*

I push the voice away and force myself to listen to more of the nurse's questions.

'And was she anxious with you and your sister when you were young children?'

The nurse has given up on getting answers from Dad. She is looking at me with a very level gaze.

I nod. I answer, I hear myself talk as though someone else is speaking. I feel suddenly so weary. It's too much, this vomiting up of the past. I had wanted this, I know; to be heard, to be validated. To be believed. But do I really have to go through every detail? Haven't I said enough? There are too many stories. Too many ways to betray my mum. To upset my dad. Too many rules from childhood and too many mantras to relate and explain.

Don't go to bed with your hair wet. Always wear a vest. Don't eat eggs unless they are cooked all the way through. Call me when you get there. Call me when you are about to leave. Sit still. Be quiet. Tidy up. No wet towels. No marks on the wall. Go to your room.

Mum in a heap at the bottom of the stairs, her ankle swollen from falling. *You'll be a good girl and look after Mummy, won't you? You're naughty. I'm taking you to Grandma's. I can't cope. Bloody kids, bloody kids, bloody, bloody, bloody kids.* And that poem she would quote at me when I had been naughty – about the girl with the curl who 'when she was good she was very, very good, and when she was bad, she was horrid'. *You are being bad right now, Anna. Bad and horrid. A horrid little girl.*

I want to leave. I want to go home and pull the duvet over

my head and sleep and sleep and never have to answer another question or have anything to do with Mum ever again.

'Would you say that anything had precipitated this recent change in Gillian's behaviour?' the nurse is asking now.

I glance at Dad. No? OK . . .

'I think it started with her mother – my grandmother – dying,' I say. 'That was about five years ago. Two thousand and eight. Grandma was her support system. Mum's behaviour became very aggressive when Grandma was dying. Then her sister-in-law died unexpectedly, very soon after Grandma. And then shortly after that Mum became fixated on the idea that she might have prolapse.'

The nurse is not saying anything any more. She is writing, writing, writing. I plough on.

'Mum was advised not to have the operation for prolapse, but she went ahead anyway. Her anxiety levels definitely increased after that operation.'

Can we go now? Please? I have gone over this so many times with Dad and Carrie already. We tried to get Dad to talk Mum out of that operation when it was clear that the consultant didn't want her to have it and when my cousin Gemma had advised her against it as well. Dad had resolutely taken Mum's side. Afterwards, when Mum's anxieties escalated over non-existent infections and then problems with sleep, both Carrie and I tried to tell Dad that Mum was sliding down. He did then take her to the private psychiatrist, admittedly, but even then he would not use the words 'mental health' or 'depression' or 'anxiety'. Three elephants clogging up every room we walked into.

The woman stops writing at last and looks up. 'Has she ever been violent?'

The question bolts through me. A crack of blue light. I don't dare glance at Dad. I stare down at my hands. I see

the red and white marks left around my wrists after Mum
has stopped shaking me. I see the bruise of blue ink on the
bedroom carpet. Please no. Not the carpet. Don't make me
talk about that now. Not in front of Dad.

'Well,' Dad says slowly. 'There was that time with the
carving knife.'

I snap upright and look at him, then at the nurse. He's not
going to tell her about that? Now? But he always thought it
was funny. Didn't he?

The nurse is holding Dad's gaze.

Dad gives a small sigh. 'It was Christmas. I gave Gilly two
unusually shaped presents . . .' he begins.

I can see it now. His little-boy excitement as he handed
them over. Mum's beaming face. Dad was notoriously 'bad
at presents', but this time it looked as though he had come
up trumps.

Mum was giddy as she took the gifts. 'Oooh, this one looks
like a bottle of liqueur,' she had said, examining a long-necked
parcel with the bulbous end. 'And this one – I have no idea
. . .' She ran her hand along a long, thin, carefully wrapped
package.

Dad had looked so pleased with himself. 'I think you'll
find them both very useful,' he'd said, as Mum had unwrapped
first a sink plunger and then an electric carving knife.

Even before Mum's expression had changed, Carrie and I
were concentrating on doing our invisible act. We were both
very young, but we both knew that these were not good
presents. Not good at all. And when things were not good,
Mum got angry.

For a beat Mum stood there, holding the knife and staring
at it.

Her face hardened into the glinting mask of fury we knew
so well. Her green eyes flashed, she bared her teeth, she

snarled, 'A sink plunger?' Then she roared, 'And a CARVING KNIFE?'

She rushed him. An implement in each hand.

Did we scream?

Did we jump up to try to stop her?

I don't think so. I can't remember. All I can remember is that face and the knife and Dad looking shocked.

Probably we shrank back and stayed

very

very

still.

We were good at that.

Dad was strong. He must have moved fast, grabbing Mum's wrists as she often did mine. He got the knife off her, I do know that. I can't remember what happened next. I can't remember what happened to the plunger either.

The knife was used to carve meat at family get-togethers for years after, and often the story would be told with laughter and jokes and 'do you remember's?

Dad isn't laughing now. He is telling the story slowly and deliberately. He gets to the part where Mum is wielding the knife, then he sees the look on the nurse's face and stops. She clears her throat and looks down at her clipboard and resumes writing.

At last the questions are finished. We leave the room in silence and go to meet up with Mum. As we close the door behind us, Dad turns to me and says quietly, 'I think maybe we will have to find a private home for Mum.'

I have never seen anyone look so defeated.

Twelve

'A girl with Asperger's syndrome is . . . more likely than boys to develop a close friendship with someone who demonstrates a maternal attachment to this socially naïve but "safe" girl.'[12]

'**W**hat's wrong with Mum?'

In early adulthood I would call my grandmother to ask her this. So many times. After fights. After tears. After shouting and recrimination and frustration and arguments repeated word for word for word. On a loop.

Exhausting.

'I don't know.' Grandma would sigh, exhausted herself. 'She's always been like this. You just have to forgive her.'

For 'like this' read: 'anxious', 'nagging', 'demanding', 'impulsive' – and, yes, sometimes violent too.

But that was the thing – she hadn't 'always' been like that to me. If you'd have asked the child me what I thought, I might have been able to articulate that she had been unpredictable and that, yes, I was a little frightened of her, but only to the extent that I knew I wanted to please her. And so many adults were frightening anyway – my head teacher, my piano teacher, the vicar at Sunday school. They existed in another realm. They were Authority. They were not to be crossed. Mum was just another one of Them.

I never once, as a child, thought of asking, 'Why is Mum like this?' Was it that I only noticed more now that I had left home and knew other mothers with whom to compare her? Or was it that I was the problem; that now I was an adult and less predictable – less controllable myself – that Mum found me difficult?

Yet Grandma would describe Mum as 'difficult' to the adult me. And I began to notice how she had her ways of containing her eldest child, and that mostly they were successful. Sometimes she would deliver a low 'Gillian', almost as a growl. Even as a young adult I would be impressed by the immediate effect this would have. Mum would stop, in mid-rant, when Grandma did this. A reflex from childhood, presumably; she would stop and make a little grumbling noise, flick her shoulders irritably and settle again.

Other times when Mum's mood was low, rather than volatile, Grandma would resort to treats – days out, new clothes, a trip to a café (deemed as extravagant, but worth it to appease Mum). Grandma had years and years of experience in managing Mum. I didn't appreciate it when I was younger.

If ever I tried to talk to Dad about Mum's moods, he used to say affectionately, 'She is like a cat.' Her moods were certainly feline in their unpredictability. One minute she would be still, content, smiling, affectionate, stretching and basking in a ray of sunlight; the next she could lash out, and you weren't always sure what you had done to deserve it. Sometimes there were warning signs: a change of expression as quick as the twitch of a cat's tail. Sometimes there was nothing, not a hair's breadth, between the smile and the snarl.

Mum would occasionally refer to herself as a cat. She would

say, 'I have green, jealous eyes – cat's eyes.' A cat – Ink – was
the only pet of ours that Mum gave her blessing to. 'She's
my familiar,' Mum would joke. Now that Mum is resisting
taking her numerous drugs in pill form, Dad says, 'It's like
when I had to give Ink her medication – I swear Mum hides
the pills in her cheek just as Ink used to do.'

Mum was a loner, like a cat too. She preferred one-to-one
conversations, shunning big groups unless Dad or Grandma
were by her side. She was at home with family, but often
prickly outside the nest. She was a house cat who liked the
security of her own four walls and the people who inhabited
them. She would say, 'Family comes first. Friends will always
let you down, but family will always be there.' She increasingly clung to Dad in social situations as she got older. 'People
like your father,' she used to say, with a hint of sadness. 'He's
the funny one, the one who tells jokes and stories.' And, 'He
looks after me, your dad.'

And she and Dad made one another very happy. They had
met during their first year at university and had quickly
become, in the words of more than one friend, 'a golden
couple'. Their relationship was one my sister and I came to
revere, as – I discovered in later life – did many of their
friends. It was not uncommon to find Mum and Dad locked
in a tender embrace. Mum would frequently say, 'I don't
know what I would do without your dad.' Dad would gaze
into Mum's eyes and call her his 'Gillyflower'. For years I
believed every marriage was this intense and self-reflecting.
A match made in heaven. Fairy-tale perfection. Happily ever
after.

When I was expecting Lucy, I had a glimpse of the early
days of their romance. I had gone back to my childhood
home – 'for a rest'– but Mum didn't know how to look after
a pregnant daughter, other than to worry and displace her

fears surrounding pregnancy by obsessing over other things. One rainy day, she would not stop fretting over the fact that there were still piles of my belongings in my childhood home.

'You need to decide what to do with them,' she said. 'You've got your own home now. I can't keep that stuff for ever. I want you to take everything back with you or throw it away.'

This was how I found myself on a dark, blustery December afternoon in 1998, crouched, eight months pregnant, in the loft of my parents' house, sifting through boxes and bags and old suitcases.

I had always hated the loft space, mainly because of Mum telling me and Carrie as children that, if we went up there, we would fall through the floorboards, onto the soft insulation, through the ceiling of the room below and die. I hated the ladder – the rattling metallic announcement it made as it came catapulting down from the hatch. I hated the way that every noise was distorted up there, so that voices from the road outside could sound as though they were somewhere much nearer, lurking in the rafters with me. I hated the smell: the fusty, dusty, mildewed smell of old cloth and paper. I hated the dark and the piles and piles of stuff, thrown up there, willy-nilly – a graveyard of possessions.

This time, though, the graveyard revealed itself to be a treasure trove. The things up here were not only mine: here, in old trunks and cases and files, were remnants of my mother's experience of being an excited and fearful first-time parent too. I pulled out a tiny, moth-eaten, hand-knitted cardigan, a smocked Viyella dress, a teething ring and a plastic bag full of cards congratulating my parents on my birth. I thought of the items I was now amassing in preparation for my own daughter's arrival. Would I be hoarding them in twenty, thirty years' time? I marvelled at Mum's decision to keep these things; for they were things she, not I, had decided to keep. I had never had her down as a sentimental woman – emotional, yes, but not soppy about objects, certainly not objects connected with me. After all, hadn't she just spent the past couple of days telling me to get rid of all my childhood possessions?

While I was sorting through my old toys and clothes and school books, I began to get leg cramps and sat down heavily on a grey metal-framed suitcase. There was a crunching sound, and I looked down to find that I had crushed the case under the weight of my advancing pregnancy. Paper was spewing from its sides, like jam oozing from a doughnut. I pushed myself up, tried to shove the contents back inside – then stopped.

The paper was in fact envelopes: hundreds of them. I shone the torch I had with me on to my dad's immediately recognisable italic hand. Mum's equally inimitable scrawl was on the rest. I knew what these envelopes were, of course. Knew I shouldn't open them. I couldn't do it, could I? Read those words while my parents were, at that moment, downstairs watching TV, drinking coffee, waiting for me. And yet here I was, at my mother's command, holding in my hands her and Dad's youthful promises of love and devotion. It would have been wrong, to start sifting through their intimate words, written under the assumption that they were for their eyes only. Wouldn't it?

In the end, the temptation was too great. I started reading. They would never know.

$\sim$

I have all these letters in my possession now. I have taken them from the suitcase and organised them so that I can read them in the order in which they were sent. There are letters for almost every day from May 1963 to July 1966. Almost three whole years of conversation – conversation that normally would be lost to the tides of time. Among the records are the minutiae of a life that had to be planned in pen and ink and not down a phone line or via the worldwide web or cursory texts or Snapchats with emojis and GIFs. Details of train times and plans for weekends are noted alongside tentative dips into the waters of romance. These quickly develop into full-blown love letters when Mum asks Dad to write to her in Latin. Soon he is calling her 'O lux et vita mea': Oh, my light and my life.

This shared knowledge of the Classics was a deep bond, undoubtedly one of the reasons they fell in love. They met while performing in a Greek play. As kids, Carrie and I found the whole thing embarrassing, especially when Latin and Greek would be regularly quoted. We felt barred too, kept out of these private, coded conversations. It was weird, wasn't it? Having parents who spoke dead languages that no one else understood?

Our only entrance into this mysterious world was through Dad's bedtime retellings of Greek myths. Whether the story was of Persephone, trapped in the Underworld with wicked Hades after giving in to the temptation of six pomegranate seeds, or strong, courageous Heracles, forced to perform twelve impossible labours, or Odysseus, hiding his men inside a giant wooden horse to trick the Trojans, or poor, chatterbox Echo who fell in love with the beautiful Narcissus but was doomed only to repeat the words he called out and so never met him – all these stories found their way into our DNA, despite our resistance.

Those letters, though: they offer me more than an insight into a shared obsession. They show me just how deeply Dad

understood Mum and how much they had in common: this
unlikely coupling of the serious, anxious young woman with
the funny, calm and kind young man. They adored one
another. Still do. Oh, my light and my life.

Until very recently they were still taking holidays in their
beloved Italy. They were taking conversation classes too, so
that they could embarrass us in Italian as well as Latin and
Greek. They had set their satnav to Italian, programming it
for even the shortest, well-known journey just so that they
could hear 'Giovanni' advising them, *'Girare a destra'* in his
dulcet tones.

Dad *got* Mum from the start. The letters prove it. Mum
asks for Dad's 'adoration' very early on. She tells him, 'I need
to be cherished'. So perhaps there had been warnings of
what he was getting into. She is open and honest in her
letters about how terrified she is of losing him, this young
man who is everything she's not: steady, in control, confident.
She tells him, 'I feel safe in your arms', and when she writes
a scrawled, high-octane letter, full of panic about exams or
travel arrangements or not knowing what to wear to a party,
Dad always replies in a measured, loving way. 'I am here for
you', he tells her, over and over. 'I am yours. I will never let
you down.'

Mum could be anxious and 'difficult', yes. But that is not
the whole story; she could also be beautiful and funny and
intelligent and loving, and Dad saw all that. He was her rock,
just as much as Grandma was. Her close friend and companion.
Her other half. These are important things for me and the
rest of the family to hold on to, now that Mum is so – so
other – so hard to reach. And so frightening.

These are not the things, however, that a mental health
nurse notes down when taking a person's medical history.
Not the things that count when trying to find a diagnosis – a

label to peel back and stick firmly in place so that everyone knows, once and for all, what is 'wrong' with you.

Oh, my light and my life. What would Mum be without Dad?

Thirteen

'Anti-depressants such as fluoxetine (Prozac) have been used to reduce repetitive behaviour. But there are concerns about the use of these drugs . . . because of the side effects (such as agitation) . . . anti-psychotic drugs . . . have also been used as a treatment for irritability and hyperactivity in autism or Asperger Syndrome but again carry risks of side effects (such as mood swings).'[13]

Dad and I are now reunited with Mum, who is being seen by a consultant psychiatrist. I can't help noticing how young and handsome he is. *What am I thinking?* I look away, telling myself to get a grip. It's just such a relief to look at something beautiful.

The consultant takes us through a new regime of drugs and explains that citalopram, the anti-depressant that Mum was prescribed, should be taken in the morning, not at night as her previous psychiatrist had instructed.

'It has the side-effect of waking you up,' he explains, 'hence your mother's agitation at night. I have already explained this to her.'

I look at Mum, who is breathing shallowly and staring

ahead. I can't believe that she has taken in a word of what the doctor has told her.

'She should also stick with the citalopram for at least six months,' he is saying, 'and not give up after one week as she has been previously advised.'

My head fills with red-hot curses. That bloody psychiatrist! Signing her off with an incorrect prescription! That idiot! That bastard!

I say nothing, however. I try to focus on what we're being told, while repeating to myself over and over, *Please say you'll keep her in hospital. Please don't send her home with us. Please. Please.*

'I'm going to give Gillian olanzapine for her psychosis,' the psychiatrist is saying.

Psychosis! He has said the word. He sees this for what it is. At last. Not a urinary tract infection, then? Surely psychosis is serious enough to keep Mum in?

I know, even as I hope this, that it won't happen. We are in A&E. You only get admitted if it's a case of life or death. Mum has us. And she's not dying.

'A mental health team from Maidstone will come to the house every day to monitor her progress,' the doctor says. 'They'll be able to keep an eye on how you're coping as well, Martin,' he tells Dad.

Mum says nothing. The psychiatrist is no longer looking at or speaking to her. He is directing all his comments to me and Dad. It is clear we are responsible. We always have been. It was folly to think that anyone else would take the baton from us. There is no magic wand. No miracle cure. We have to take her home with us. But, still – a team! A whole team, dedicated to Mum!

Dad looks hopeful. 'That's wonderful. Thank you,' he says.

We'll have to wait for them to visit, though. And in the

meantime we still have an extremely distressed woman on our hands. Mum has found the ordeal of the tests and the questioning too much. On the way back to the car she is agitated again, trotting, whooping, panting, drawing unwanted stares as she did when we arrived. It's only two o'clock and we still have the rest of this day to get through.

Mum is not allowed to start some of the new drugs until 9 p.m. When we get home, Dad and I resort to what all stressed-out parents do when caring for a wired and noisy child – we put the telly on. We find a documentary about British sketch shows, which includes clips from *The Two Ronnies*, *Monty Python*, *Not the Nine O'Clock News*, *Fry and Laurie*. I know Dad is thinking what I'm thinking; how, thirty years ago, we sat on the same sofa and watched these same shows together, Dad and I hooting with laughter, Mum not understanding the humour and having to have the jokes explained. No one is laughing now.

At long last it's time for the life-saving pills. I'm not letting myself think of the implication of chucking so many highly potent chemicals down my mother's throat. I just cling to the idea of her falling asleep.

Dad and I tuck her into bed, and I send Dad downstairs for a glass of wine and a break as I sit with Mum, stroking her hand. I find myself wanting to sing the only song she ever sang to me when I was small: 'Golden Slumbers'. I contemplate reading to her. She didn't like reading us bedtime stories. She didn't really like stories – didn't see the point of them. 'I prefer facts,' she used to say. Dad was the storyteller, the crooner, recounting tales by heart, remembering the words to every Beatles song, every folk song and nursery rhyme and poem.

Before I can test the tune of the lullaby to see if I can manage to sing without crying, Mum is asleep, snoring gently. I leave her to go back downstairs and sink a glass of wine with Dad. Our own drug of choice.

Fourteen

'*Anything that occurs in an unpredictable way is likely to throw the person [with AS] into a panic and may trigger a withdrawal or an avoidance, or a desperate attempt to re-establish predict-ability by imposing a fixed pattern or sequence of behaviour.*'14

I have to get Tom and his friends to the other side of town. I've been in hospital but he needs me to take them. I can't drive. We set off on the bus. I'm wearing a dressing gown with dirty, frayed cuffs and a flappy belt, which keeps getting in the way. I clutch the gown to me, worried it will fly open and reveal the fact I'm wearing nothing underneath. The bus speeds along. I look out of the window. I don't recognise the roads. We are too far out of town and will have to walk a long way to get home. I leave the boys to head back and find myself lost, wandering along the canal. I am in Amsterdam now. I need to find the boys. Where did I leave them? I walk and walk until I am climbing a steep paved path, which takes me to the castle walls in my home town in Kent. I climb until I reach the ramparts. I look down. Can I spot the boys? I am standing on a cliff edge. My dog is at my feet. I can't get over the cliff and down the other side to where the boys are. I look up. And up.

The cliff climbs behind me. I know what I must do. I must scale the cliff's sheer side to make it to the top. Then I'll be able to see the boys. A friend appears at my side, urging me on. It's the same friend who has been texting me recently, telling me to 'hang on in there'. She gives me a leg up. I scramble my way to the summit. I look down. I still can't see the boys. 'I may as well jump,' I think. 'I'm probably going to die anyway.'

⁓

I wake up. In a cold sweat. Again. I call my husband, who really is in Amsterdam, and tell him my dream, and he gives a hollow laugh. 'God, your dreams are transparent,' he says.

I drift back to sleep, hoping, praying, that the drugs will have produced a magical cure overnight.

Of course they haven't. How long did the psychiatrist say Mum had to stay on the anti-depressant? Six months at least.

Mum is pacing and talking and whooping from the moment she wakes. She knows that I will be leaving later today to get back to Lucy and Tom, who are being looked after by my in-laws. Is this why she comes into my room at 7.30 a.m.?

'Time to get up,' she says in an expressionless mumble.

I sit up, irritated. She was never a mother to allow her teenage children to lie in, but this is ridiculous. I am in my mid-forties; I have had an exhausting couple of days and nightmare-riddled nights, looking after her. And now she wants me to get up on the dot of seven thirty?

'Mum, can you leave me alone for a bit? I've got a long drive ahead of me.'

Mum's face floods with panic. 'No,' she says. 'No!'

I shouldn't have said it was a long drive. She gets anxious about me driving on the motorway, because she gets – got

– anxious driving on the motorway herself. She also gets anxious about how far away I live. She often tries to prevent me from leaving altogether. In the past she has become aggressive in the hours before I have to leave her house. Not today, though.

'I want to strip the bed,' she says, her voice a monotone, the panic suddenly gone. 'Get up – I need to get the sheets in the wash.'

I stumble out from under the duvet, grumbling that she's got all day to do that. I immediately chastise myself for being moody when Mum is so ill.

'Why don't you let me do the laundry, Mum?' I say. I am forcing myself to sound kind. 'Your hand is still bandaged.'

She's not having any of it; the sheets and duvet cover and pillowcases are wrestled from me and she trit-trots off at speed; a puppy, determined not to let me take a bone from its jaws.

∽

In the end, doing the laundry is the only thing that calms her down – and keeps her away from Dad, who looks close to collapse again by lunchtime.

As soon as the linen is almost dry, Mums wants to iron everything. I don't want to let her handle a steaming hot iron. Her hands are shaking. She's still bandaged from the burns she gave herself trying to clean the oven.

She is insistent, however, and I relent. Ironing has always been a pastime Mum enjoys. I have never been able to understand it, personally, finding it pointless, mind-numbing and a waste of time.

'Help me fold the sheet,' Mum says.

We take two corners each, moving to and fro, partners in

a strange sort of country dance, touching the corners of the sheet together, taking up the bottom edge, moving apart, touching the corners together again.

It reminds me of the barn dances we used to go to as a family, and the one at my wedding. All ages joining in, Grandma in her eighties, dancing with my old school friends, the caller encouraging us to turn our backs to each other in a 'do-si-do'. Mum on Valium and champagne, dancing and smiling, and smiling and smiling.

Mum lays the sheet on the ironing board, smoothing it out. She starts to iron. I watch the flex like a hawk lest she trip on it or get it caught around her wrist.

I needn't worry, though. The minute Mum begins to sweep the iron over the sheet, it is as though a spell is cast. With the rhythm of the movement there is a transformation; as she concentrates, she calms. The iron goes back and forth, back and forth, and she is concentrated on its every move. She is no longer trotting, no longer making strange noises. She is not panicking over anything, has forgotten about the noise the fridge is or isn't making. She seems even to have forgotten I am there. Her breathing has softened and deepened and become more regular, almost in time with the ebb and flow of her hand. Mum's focus is entirely on the task, she is present, in the moment, even – is this possible? – enjoying herself. Mindful ironing. Who knew?

Mum's airing cupboard. A constant source of jokes and frustration for me and Carrie. Even now. Until the day I met my husband I had thought it was the case in everyone's house that the mother ruled the airing cupboard. Our mother made sure she ruled hers with her shelves of perfect laundry: sheets folded and smoothed to crisp perfection; shirts as neat as the day they had emerged from their packaging; pants and socks as sharp and fresh as the day they'd been bought.

Her airing cupboard has a system and it is a system only she can control. She does this by keeping everything inside neat – and by keeping everything and everyone else out. As teenagers, we would open the door quietly, slowly, so as not to alert her as we fished out a favourite top for a party. We rarely got away with it. She would notice that something had gone and that barked phrase – 'No rootling!' – would explode up the stairs.

Dad used to tease her with one of the many folksongs he knew by heart.

. . . And there I saw my darling!
She looked so neat and charming
in every high degree.
Dashing away with the smoothing iron!
She stole my heart away . . .
'Oh, go away, Martin!'

He would grab her around the waist and steal a kiss, even as she scowled. No interruption was welcome while Mum was concentrating, especially when concentrating on ironing.

~

Mum's brow smooths along with the linen. This laundry-control is part and parcel of a larger system: one Mum has tried all her life to construct in order to control life in general. A system that is now falling apart altogether as Mum's hold on rationality slips. Those cracks in the wall. The noise of the fridge. The rumpled linen. Order must be imposed on disorder.

Until disorder is everywhere and all that is left for you to hold on to is the soft hiss of an iron.

It's soothing. Hypnotic, even. I have fallen under the spell myself.

But then Mum finds a tiny needle-sized nick in one of the sheets, and the trance is broken.

'Look! A hole! Oh, no. What am I going to do? A hole! The house is filthy – can't you see? And there are cracks in the walls! I'm useless, useless, useless . . .' Her face crumples. She is off on her loop of worries.

'Mum, it's OK, let's fold the sheet over and you can iron the other side.'

I manage to bring her focus back for a few moments, but the damage has been done. Now that Mum has lost concentration on the physical task in hand, she is back to panicking and obsessing again. Off she goes, trotting to the kitchen, panting, calling for Dad, listening to the fridge, making me listen to it, trying to convince me.

'It's broken, can't you hear, can't you see? BROKEN!'

Yes, I do see. I see what it is you are saying. I understand, I do.

But it's not the fridge that is broken, poor Mum. It's you.

Fifteen

'When [anxiety] is at a high level the [person] may need to burn it off. This can be done by going for a run or doing some other high energy exercise [. . .] If [she] starts to get stressed and begins repeating things or gets stuck doing a routine, gently divert her attention.'[15]

In the end I take her out – force her out – for a walk around the park over the road.

'Let's get some fresh air.'

There I go, mothering Mother again.

I used to take Lucy and Tom and the dog over the road to get some air. Usually when they had become 'too raucous' and Mum could no longer bear 'the noise and the jumping and the dirty paws and the hair on the carpet!'

Neither my dog nor my kids have so much of that excess energy any more. But I can't let myself think of them – of the fact that I should be exercising my dog down by the canal back home then rushing to pick up the children from school, hugging them, hearing about their day, carrying their bags to the car, going back home again, to my home, to my own chaotic life.

I can't help thinking of them, though. I should be there, not here. I shouldn't be walking around and around a patch of grass with my manic mother. Jogging, actually. Mum is walking so fast. She's seeing things that aren't there. She's talking and talking all the while, telling me she doesn't want to be outside, she wants to go back home, but the walls are cracking up in there, haven't I seen? The wallpaper is moving.

'Look up, Mum,' I say at one point, in a bid to distract her. 'Look up at the sky, at the clouds.'

'I will lift up mine eyes unto the hills,' she says, her unfocused gaze flitting to the clouds.

From whence cometh my help, I finish the verse automatically in my head.

What is this? My mother, quoting scripture? This is new.

Mum turns on me, wild-eyed. 'I have cried out to God, you know. He won't listen. Sometimes I think I see him in you.'

I don't know what to say to this. In the past the mere mention of religion has been enough to spark an apoplexy of anger in Mum. *How can you believe? What has God ever done for me? He wasn't there when my father died! He's never been there! He doesn't exist.*

'Don't abandon me, Anna!' she cries out suddenly, her eyes liquid with fear.

Lord, do not forsake me.

Do not be far from me, my God.

I'm crying now and trying to hold her while she pleads with me not to leave her. I make promises I can't keep. I say I won't leave, knowing full well I must. My children need me; although right now I doubt they need me as much as Mum does. I tell her that if God is here he's in her too, that he's in the washing of her hair, the ironing of her sheets. I don't know what I'm saying any more. I certainly don't know what I believe in any more. Maybe I am going around the twist as well.

∽

We don't last more than a couple of laps of the small park. We go back inside to find Dad preparing an elaborate lunch. He loves to do this. He likes to spend all day prepping food for a meal if he can. He loves spending time on things in general. He is a thoughtful, slow, methodical, meticulous person. This is no doubt why he was such a good lawyer, such a precise translator of Classical texts. I see him pottering and am about to stop him, to tell him Mum is delusional, that he shouldn't be wasting time like this.

Then I see that in the split second between him looking down, half-smiling, at a marinade, and us entering the room, any pleasure he was experiencing has vanished. I feel a hot rush of shame for snatching this moment away from him. He has not been able to spend time on anything for himself for a while. And Mum is not about to allow him to do so now.

'Martin! Martin!' Mum is rushing at him, plucking at his sleeve, begging him to stop cooking. But to do what instead? It's not clear.

'Dad, I think maybe you should let me cook,' I offer.

He sighs, nods, steps away from the chopping board and the bowls of ingredients. Goes to Mum with a small smile and soft words, approaching her as though she were a frightened animal.

I take over the preparations. And instantly know that I have done the wrong thing. I should have been the one to take Mum away. I should have allowed Dad to cook. To spend all day doing it if necessary. He needed this.

I shake the thought away and tell myself crossly that what

Dad *needs* is to rethink daily life. He needs to get ready meals in. He needs to put all his focus on to getting Mum professional care. He needs to stop fiddling while all around him blazes and rages and burns to the ground.

Then I think that what I need is to stop trying to tell my father what to do.

⁓

The nurse from the mental health team arrives on the stroke of five, a trouser-suited fairy godmother, just as Dad and I have given up hope of the promise of her appearance ever being fulfilled.

The next forty-five minutes are the calmest we have experienced since I arrived – even calmer than the ironing session. The nurse, Sam, talks softly and slowly, gently tackling Mum's anxieties about the house head on, asking her what her concerns are. She says it's good we've been for a walk.

'Try to do this at least once a day,' she says.

Her voice is so low and quiet that I feel my heart rate settle for the first time in days and watch in wonder as Mum smiles for the first time in months – years, it seems. And with that smile, some of her youthful beauty shines through.

Mum looks at Dad while Sam talks. She has such love in her eyes that it breaks my heart. He gazes back at her with equal tenderness, with the same world-excluding focus they used to have, before this nightmare took hold. Everything will be all right. Mummy and Daddy still love one another.

I thank the nurse and say goodbye to Mum and Dad before starting the long drive back to Wiltshire. Back to reality, back to the safe shores of family life. Back to sanity.

Sixteen

'The family are all too aware of quick mood changes, especially sudden rage, and try not to antagonise the person, due to fear of the intense emotional reaction.'[16]

When Carrie and I were young, Mum's need for a calm, ordered, structured life was a good thing. Most of the time. The routine way in which she led us through our early years was reassuring and confidence-giving. Everything had its place and Mum's chosen place was at home, waiting for us after school with tea and a clean space in which to sit and do homework.

She was strict about homework – it had to be done before television or reading or piano practice. But I welcomed this routine and her interest in my work. I wanted nothing more than to please her by trotting out a perfect column of spellings. She would test us every week, making us sit and write out the words in my grandfather's old desk diaries in which I later started to write my first stories. If we got one word wrong, we were to copy it out correctly three times. If we kept getting it wrong, we were 'care-*less*', the displeasure meted out in those two hard syllables.

I revelled in her hard-won approval when I read out long words correctly or recited a times table perfectly or learnt some poetry by heart. I loved to see her smile when I mastered a new piece on the piano or could say a new word in French or when I won a handwriting competition or first prize at the end of the school year. She was my lodestone. She was the yardstick by which I measured my own achievements, my own sense of self-worth. I had to work to earn her praise, as it was something Mum struggled with. She would often couch it in terms of 'could do better'.

And more often than not, we couldn't. There would be something we did – or did not do – that would set Mum off. Sometimes unintentionally, sometimes deliberately. Even the most nauseating of teacher's pets can have enough of playing the 'good child' day in, day out.

In any case, all children are capable of pushing the wrong buttons. It is in the natural way of things to test a parent or carer. It's how we learn to break free, to grow up, to learn how to navigate the world for ourselves.

It's just a shame it wasn't Mum's way to allow this to happen. It was too scary for her to see us make mistakes, or break the rules; to bring disorder into her home. If we did, then something would happen to us, something terrible. She would lose us forever and it would break her heart. And so we kept coming back, we kept accepting apologies for the screaming and shouting and slapping and shaking. We kept saying sorry for our own behaviour and promised not to upset her again. We loved her, and hated to see her unhappy, hated to think we had caused her grief. Any child would hate to see this.

Most children, however, do not have a mum who reacted as violently as ours did when we let her down. I know this now. Sure, we all 'lose the will' sometimes. We all scream and shout. We all threaten punishment – no treats, the naughty step, no playdates. We all say things we later regret.

We don't all take our children by the wrists and shake them until their teeth rattle, ignoring their cries of, 'No, Mummy! Please stop!' We don't leave red bracelets of pinched marks around those tiny wrists. We don't clench our teeth and stare, wild with fury, into the mirror and chant, 'Bloody kids, bloody kids, bloody, bloody, bloody kids!' over and over while our small children cry and beg for us to stop. We don't go to our rooms and shut the door and ignore our crying children. We don't put them in their cots and leave them there until they wear themselves out screaming for us.

'Has she ever been violent?' the nurse had asked during our visit to A&E.

Yes. Too many times to mention. Too many times to clearly remember all the details of every occasion. But the worst time will always be remembered. By me, by my little sister, who witnessed it, hiding under the table on the landing, and by my father, who came home to see the bruises on my arm.

I am excited. I got my first fountain pen today. It's a turquoise Osmiroid one. I had to go to Mrs B's office at school to buy it with the money Dad gave me this morning. You are only allowed to do this if you have learnt to write Italic properly. Mrs B makes you write in pencil until she thinks you are doing it right. Yesterday she said I was finally doing it right. I should think so. I have been practising and practising, doing my 'ascenders and descenders', my 'x-height' letters and my 'upstrokes and downstrokes'. I have written lots and lots of rows of ns and ms and ds and bs and ps and qs in my rough book and I have copied out the sentence: *the quick brown*

fox jumps over the lazy dog loads of times. That sentence is
called a 'pangram', Mrs B says, because it has all the letters
of the alphabet in it. Dad says 'pan' comes from the Greek
and means 'all'. I suppose 'gram' means 'letters' but he didn't
say. Anyway, that's not important. What is, is that Dad was
proud of me yesterday because I had got a special mention
in the Italic Handwriting Society's magazine for a competition
we did. He says my writing is beautiful and agrees with Mrs
B that I can now have a proper pen. I am dying to use it. I
am in my bedroom and I am going to write something important and show it to Mum. I want her to be proud, like Dad.
But first I have to fill the pen with ink. Mrs B showed me
how. She gave me a lesson in how to do this. You have to
use Quink ink, which is precious. You mustn't be wasteful.
And you mustn't spill a drop.

I can see why. The ink is beautiful. It is dark, dark blue in
the bottle, but when you write with it, it comes out lighter.
It's called Royal Blue. I expect the queen uses it. The pen is
beautiful too. It's chunky and heavy. I love how it feels in my
hand. Smooth and important. It has a gold-coloured nib,
sharply cut so that you can make thick and thin lines to do
your Italic. And the best thing is the little lever, tucked neatly
into the side. When you lift it, it sucks the Quink ink up
magically into the pen.

I haven't shown the pen to Mum yet. I'm going to write
her some shopping lists. Or maybe some spellings. Or a story.
Or a poem.

But first, the ink.

I pick up the bottle and put it on my desk. Take off the
lid. Very carefully. Then lower the nib into the top of the
bottle and—

NO!

My hand has slipped!

The bottle is falling.

Onto the new green carpet.

Nonononono. I can't let it . . . can't spill . . . can't make a mark!

I reach to grab it but I can't.

The bottle is tipping and rising and a Royal Blue arc of ink is flying through the air and

falling

falling

falling to the floor . . .

The Royal Blue is pooling on the carpet of green. Sinking, sinking . . .

And leaving a stain. Like a bruise.

I have wasted it.

I have spilt every drop.

No time to think. No time to try to clear up the mess. I can't hide this. All I can think is, *I must tell Mum*, even as I know that this is the worst idea. I am going to be in so much trouble. *So. Much. Trouble.* The words beat like a drum in my chest as I run out of the room, on to the landing, crying, crying out to Mum, who comes running up the stairs.

My ink, my beautiful blue ink! Wasted! I want Mum to make it right, to say she knows what to do. To take me into her arms and stroke my hair and say, There, there, like Grandma would. But of course she doesn't. I am in trouble. So much. So much trouble.

I can see at once that Mum doesn't care about the ink. Her mouth is a giant black 'O'. Her eyes flash. She doesn't care about making me feel better. She cares about the carpet. She grabs my upper arm, her fingers sinking into my flesh.

What.

Have.

You.

Done?

She screams and hits my arm with her fist, over and over and over again.

Each.
Punch.
Tells.
Me.
How.
Stu-
Pid.
And.
Care-
Less.
I.
Am.

∽

I don't remember the pain from this beating. I don't remember the fear. I certainly don't remember my six-year-old sister watching from a safe distance as I was hit, punched, pummelled, although she says she was there. I remember only shame. Deep, hot, dark shame. For being stupid. For being clumsy. For being a clumsy, fat, podgy, stupid child who had made the worst mess imaginable. For getting ideas above my station, thinking that it was appropriate for a nine-year-old child to keep a diary written in fountain pen.

For thinking that I could in some way impress my mother with my stupid, stupid, ideas. Useless. I am useless, useless, useless.

Seventeen

'The person with Asperger's syndrome usually needs reassurance, but may rarely reassure family members, has little interest in the events of emotional significance to others, and can often criticise but rarely compliment.'[17]

I leave Mum and Dad on 16 May 2013 with the following regime typed out and Sellotaped to the side of the kitchen cabinet:

Mornings: take ONE citalopram (anti-depressant) until further notice. MUST BE TAKEN IN MORNING. May wake Mum up otherwise.

Nights: Around 9 p.m., or an hour before bed, take ONE olanzapine (anti-psychotic) until further notice and TWO zopiclone (sleeping pill) until further notice.

Do not take diazepam unless instructed as this is a tranquilliser.

I give this information to John by email as well, in case Dad panics and can't remember what to do.

I spend the next fifteen days trying to reinsert myself back into my own life. It's not that simple, though. My body may be standing in my kitchen, facing my kids as they talk to me, but my mind is back in Kent, picturing what Mum might do next. I'm not listening when Tom tells me about his chickens and how many eggs they're laying and could he please have another bantam? I'm not engaged when David calls from Amsterdam for a nightly catch-up on things. I'm not concentrating when Lucy tells me about her GCSE choices. I'm not focused when I sit at my desk and try to write the children's book I'm supposed to be delivering to my agent this summer.

More often than not, I am on the phone. To Carrie to try and paint the most accurate picture I can of how bad things have got. To John to offload and ask for support. Carrie's children are very small: her youngest is two years old. She can't drop everything and go and help Mum and Dad. I know this, but boy, do I want her to. I can't do this on my own.

In calmer moments I think of the drugs and the mental health nurse, Sam, and I think, 'It will be OK. We just have to be patient.'

But it isn't OK and it doesn't get better and the drugs don't seem to be working at all. Mum is stuck in a breathless, gasping cycle of obsessions. The fridge and cracks in the walls are no longer top of the agenda. Mum has now switched back to chuntering about having prolapse again. It doesn't take a psychiatrist to tell me that her anxieties about everything falling apart have now been transferred to her own mortality.

Initially I find some consolation in the fact that the mental health 'team' are checking in regularly. Then Dad tells me that Sam has not come back. Because of staffing problems, it's not possible to guarantee that the same nurse will come to each visit. This upsets Mum.

'And they won't come at a regular time,' Dad complains

during one of our stereophonic phone calls, in which Mum breathes heavily down one receiver and Dad speaks down the other. 'It's impossible to plan anything,' he says. 'They say they'll come "sometime in the morning" and even then they might come in the afternoon. Or not at all, if they are really busy that day.'

This lack of a routine upsets Mum even more than not seeing the same nurse each time.

'You don't like it, do you, Gilly?'

'No.'

'Your mum gets very anxious waiting for the nurse to arrive.'

I bet she does.

∽

Mum has had a problem with people not calling or turning up on time for as long as I can remember. Things have always had to happen exactly as she expected them to, otherwise she was liable to fly off the handle. It didn't matter that traffic jams, lack of money for a phone booth or acts of God might have contributed to me not arriving or calling on time; I would still feel the full brunt of her anger if I didn't meet her expectations.

When I was living at home I don't think I noticed it so much – it was yet another thread in the fabric of childhood, and both Carrie and I had found strategies for managing Mum's anger over these things without really thinking about what we were doing. We have talked about this a lot. We came of age in the Eighties and early Nineties, well before mobile phones were around. I think now that the reason I survived my teens without too many battles was that I was unable to contact Mum much of the time – and she was unable to contact me. She didn't always know exactly where

I was or what I was doing, and my strategy was to call just regularly enough that I could maintain this freedom. Carrie adopted a different tack, never going out without a stack of loose change for a call box.

'I knew if I had money in my pocket, I could call Mum to let her know if plans had changed – to let her know where I was and when I was coming back,' she told me.

I preferred to stick to arrangements so that I could at least enjoy the time I had before having to go home. I would make sure I was back before curfew and always came out of events early. It was better that I was the one waiting for Mum rather than the other way around. Friends would query it, even tease me about it, and try to get me to stay on at parties. I would always say, 'No, Mum wants me back.' I was more worried about getting into trouble with Mum than about friends thinking me 'square'.

Since leaving home, though, anxiety and aggression around issues of timing have become one of the biggest things Mum has argued about with me and Carrie.

The first time it was really bad was during my first few weeks at university. In those days the best way of keeping in contact was to write. It was the only way to stay in touch when phone calls were expensive and you were liable to have any conversation interrupted by a parent grabbing the receiver and shouting, 'We're not made of money, you know!' or, 'Why don't you just come round and have a conversation here instead of wasting good money?' Or Mum's chosen method of disruption once we had a phone installed upstairs: pick up the receiver and breathe heavily into it before barking, 'That's enough. I need to use the phone now.'

I fully intended to write home when I was at university, but in those initial few weeks I was so giddy with my first taste of freedom, not to mention anxious about the terrifying new workload, that I didn't know what to do with myself. The only thing I did know was that I would write home when I felt like it.

Mum had other ideas.

∽

I went up to university on Sunday 9 October 1988.

On 11 October Mum wrote a chatty four-page letter, filling me in on what she had been up to and telling me I had left a shirt in the airing cupboard. (Presumably because I forgot to ask her to get it out for me, as I would not have been allowed to fetch it myself.)

On 15 October she wrote another four-page letter, which began by saying, 'Dad and I are surprised that we haven't heard from you, apart from that rather short phone call. We do want to hear how you're getting on. I think it would be a good idea to phone on Sunday evenings. You probably won't have time to write to many people, but I think your family should come first.' She finished the letter by repeating the wish that, 'We would like to hear from you.' This was underlined heavily. She added, 'Use a first-class stamp when you write – second-class is unreliable.'

On 18 October she wrote a one-page letter, which said, 'We are really rather upset that you haven't bothered to get in touch by phone or letter. You know we can't phone you and we are obviously wondering how you are getting on. Will you please phone us one evening after 7.30 p.m. (not Friday)? Surely you have time to write once a week.'

I don't remember how I felt on reading any of those letters. Re-reading them now brings Mum's voice back, as though she is standing in front of me, glaring, hands on hips.

I can look back to what happened two days later as if I

am opening a wardrobe door and stepping directly into my own personal Narnian winter.

∽

It is 20 October 1988. After morning lectures, I go back to college and go automatically to the fusty wooden pigeon holes in Front Court. I have learnt quickly that this is how students communicate with each other – leaving notes asking if you're free for coffee, arranging to meet in the bar later. (We check our pigeon holes almost as many times a day as my teens will be checking their mobile phones in the next century.) Notes in pigeon holes, notes pinned to doors; in these pre-internet times our days are punctuated by little hand-delivered messages and we get to recognise one another's handwriting at one hundred paces.

The note I see in my pigeon hole this morning is written in a hand I would recognise at one *thousand* paces. It is a messy scrawl and the writer has pressed heavily into the Basildon Bond with a blue Bic biro. I am disappointed. It is not a note from one of my new friends. It is not even a letter from one of my old friends, which would at least be entertaining. It's another letter from home. From that place I am doing my best to put behind me as I reinvent myself with new people, new ideas, new experiences.

I think about pushing the letter into my bag and saving it for later, but something makes me decide against it. I slide my finger under the gummed-down flap of the cream envelope and prise it back. A card slips out and falls to the floor. I bend to pick it up, but the message has already hit me between the eyes.

'RING HOME IMMEDIATELY!'

That is all.

Three angry blue-biroed words, carved into a postcard.

Fear rinses through me. What has happened? Is Grandma ill? Is Carrie hurt? Dad? Not Dad . . .

I run to South Court, to the payphone in the corridor outside the student bar. Thank God, no one else is using the phones. I wrench open the booth, pull the glass door shut behind me and grab the receiver off the hook. I push my finger into the rotary dialler and pull it around. It takes for ever for the dialler to circle back after each number.

0

7

3

2

COME ON!

3

5

0

BLOODY HELL!

6

4

8

I listen to the ring. As I wait for someone to answer, my heart skittering, I picture my parents' phone on the narrow white shelf above the radiator in the sitting room. I see Mum come to answer it. I start to imagine terrifying scenarios. What if Carrie's been in a car crash? What if Grandma's in hospital again? What if Dad is dead—?

'Tonbridge, three-five-oh—'

The sound of my father's calm, measured voice makes me jump. I wasn't expecting him to be at home. I don't let him spell out the rest of the number.

'Dad! Thank God . . . It's me, Anna – I got this awful note from Mum—'

'I'll just get her for you.' Dad sounds as he always does on the phone – overly formal, as though I am one of his colleagues at the bank. He is keen to pass me over to Mum. There is no hint of panic or any other unusual emotion in his voice. There is nothing to suggest that I should be fearful of what Mum will say.

Still, those three capitalised words swim before my eyes as I hear the clatter of Mum picking up the receiver.

'Hello.' Her voice is clipped. It has a familiar edge to it.

My shoulders tense, bracing for the blow. A well-rehearsed reflex.

She is angry.

My whole body fizzes with dread, but I force myself to sound bright and breezy.

'Hi, Mum! How are you?' I sound more brittle than bright. 'Everything all right?' My voice rises in a squeak.

Of course it isn't. I know I am for it. I am about to be verbally attacked.

So, why do I stand there and take it? Why do I keep feeding coins into the phone, which only serves to feed her rant? Why do I allow her to call me back to continue the harassment long after I have run out of ten ps? Why do I let her go on and on while people queue up outside the booth and start hammering on the door for me to get off the phone?

The next day, 21 October 1988, I get another letter from Mum.

'I am sorry I upset you with my nags about not hearing from you. I was missing you and worrying about how you were.'

It is a sweet, kind letter, telling me not to worry about the

work, which I am already feeling is threatening to overwhelm
me. She understands. She found the workload onerous too
when she was a student here. It will get easier, she tells me.
I must remember to have fun too. She finishes, 'Don't have
an inferiority complex. Just relax, enjoy yourself and don't
worry.'

'Relax . . . don't worry.'

She meant it, every word. There were many letters after
that, pouring out her love and telling me how much she
missed me. I missed her too. But telling her that, that I loved
her, that I was looking forward to seeing her, was never
enough, and so I never could relax where Mum was concerned.
There were just as many letters over the next few years that
harangued me – for having moved on, for growing up. For
leaving her. And there would be so much more panic,
displayed as anger, communicated through phone calls, letters,
emails, texts and face-to-face rows, over what Mum saw as a
lack of care and a lack of regard for her feelings on my part,
and a huge need on her part to know where I was and what
I was doing – to not let me go.

I will spend a lifetime trying to reassure her, to make her
feel better, to assuage her anxieties. And I will fail at every
turn.

There is simply no way that I can relax.

Eighteen

'Spending time in green space or bringing nature into your everyday life can benefit both your mental and physical wellbeing. For example, doing things like growing food or flowers, exercising outdoors or being around animals can have lots of positive effects.'[18]

By the end of May 2013, two weeks after Dad and I took her to A&E, Mum is under the care of a new psychiatrist who seems to have the measure of her.

'She doesn't like him, mind you,' Dad tells me.

'He's South African,' Mum says.

Dad is convinced that the man's straight-talking manner is an answer to our prayers. The man certainly doesn't seem to pull any punches when it comes to trying to persuade Mum to go into respite care.

The background to this is that Dad and Mum have had a holiday booked for a while – to their beloved Italy. Dad booked it thinking it would do Mum good after the last psychiatrist said that all Mum needed was rest and loving care from her family. Mum is now doing everything she can to scupper Dad's chances of getting away (because it is really he who needs the holiday, as far as Carrie and I can see).

This has become Mum's new loopy rant when I phone.

'We're supposed to be going to Italy . . . I can't.'

'But Mum, it will do you good.'

'Yes, Gilly. Anna's right. You love Italy. It'll be warm and sunny—'

'No! I can't! I haven't got any clothes!'

'We'll get you some clothes.'

'No! I can't go out. I've got prolapse.'

Nothing we can say will reassure her.

She can't go, the house is cracking up and falling down, she can't go, her body is falling apart, she can't go, she has no clothes, she can't go. Can't. Can't. Can't.

Dad needs this holiday badly. He needs to get out of the prison he shares with Mum. She is not letting him go anywhere without her any more, and she doesn't want to go out herself, so his Sunday outings on the river in his canoe have stopped, as well as his walks with friends and Friday nights in the pub. He needs to go away. To feel the sun on his face, eat good fresh food and drink dark red wine. He will be the one cracking up and falling down if he doesn't go.

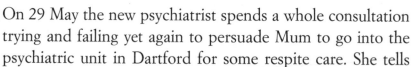

On 29 May the new psychiatrist spends a whole consultation trying and failing yet again to persuade Mum to go into the psychiatric unit in Dartford for some respite care. She tells him that she doesn't need to go, that she will go to Italy instead. Dad smiles, breathes, says thank you, and my parents leave the room.

The minute they are out in the corridor, Mum turns to Dad and starts on again in a panicky loop about not being able to go on holiday. The door to the psychiatrist's room swings open. The doctor steps out, startling Mum into silence.

'Gillian, I can hear what you're saying,' the psychiatrist says. 'Either you go to the unit of your own free will or we will send some people around to collect you.' His clipped, firm vowels leave no room for doubt.

Dad tells me this over the phone. Dad and I both know what 'some people collecting Mum' means, but that doesn't mean we're ready to speak the words aloud. To do so would be to admit our part in this. Our part in depriving Mum of her liberty. Our part in having her sectioned.

Straitjackets.

Restraints.

In the end we don't have to play this part.

'Mum has agreed to go of her own accord,' Dad tells me. 'I'm taking her there today and then I will go to Italy without her.'

Mum and Dad have been married for nearly fifty years. They have never been on holiday without one another. I can't allow myself to think what either of my parents must be feeling right now.

I call Carrie and tell her, 'I don't think we'll ever get Mum back. I feel as though this is the beginning of the end.'

'Yes,' Carrie says. 'I feel the same.'

While Dad is in Italy, I escape to Cornwall with my family. I am in need of respite too. I need to put Mum out of my mind. And I need to write. I have a new book brewing, but I am blocked. The words whirlpool. I can't pin them down. I need to get outside, to breathe in fresh air, to move my limbs. It is an impulse I can't ignore; as natural for me as

Mum's instinct to do the exact opposite. She has not taken the advice Sam, the mental health nurse, gave her, about exercising every day. It is no surprise. She has never taken this advice, even though it has been meted out for as long as I can remember. She has always been hopeless at sticking with any form of exercise, quickly dropping classes when the effects do not show immediately on her physical or mental state. Even the tennis she used to play with friends fizzled out once she became impatient with the other women. They had wanted to enter tournaments and she was contemptuous about most kinds of competition in sport.

'I hate sporty people,' she used to say. 'They are so boring.'

Add to that the fact that most sport takes place outdoors, which is a space Mum equated with dirt and chaos, and the fact that sport was something that, according to her, interested 'people with low intellect', and Mum was not to be persuaded. She was scathing about friends who were passionate about golf. She couldn't bear to hear them talk about it. The one sport she did care about was cricket. Neat, orderly, rule-bound, white-clothed cricket. She could watch it for hours and talk endlessly about the scores. She could talk about cricket for almost as long as she could talk about history, politics or the ancient world. Her memory for cricket scores was every bit as impressive as her memory for dates and declensions.

I have never bothered to learn anything about cricket, not even when Tom was playing at school. On the other hand, I have thrown myself into the dirty, chaotic, great outdoors ever since meeting David. Ever since discovering this place.

In Cornwall I like to get up every morning before the rest of the family has stirred. I make a coffee and call my dog from her basket and we walk down through the woods to the sea. The lime-green trees filter warm light. The moss and lichen speak comfort. The smell of the earth rises up to greet me. The coast path wriggles and writhes its way over granite and roots and through leaf mould and mud. It takes me faithfully to the sea.

The low sunlight glistens on the water. I stand on the rocks and stare out at a seal. He stares back at me. I take my clothes off and fold them into a small pile. I ignore the reproachful gaze of my Labrador and the quizzical look from the seal and I lower myself into the crystal sea. The water laps gently at my arms as I push forward. The grip of the cold on the back of my neck is iron-hard. I gasp. I breathe, I kick. I push out with my hands. I am alive alive alive. And miles away from Mum. And free.

∾

Mum has always resented my love of this place. She has been angry about us taking our summer holidays here ever since Lucy was born, taking it as a rejection of her and of Kent, my home county.

'Aren't you proud of your roots?' she would say, if I dared to mention how much I loved Cornwall.

At this point in time I am not, actually, no, I would like to tell her. At this point in my life, Kent equals claustrophobia. It equals being stuck indoors, being nagged. It equals a closed-in, net-curtain-twitching, pavement-lined, hide-bound childhood. It equals family troubles and fear and panic and worry and pain.

Cornwall is the opposite of all that. It is big sky and big sea. It is swallows under the eaves and swifts screaming overhead. It is rooks calling out as the sun sets. It is jackdaws nesting in the kitchen wall. It is tangled woods and Celtic stone circles and light and clean air and freedom. And it is where my husband was born – it is where his roots are, which is part of the problem as far as Mum is concerned. Anything that takes me away from her is a problem.

As I swim, I think: even if I brought her here so that we could be together, she wouldn't be happy. She would hate it here. She would not see what I see. She would hate the mud, the uneven ground, the hard, unforgiving granite, the ice-cold water. She would be frightened of the big swims I do with David and the kids, crossing the bay, bobbing on waves, jumping off rocky islands. She would be terrified of the idea of what we might be swimming with: fish, lobster, crab, jelly-fish.

'I hate wildlife,' she told me. 'I just don't like nature.'

Once I told her of a time when we arrived at Porthcurno beach early one morning. The kids were still small and prone to waking early, so we'd upped and we'd offed straight after breakfast. There was one other person on the beach, a man getting changed for an early morning swim. As we walked down from the lifeguard's hut, the man waved to us and pointed out to sea. We followed his gesture to see – DOLPHINS! Five or six of them, arcing out of the water, not far from the shoreline. We didn't stop to comment or think; we ran, shedding our clothes down to our swimmers as we sprinted into the water. Even Tom, who at that age was so small and skinny that he found the cold hard to bear, followed us out into the bay. And the dolphins came to greet us! They jumped and they twirled and they whistled and they clicked. We oohed and we aahed and we clapped in admiration – they responded by jumping and twirling higher and higher, their smiling mouths reflecting our elation.

'It was so exciting!' I told Mum. 'I have never been that close to a large sea creature. I might never again.'

'You were so foolish!' she said. 'Tom and Lucy could have drowned.'

Yes. Yes, they could have. But they could also have missed out on an experience that will have added to their lives in an unquantifiable way.

∾

I will never get through to Mum that life is sometimes about taking risks. Risks are too scary. They are to be avoided at all costs. Risks are the unknown, the uncontrollable. And since her breakdown . . . since that call from Uncle John . . . everything outside – even the High Street, even the corner shop, even the garden – is a risk. It's no wonder she tells us that she can't go to Italy.

John tells me now, 'I'm afraid Gillian should have accepted help earlier in life to learn how to cope with her fears.'

Maybe she had thought she was coping. Maybe all her risk-averse behaviour had worked for a while. Had kept her fears at bay. Not any more. And now it's too late to learn new strategies. Mum can't cope any longer. She is the one who is drowning, and it is happening too fast for any of us to reach her.

Nineteen

*'Some autistic people can display challenging behaviour.
It includes what would normally be considered physically
aggressive behaviour, but can also include other behaviours, if
they are having a negatic impact on the person or their family.'*[19]

By 9 June 2013, Mum is back at home after a short stay
in the mental health wing, but she is no better. She's
constantly calling me and Carrie again, sometimes three or
four times a day, wanting us to fix her, to listen to her, to
help her. She is now convinced she has dementia and that
her bowels have ceased working. We are wrenched back on
the emotional bungee of Mum's far-reaching apron strings,
just as we were enjoying a bit of time, hanging free. Thank
God Dad has had his holiday. He will need all his reserves
of energy again now that Mum is home.

The drugs, the mental health team, the psychiatrist, the
mental health hospital: nothing has had any effect. Why am
I surprised? It's not as though we haven't been here before.
Earlier this year, after I had that panic attack in February, I
had reached a point where I felt I could no longer talk to
Mum. Her regular phone calls and repeated cries for me to

fix her had broken me. I had tried to explain that I had to get on with my own life and look after my own family, all to no avail.

That's when, on 12 February 2013, I had resorted to old-school tactics of writing a letter to Dad, the pen being mightier than most things, and certainly mightier than my ability to express myself orally. It was one of the hardest letters I have ever had to write. I told him I needed a break. A break from talking to Mum, from the constant coaching she needed. I told him I couldn't stop crying, I was having trouble sleeping, I was experiencing all kinds of physical problems, including back pain, eczema, nausea, all due, I was sure, to stress. I was also having vivid flashbacks to things that had happened between me and Mum in the past. And then I had the panic attack, resulting in my driving the wrong way down a one-way street.

I told him that I had tried all my life to make Mum happy, but now I knew that no one could do that other than herself. I wrote that I had tried everything: I had tried being 'good', tried working hard, tried achieving the ambitions she had for me at school and university – even in marrying a good man and having children, I thought I might finally win her over. And in smaller ways – planning nice things to do when we are together – I had also tried to make her happy. These things had only ever worked momentarily, I told him, and they had had no lasting effect.

I wrote that I was sorry to have to tell him, but that I could not do this any more: talking to Mum (or rather listening) so many times a day and thinking about her constantly. I had to give myself to my own family. Something I was not doing at that moment because of my preoccupations with Mum.

I ended by saying that I just could not face seeing or talking to Mum while she was refusing to take responsibility. Once she admitted that she needed psychological help, I would be able to gladly support her through that, but I could not be her mother. I could not be the person she wanted: 'just someone to talk to'. I could only suggest that she seek a new psychiatrist – someone to help navigate her way through her dark times. I was not that person.

I signed off, assuring Dad this didn't mean that I didn't love Mum. It was just that I couldn't waste any more of my life feeling this much turmoil. I wrote the letter in floods of tears, feeling as though I were signing a divorce settlement.

On 27 February Dad replied in his beautiful even calligraphy, and his reply infuriated me and saddened me in equal measure. His language was mostly quite formal, possibly in a desire for clarity, probably because that was always how he spoke when backed into a corner. In his letter he praised the private psychiatrist, who, three months after this, had signed Mum off, exasperating the GP and making me and Carrie spit tacks whenever we heard his name. He assured me that taking Fluanxol was going to be the answer to everything, but when I read that Fluanxol is prescribed for schizophrenia I was not reassured – Mum had never suffered with that. He gave long and wordy explanations, which read as though he had cut and pasted a description of the drug and its effects from an NHS website.

'It helps the brain generate serotonin. This acts as a neuro-transmitter that helps relay signals from one area of the brain to another. It is believed to influence a variety of psycho-logical and bodily functions by facilitating the operation of brain cells related to mood, appetite, sleep, memory and learning, temperature regulation and some social behaviour,' he wrote. 'Fluanxol assists a natural brain function to develop and take over without help after six months or so. Mum is making remarkably good progress.'

He ended in an uncharacteristically emotional manner, telling me I was 'a loving, caring, brilliant daughter'.

His letter came with one from Mum asking me to 'accept my profoundest apology for being such an ogre of a mother' and for 'being selfishly wrapped up in myself physically and mentally' and begging me to 'give me another chance to show how I can be a cheerful friend as well as your mother'.

I still insisted on a break. I couldn't handle Mum's challenging behaviour. It was too much. I didn't speak to my parents for three months, until that day in May when John called to break the silence. And now it's June and all those promises have been forgotten, anyway. Mum is incapable of keeping them. I know she is and I should feel sorry for her, but instead I am angry. She has just persuaded the hospital to reduce the dose of her anti-depressant. And they have agreed.

My heart breaks into ever smaller pieces. I love her. I don't want to leave her. I hate her. I wish I never had to see her again. The drugs don't work, and even if they did, Mum has to stick with them and she won't because she has never stuck with anything. There is no solution to this. No cure. In any case – a cure for what? At this point we have no diagnosis that makes proper sense. No clear medical explanation for how Mum has got to this point. We are simply agreeing to drugs and drugs and drugs and drugs, none of which seem to make Mum feel better, many of which I fear are making her feel worse. In moments of compassion and empathy I weep for Mum. She is in hell. She is in the bell jar. Her world is a nightmare.

In my darkest moments, I wish her dead. I tell Carrie and she quietly agrees.

'I'm more worried that this is going to end up killing Dad,' she says. 'Mum will kill him in the end – from stress, I mean.'

Twenty

'With each passing year I find my birthday more of a struggle. It's not the day per se or the fact that I'm getting older, but I find all the attention I get on my birthday rather over-whelming and sooner or later I wish that everybody just leaves me alone. I also don't like getting presents and surprises in general. I hate having phone calls and usually everybody phones on that day and that just stresses me out a lot. It makes me feel uncomfortable and anxious and I generally just feel very, very exhausted in the end.'[20]

Early summer is a flashpoint for Mum's anxieties. This is because it's her birthday on 12 August. She likes to know well in advance what we are planning for it and what gifts we will be giving her, so she starts obsessing about it around June. In the end it doesn't matter how much fuss we make, whether we give her the gifts she has asked for or whether we take her at her word to 'surprise me' – we always get it wrong. The build-up is getting worse as she gets older, and 12 August 2013 has particularly loud alarm bells attached to it as it's Mum's seventieth birthday.

The emails and phone calls about this birthday started not

just months in advance, but years. In 2011 Mum got it into her head that she wanted to take 'the whole family to a nice villa somewhere for my seventieth' and made sure to tell us repeatedly that it was what 'all my friends have done'.

Carrie and I were both adamant that this wasn't going to happen. Since getting married and having children we have tried these adult family holidays, each time thinking 'it will be fine', each time vowing we'll never do it again. They have all been unmitigated disasters. Mum has never been an easy person to go on holiday with as everything has to be planned down to the last detail, but when we were kids, we just thought everyone's mum was like this. After all, she had to do all the packing, all the laundry, get the sun cream and the insect cream and check we all had the right clothes and sun glasses and swimming costumes. She was the one making lists and ticking them off and laying all the clothes out over the spare-room bed weeks before we were ready to go, shouting at us if we crept in to grab a T-shirt we wanted to wear. 'Leave it! It's for the holiday!'

It certainly all looked stressful.

Any last-minute changes to a day's plans, including what we are going to eat where and when, could throw her into a rage. Small children with their own, sometimes unpredictable, needs didn't tend to fit well into this kind of regimented approach to holiday-making. We've been there, done that and we're not keen to do it again.

It's not even as though Mum sounds happy about the idea when she brings it up. It's as though she knows what a seventieth birthday celebration *ought* to look like, but she has no concept of what it is that she actually wants or would enjoy.

Carrie and I have avoided the issue for as long as we can. It is now, selfishly, somewhat of a relief to see that Mum is too ill to go to a nice villa somewhere. However, the occasion must still be marked and Dad is determined to give Mum a good day. So David and I agree to take the kids to Kent for a barbecue even though we have only just come back from a blissful two-week holiday during which we did not have to answer the phone once to Mum or Dad. I am not looking forward to it one bit.

Then something incredible happens.

At the beginning of August, the South African psychiatrist tries Mum on a different drug: pregabalin.

'It's a miracle,' Dad whispers down the phone. 'She's transformed! I've got her back again – she's more herself than she's ever been!'

He is so happy. So bright. So Dad. I've got *him* back again. I can't believe it.

'You shouldn't,' John tells me in an email. 'These neuropathic pain relievers have a cruel habit of easing anxiety for a short while in a geriatric patient and then the effects start to wear off. The best you can hope for is a period of good effects, followed by a step backwards, followed by a mild improvement when the consultant tinkers with the dose and so on. It's like a staircase that will take you back to where you started. Or worse.'

Dad refuses to listen to such negative spinning. He is no longer talking to John, the younger brother-in-law with whom he shared so many jokes, so many good times. He is angry with what he sees as a lack of love and support.

And it is difficult to ignore Dad's euphoria, to not be carried along with it. Mum does sound like a new woman on the phone.

We go to Kent full of trepidation, worried that Dad is over-egging things. But we find that he is not. Mum really is a new woman. Or a new version of the best ever version of herself so far. She is consistently loving and gentle and kind, with no sign of any mood swing brewing. She has made an old family favourite, a fruit tart, and she has planned a lovely day. She smiles and kisses and hugs us. She even lets the dog into the house with no comment about muddy paws and hairs on the carpet.

She says, 'You look thin, Anna. Is that my fault?'

I shrug. I've lost a stone since May.

'I'm sorry,' she says, hugging me. 'You shouldn't have to look after me. I'm the mum, after all.'

I hold back tears. This is a dream. I'm going to wake up soon, surely. But, no. Mum's delight in seeing us is real. The heat from the sun is real. The food is real. And there's so much of it. Dad has prepared one of his legendary barbecues, with enough food for four families. We sit in the garden and drink wine and eat falafels and *keftedes* and grilled aubergine. After we have demolished the fruit tart, Dad takes the kids out in his canoe. We all swim in the town's open-air pool and David and I go for a walk along the river with Mum and the dog.

In the car on the way home we can hardly bear to speak in case it breaks the spell.

'They were nervous,' David says. 'They wanted it to be perfect.'

It was.

A couple of days later I receive the most beautiful letter from Mum that she has ever written me. I keep it in my diary for months and months, reading and re-reading, still not believing that this is really my mother. That she has managed to say all these loving things without couching them in self-pity or recrimination or criticism for a birthday that hadn't lived up to expectations.

Dear Anna,

Thank you so much for coming for the weekend. We had a
lovely time playing cards, swimming and canoeing with you all.
Thank you too for all your presents and cards, especially the
handmade ones and the poetry selection and illustrations.
Thank you also for all the support you've given me this year. I
do feel better and will try and face the future more calmly. It
was lovely to see you all and I look forward to many more
family gatherings and activities together.

    Much love to you all,

    Mum, Grandma, Gillian

It is a letter from the mother I remember from days when I
had done the right thing, when I had earned her approval
and cuddles, when I had been a good girl and felt safe in her
arms. It is a letter from the mother I had almost forgotten
existed.

Suddenly I don't want to hear John's doom-laden words,
either. I don't want to think of the Escher-style image he has
painted of downwards-spiralling, never-ending staircases. I
just want this woman, this mother. This real mother, not the
evil step-mother revealed by anxiety and depression. We cling
to hope. We make wishes and say prayers. Make her stay like
this forever and ever, Amen.

We have a damn-near perfect four months after this, with
enjoyable family get-togethers and loving phone calls, during
which Mum is calm and seems happy, even if she is a little
more fragile these days. My kids notice the change and are
visibly more relaxed around her. She still clings to Dad and
relies on him to make any decision, even at times down to

what to eat, but she smiles all the while. There are a couple of occasions when I catch myself thinking that she looks a bit wobbly on her feet, or she shows tiny signs of old anxieties creeping in. I mention it to Carrie, but on the whole we have managed to convince ourselves, as Dad has done, that Mum is one hundred per cent cured.

It is only four months of happy delusion, though; John's warnings turn out to be well founded. We should have known it really. All enchantments have a shelf life. By Christmas 2013 the pregabalin is no longer having any effect at all, and we are at the bottom of the staircase once again.

Twenty-one

'Anti-depressants . . . have been used to reduce repetitive behaviour. But there are concerns about the use of these drugs . . . because of the side effects (such as agitation).'[21]

W e should have seen it coming, that slide back to the bottom of the staircase. It should not have come as a shock. There were lots of signs on top of John's warnings. People don't always stop to read the signs, though. Especially when they think they know where they're going. And Dad, Carrie and I were convinced that the only way was up during that pregabalin Summer of Love.

So when in October 2013, Mum and Dad decided that Disneyland Paris would be the place to belatedly celebrate Mum's seventieth birthday, we didn't stop to think how destabilising it would be, taking her away from the secure rhythm of her home life. She was gentle and smiling on the Eurostar and still seemed heavily under pregabalin's spell. Even when we entered the noisy, crowded theme park, Mum showed no immediate signs of distress. She had been there with me and my kids years before, and knew what to expect.

What she didn't expect was that a violent storm would

envelope the park the next day. Mum immediately began to worry about Carrie's kids getting wet.

'They'll catch a cold. You can't stay out in this. Take them inside.'

Dad reassured Mum that he would help Carrie back to the hotel with her small daughter. The rest of us told Mum we would find shelter in the park.

'Come back straight away, Martin,' she said. 'In case you get lost.'

Did she mean, 'In case I get lost'? Even this didn't alarm us as Mum had always worried about where we were and how we'd get back.

The next day Carrie and I took Mum to have a sit-down in one of the cafés. She went to the Ladies and was gone for an unusually long time. I began to wonder where she was and went to look for her. I found her wandering, panic-stricken, having taken the wrong turn out of the toilets.

'I didn't know where you were. I couldn't find you.'

It took us a good few minutes to calm Mum, to reassure her. Still, we didn't see this as a sign.

We should have done: the shuttlecock phrase that is batted between Carrie and me, back and forth, back and forth over the months that follow this trip.

Why didn't we see what was happening? Was it because Mum was actually very gentle and sweet in between these panic attacks and seemed happy when we were all having meals together or sitting on the quieter rides such as the Mad Hatter's Tea Cups or the Magic Carpets of Aladdin? Or was it because Dad was having too much fun with his grandchildren? Either way, it was a joy to see them both smiling.

And that weekend Dad was the smiley-est of all of us; whether it was while getting competitive with his grandsons

on Buzz Lightyear Laser Blast or screaming with glee on the
Rock 'n' Roller Coaster or singing his way around It's a Small
World, it seemed clear that the only way was up, up, up to
the heavens above. The signs could go hang themselves somewhere else, thanks very much.

On the last day, determined to pack in one last bit of fun
before catching the train home, Dad and I had decided to
go to The Twilight Zone Tower of Terror: a 'haunted' hotel
in which you enter a lift and then plunge thirteen floors at
speed, the doors opening and closing on to various apocalyptic
scenes along the way. We knew Mum would hate it, so we
went with Tom and Lucy, even though it meant we would be
running to catch the Eurostar back. Mum didn't want us to
go.

'Don't do it. It sounds dangerous. We haven't got time.
You'll miss the train. What will we do if you miss the
train?'

We ignored her. We went on the ride, screaming and
laughing, acting like kids, Dad forgetting he was nearly
seventy, Lucy and Tom forgetting they were cool adolescents.
And afterwards we ran all the way through the park to the
station, arriving with minutes to spare.

We didn't miss the train. But we missed most of the performance Mum made as the time of departure got nearer and
nearer and we still weren't at the station. David told me
afterwards that Mum was extremely anxious. 'She was very,
very stressed – pacing up and down, checking her watch,
repeating over and over that you would be late.' I remember
feeling a stab of guilt, but mostly I was cross with her. Dad
had been having the time of his life. It was as though he knew
he had to squeeze every last ounce of joy out of that trip, in
case he never got the chance ever again.

It was as if he could see into the future, a future in which

Mum was to spiral down and down and down – faster than any funfair ride and a hundred times scarier.

∽

By Christmas 2013 she was back to being clingy, panicky and agitated pretty much 24/7. She and Dad came to stay and I took her out for a walk in the sunshine. It was one of those mild December days where the low light casts long shadows and the air is still. We made it down to the canal, a ten-minute walk from my house. Mum gripped my arm, saying she wanted to go back, she didn't want to be outside, she didn't want to walk.

I tried to distract her, pointing out early hazel catkins, ducks, buzzards, cormorants, as Dad had always done. I wanted to show her beauty and life and hope.

'Let's go back,' she kept saying. 'I want to go back.'

I had the tiniest inkling then of what it must have been like for Dad – a man who all his life had drawn comfort and relaxation from being outdoors, who loved nothing more than to get on the river or go out looking for birds, who had dealt with years of commuting and office work by balancing it with time in nature. How was he managing, being forced to spend every day cooped up inside with Mum?

'But it's a lovely sunny day,' I said, trying to keep Mum going.

It didn't work.

'All I can see is misery,' she replied.

Twenty-two

'For [people] with ASD, the Christmas holidays can be a stressful and anxious time. Meeting family demands can be especially nerve-wracking, particularly if you want to break with time-honoured traditions that just don't work for [someone] with autism.'[22]

The next day she is literally at the bottom of a staircase. I hear a cry, a crash, a rumble, another crash and go running up to the landing. Mum is lying in a heap, hugging her knees and moaning. She has fallen from the top floor of our house down a full flight of stairs. The real tragedy is that no one can honestly say that they believe it was an accident.

Mum always hated Christmas and would have done anything to make it go away. Maybe even something as drastic as throwing herself down the stairs. Her attitude towards Christmas was the same as that towards her birthday: panic about planning, needing to know every detail in advance, worrying about presents. Except that Christmas was far more complicated for Mum, because the day was not all about her. There was far more to worry about; more to try to control. She would call me and Carrie and John at the beginning of

September to ask us our plans, and if we didn't know or couldn't commit she would call and write and beg and plead and nag until we capitulated. She needed to know precisely where we would be convening and who would be invited and exactly what we, our partners and our children wanted as presents before September was out. As she got older, the Christmas-related phone calls would start almost as soon as her birthday in August had passed.

∽

It is Christmas Day 1977. We are at Grandma's house. I love coming to Grandma's. We come here a lot, especially when Mum is tired. Grandma makes sticky Bakewell tarts and lets us make our own creations from the left-over pastry. She lets us use her beetle-black sewing machine to make pin cushions and hankies. She plays games with us like Hunt the Thimble and Hide and Seek. Grandpa sits in his big armchair in the corner and smokes while we sing him the songs I've learnt at Brownies and taught to Carrie. We do the actions as we sing, 'If I were not a Brownie Guide, a bus conductor I would be!' We are spoilt here, Mum says. It doesn't feel like spoiling. If you spoil your dress, you can't wear it again because you have made a mess on it and it is ruined. Grandma is not making a mess and nor are we. And even if we did, I don't think Grandma would mind. She would say, 'There, there' in her kind voice and it would all be forgotten about.

She lets us watch telly in the evenings after we have had a bath. Carrie and I sit on the soft gold-coloured sofa in our pyjamas and dressing gowns, sipping hot sweet cocoa and nibbling salty Tuc biscuits while we watch *The Generation Game* and *Benny Hill* and *The Two Ronnies*.

This Christmas is extra-special because we have a new baby

cousin – our own baby Jesus, wrapped in a white holey knitted blanket. He is called Simon and has curly yellow hair like an angel. He gurgles and smiles and he's very cuddly. My Aunt Euphan lets me help to change his nappy. I hope I have a baby like him one day.

Mum has already told me what I'm getting for Christmas. I wish she wouldn't. I like surprises, like the ones that Father Christmas brings. Grandma has let us leave a glass of whisky and a mince pie on the little stool next to the electric fire. Uncle John says we should leave a carrot for the reindeer. He makes us laugh, balancing Christmas decorations on his glasses and pulling funny faces. He and Dad tell jokes and speak in funny voices, doing something called 'The Goons'. Mum doesn't think they're funny. She says they are 'facetious'. I don't know what this means, but she curls her mouth as she says it, as if she's swallowed something nasty, like the slimy skin off the school custard. Mum helps Grandma in the kitchen. She doesn't join in with the games. She likes cuddling Simon and tell us that she likes little boys. I wish I had an older brother. I don't like being the oldest.

Those Seventies Christmases were cosy and simple. I was very small, so I remember little of how the day passed; the gaps in my memory are filled by family anecdotes and the orange-tinted Polaroids in the family photo album. Mum doesn't feature in either my memories or the photos from this time. This is possibly because Mum was happy to take a back seat. Grandma was the hostess, and we were in Mum's childhood home, so Mum could relax and disappear into the simplicity and structure of a tried and tested routine.

But things were about to change. By the time Simon's sister,

Gemma, arrived in 1979, Grandma's small semi-detached house had to admit defeat: there just wasn't enough room for us all. Besides, Grandpa's health was declining – emphysema was creeping through him, stealing his breath and his energy due to years and years of smoking. Also John had recently bought a beautiful, romantic tumble-down house near Winchester. All in all, it made sense for Christmas to be moved to a new location with a new generation to host it.

From that point on, the memories of family Christmases loom large. They are in high-definition with the volume turned right up. This is partly because of how much my Aunt Euphan loved Christmas, partly because of how very different it was from those smaller, quieter affairs at Grandma's. In temperament, she was Bob Cratchit to my mother's Scrooge. Christmas to her meant fun and noise and laughter and lots and lots of people. It meant dressing up for a lavish Christmas Eve supper. It meant every room in the house decorated to the hilt, Christmas music playing and the largest tree I had ever seen. It meant 'tree presents' as well as 'main presents', midnight mass in the local cathedral, and food, glorious food. If there weren't enough beds for everyone, beds were found or made up out of whatever was available. Euphan's mother and Grandma shared a room, uncomplainingly. We played large, raucous games of charades, went for long, frosty walks with John's two faithful Labradors, watched films on the largest telly I had ever seen, which had a room of its own in the converted attic. We drank champagne long before we were allowed to.

And Mum could not cope with any of it.

She would hold it together for the first twenty-four hours. She would play the games and join in with the chatter and we would all think, 'Maybe this time it will be all right. Maybe this time we'll have a trouble-free Christmas.' Then a black mood would kick in sometime late on Christmas afternoon. If was as if twenty-four hours was Mum's limit. Perhaps we should have realised this and planned to leave early. Perhaps we should have seen that the large group of people, the noise, the merriment, the excess of food was too much for her.

No doubt alcohol played its part, serving to deepen and congeal an already depressive personality. Mum's hot rage would have been cooking slowly along with the turkey since our arrival on Christmas Eve. So slowly, that no one was ever prepared for the explosion. No one ever knew exactly what would trigger it, or how it would manifest. So every year we would play the game of pretending that this time it might not happen, that this year we might get away with it. We never did.

One year Euphan comes into the dining room carrying a large platter of roast potatoes. They are piping hot, perfectly crisped. They smell so delicious it's all we can do not to reach up and pinch one from the plate. Euphan is beaming. She loves to entertain. She loves to cook. She has worked hard for weeks to make this Christmas special. She once told me that it was because her own childhood Christmases had been lonely. She was an only child and had yearned for a picture-book Christmas, so now in adulthood her larder is full to bursting with cakes and biscuits and pies and pickles and packets of fancy Christmas crackers and party poppers and special paper napkins. It's magical. Carrie and I can't stop smiling. John is pouring champagne, making jokes, making Dad laugh.

Suddenly there is a snort.

'Why do you always have to cook so many bloody potatoes?' Mum spits. 'You always have to do everything to excess.'

Euphan's smile vanishes. The room falls silent. The jokes and laughter peter out. Even the light seems to fade from the room.

Grandma says, 'Gillian,' in a low, warning tone.

But it's too late.

'It's so wasteful. So greedy,' Mum says. The dangerous glint is in her eye. Why doesn't someone stop her?

Euphan puts the dish down heavily. 'At least I'm not mean, like you,' she says. 'Counting out each potato: one for you, one for me.'

No. She shouldn't have said that. Even though it's true. Mum cooks only the precise amount of food necessary. She weighs the exact amount of pasta per person, she allows a maximum of four potatoes for Dad, three for each of us. If we're still hungry, tough. There's never enough for seconds. That would be greedy. And wasteful if we didn't want more.

Grandma, John, Dad – they all start murmuring, trying to calm the raging beast with the snarling voice. Trying to step in between the hunter and the hunted. But it's too late, the touch-paper has been lit, there is no going back, the row escalates. Mum and Euphan's voices rise against each other, clashing like hot steel.

Carrie and I and our two cousins bolt our food and make a dash for the door, scattering to the four corners of the house to play with presents and watch telly. We don't talk about what has happened. It has happened too many times before. Mum pushes Euphan until she cracks. Euphan is not one to walk away. It's the way things are in this family, and there's nothing we can do about it. We may as well stay away and act as though Christmas is still fun. The adults stay downstairs; Dad and John rushing to clear away, taking refuge in the kitchen with the washing-up. Grandma and Euphan's mother sit quietly by the fire and nap until the storm has passed.

At the end of the day, Mum sits back in an armchair, surveying the crumpled present paper, the remains of snacks left on plates, the empty glasses abandoned to side tables, the sleeping Labradors. She looks around, taking in the evidence of the end of Christmas, and says, 'Well, thank God that's over.'

∽

When Dad and Mum arrive for Christmas at my house in Wiltshire in 2013, Dad is very tired from managing Mum. They both have chest infections and Dad is complaining of a sore leg. Mum is on antibiotics and obsessing over what time to take them.

'When are we eating? The doctor says I have to take the antibiotics with food.'

She follows me around like a lost lamb, whining and complaining and driving me mad. Even after she falls down the stairs I have to steel myself not to get irritated. I have lost all the patience and love I had back in May. It may be the season of goodwill, but I'm not feeling it. This year it will be me sitting back, surveying the scene on 28 December and saying, 'Thank God that's over.'

Twenty-three

'I am aware that grey dreary days make many people feel "gloomy" or "sleepy," but for me the problem goes far beyond feeling glum. For me, my entire body is affected, my mood, my energy, even my outlook on life itself is affected. I guess you could say that my moods quite literally change with the weather.'[23]

In January 2014 the Met Office sends out red weather warnings for impending storms and floods heading our way. Indoors the forecast is just as bad: the effects of the pregabalin have worn off completely. Mum's breathless, panicky, pacing behaviour has returned, and with it a weather front so apocalyptic it's hard not to think of the two things being related.

Outside, the storms rage and the waters rise. The Somerset Levels are flooded and people lose their homes. Inside, Mum's anxiety causes its own inundations, and Dad's anger levels rise in tandem. The prospect of Mum once again losing her grip on reality looms like the thunder clouds above.

I feel a bit under the weather. This is one of Mum's catch-phrases. She has always trotted it out with such regularity that we have learnt to ignore it. It is as though she has to speak out every mood, every physical feeling. She tells you what her bowels are doing that day and if you ask her to stop, saying you don't want to know, you are accused of being uncaring. When she insists on giving regular updates on her 'downstairs problem', Carrie and I begin to refer to it as 'Mum's Vagina Monologues'. We know we are being unkind, but sometimes black humour is the only antidote to Mum's catalogue of obsessions.

She is obsessed with the weather, and it seems to have a direct bearing on her moods – much more so than with other people. She hates the rain and the mud and mess that comes with it, but equally she can't stand intense heat or cold. In the days when we still joked about these things, we would tease that there were only two days a year that suited her: one in spring and one in early autumn, when the days could be balmy and Goldilocks-perfect in their balance of just-right temperature, sunlight and blue skies.

Carrie and I have said more than once that bad weather seems to follow in Mum's wake. Yet again, we know we are being unfair, but there are an alarming number of occasions on which the sun has been shining right up the point of our meeting Mum, then, at the eleventh hour, the skies have darkened and a chill has set in.

When I first went back to work after maternity leave with Lucy, Mum came to look after her one day a week. I had been worried that this would be too much for Mum as she would have to come up from Kent to Hammersmith with Dad, who was still commuting to Docklands. It was a long journey in heavy rush-hour traffic, and there would be no time for me to make sure Mum was comfortable and happy on arrival as I would have to run out the door the minute she arrived.

She was adamant, though.

'I want to be an involved grandparent,' she told me. 'Like my mother was. I only wish you lived nearer.'

When she discovered that my mother-in-law had also offered to help one day a week, this increased her determination. She was not to be outdone in the grandparenting stakes.

I relented, thinking it would be good for Lucy to get to know both her grandmothers equally, and that it would be better for me to leave her with family than worry about the other options available to us.

My mother-in-law would come on Tuesdays. She would take over with a gentleness and ease that was relaxing and reassuring, and I would go to work feeling calm and ready to face the day. Every Tuesday afternoon I would come back to find Lucy happily tootling around the sitting room with my mother-in-law, playing at 'kitchens' with wooden spoons and saucepans, playing at 'doing the washing' with my real, out-of-control laundry pile or sitting on the sofa quietly working her way through a stack of picture books, which I was sure my long-suffering mother-in-law had read at least ten times already that day alone. The sun would be streaming in through the tall window at the front of the house, and both daughter and Granny would look up and smile as I walked in.

'We've had a lovely day!' my mother-in-law would say, and Lucy would beam and gurgle her agreement.

Wednesdays could have not have been more different. Mum would arrive flustered, often angry about the levels of traffic around Hammersmith flyover. It would usually be raining, which would only serve to increase her fury.

'My hair's a state. And now I'll be stuck indoors all day, I suppose.'

She would want to talk to me and have a coffee, meaning I had to run to the office on the Fulham Palace Road, arriving late, out of breath and in a state myself, far from ready to do a day's work.

During the day Mum would often call me to complain that Lucy was 'grizzly' or that she was bored and didn't know what to do to occupy her baby granddaughter. I tried to keep the calls short, aware that I had to leave the office on time.

Still, I would invariably have to run home, knowing that if I didn't make it back on the dot of six Mum would be fuming. Likely as not it would be raining or threatening rain or have rained all day, in which case I would arrive home with soaking hair or splashed clothes or both. I would come back to find the sitting room in darkness, Lucy wriggling on my mother's lap while she held on to her tightly. Or Lucy would be sitting on the floor crying, surrounded by toys, ignored, while my mother sat on the sofa, her face screwed up in a scowl, ready to pronounce the words:

'You're late.'

Of course, I know she loved the idea of looking after Lucy. She probably – almost definitely – also had moments of happiness during the day. Mum loved babies and liked nothing more than to see Lucy wobble on to her legs for her first few steps, or mimic a character on television or try to sing a song. But she also found Lucy a 'wriggly' baby who 'didn't like cuddles' and was apparently noisier and more active than either I or Carrie had been at that age. So rainy days were hard work for her; they are for anyone caring for a small child in a small room. But for Mum, they were harder than for most.

⌒

Later when Tom was born, we were living in France. I would take the children back to England to see my parents. The train journeys seemed interminable in that age before iPads and smartphones. I would arrive, frazzled, the children hyper from hours of enforced confinement on the Eurostar and then a car journey from Ashford. Things would rarely go smoothly en route, so I came to expect Mum to greet me with those words again: 'You're late.' The sky would be darkening overhead, the temperature plummeting, both in an echo of Mum's mood.

Sometimes I would arrive to clear skies and smiles, only to find that something I said or did – or failed to say or do – would trigger a barked comment and the clouds would gather overhead as though lending weight to Mum's argument. Whenever this happened, the sun never managed to reappear for the rest of the visit.

 ❧

There was one occasion when I was staying with the children and they were feverish with pent-up energy. It was raining outside, and I had set them up with some colouring in the living room.

'Not in here!' Mum said, rushing in and gathering up the pencils and crayons. 'They'll make marks on the sofa!'

Dad was asked to set up a table in the utility room for them.

'You can sit quietly in here,' Mum told them.

Lucy and Tom managed about half an hour before breaking free and careering into the sitting room like two small puppies, shrieking and giggling. They bounded on to the sofa, wrestling and tickling one another.

'Not the sofa!' Mum cried, rushing in again.

I should have stopped the kids; no one under the age of forty was allowed on that sofa, and only then if they obeyed the rules on how to sit (without denting the cushions or leaving marks or hairs or fluff on the fabric). But a long car journey and a disturbed night and early morning had already taken its toll, and this latest outburst from Mum tipped me over the edge.

'They are two and four!' I shouted, picking up both children and ramming them into their rainproof gear. 'They cannot be expected to sit in the utility room all day while it rains!'

Mum's anger momentarily dissolved into confusion. 'You and your sister were never like this,' she said, frowning at my writhing offspring.

No, we weren't. We knew we couldn't be. We knew what you would do if we didn't behave. We would be pulled up by our wrists and you would shake us and shake us and then you would go to the mirror and pull that face and chant those awful words. So, no. Carrie and I never played roughly unless Dad was at home and taking the lead in what he called 'horseplay'.

I didn't say any of this at the time. I simply strapped Tom into the buggy and grabbed Lucy by the hand and we stormed out into stair-rod rain and gale-force winds.

Anything to get away.

Twenty-four

'As the patient ages and the environment becomes more demanding, social communication impairment may underline the development of social anxiety, especially if the patient is high functioning and aware of his/her social incompetence. Social anxiety, defined as intense anxiety or fear of being negatively evaluated in a social or performance situation, in turn leads to avoidance of social situations, therefore limiting the patient's opportunities to practice social skills.'[24]

During March 2014 Mum's anxiety escalates even more. She is no longer calling me and Carrie. She doesn't even send me a birthday card. Her anxiety is now manifesting in not wanting to go out or see anyone other than Dad. Dad is finding this very hard. He deals with it by trying to coax Mum out. He says it's because he thinks it will 'do her good', but Carrie and I both know what he really means is that he needs it for himself. The mother of my oldest school friend tells me that she saw Mum and Dad at the station one day.

'They were getting tickets from the machine and your Dad was talking quietly to Gillian the whole time. She was clearly distressed. I went up to say hello. Your dad was his usual charming self, but your mum didn't seem to want to talk to me. She kept telling your dad that she wanted to go home. He was taking her up to London for some event or other. I did feel for him. He looked exhausted.'

The psychiatrist has noticed Dad's exhaustion as well as Mum's deterioration. He suggests another short stay on the mental health ward at Dartford hospital. Mum's condition does not improve while she is there. Dad says he misses her, but when she comes back home his mood immediately plummets. He's at least talking to me and Carrie more. There's nothing to hide now. We've seen the worst, haven't we?

'She won't let me do anything without her,' Dad tells me during one phone call. 'She doesn't enjoy anything any more. She won't see friends. Won't go to any of the groups we belong to. I've cancelled our next trip to Italy; even if I thought Mum was up to it, she's not insured to travel now.'

Mum can't travel any more? She's already been locked in at Dartford. Now she can't leave the country? All of my parents' retirement plans had centred on trips abroad, on enjoying their freedom together, their sunshine years. It's not right. How can Mum's illness take such a toll on Dad?

He's still talking. 'The psychiatrist is seriously considering using electric shock treatment this time,' he says.

I don't feel the outrage I should. It is just words and words and more words about what 'might' happen, what 'should' happen. But nothing ever does.

⁓

In April Mum goes into the mental health unit again.

'She shouts at me for being late even when I am on time for my visits,' Dad says. 'It's as though she wishes for things and then believes they have been agreed, even when they haven't.' His voice is so quiet I have to strain to catch every word.

I cannot find anything adequate to say in return.

Later in April my cousin Gemma goes to see Mum just before she's voluntarily admitted on to the mental health unit in Dartford for a third time. She is badly shaken by what she sees. She rings to tell me. Her reaction shakes me. Gemma is rarely seen to lose her poise. She has seen more shocking things in her time as a junior doctor than I will ever see. And she has lost Euphan, her own mother – gone in the blink of an eye. Taken from her and Simon and John brutally fast, only a few years ago. There had been no warning, no sign of illness. At Euphan's funeral, while others had wept, Gemma had been her mother's daughter: upright, neat, smiling, the perfect hostess at the wake.

Now she is trying to keep that composure, but the waver in her voice tells a different story.

'I couldn't have a conversation with Gillian,' Gemma tells me. 'She just ranted on a loop about her current list of anxieties. Or she was completely silent.'

'I know,' I reply. There is nothing else to say.

'She is lucky to have had so much love and stability in her life,' Gemma says.

The use of the past tense is not lost on me.

So much stability: Grandma and her constant reassuring presence. Dad and his endless love and patience. 'Oh, my light and my life.'

'I have seen many people with mental illness who have not had that kind of support,' Gemma says. 'Their lives descend into hell as people abandon them.'

I stifle a sob. *Abandon.* Mum asked me not to abandon

her last year. And now she is in the unit again, broken, lost, frightened. What have I done if not abandoned her?

∾

Most days my chest is tight and I find it hard to breathe. At one point I go to the doctor, fearing an asthma attack or, worse, a heart condition. 'Stress' is the diagnosis. I bolt from the surgery, wanting to cry, to pound my fists, to rend my clothes and tear my hair. What can I do about stress at a time like this? I haven't got time for stress.

I know it would do me good to cry, but the tears won't come. On other days, I find crying comes too easily and when I least want it to. I am talking to a woman in a health food shop, asking about supplements to ease my pounding heart, to help me sleep. She looks deep into my eyes.

'You look very tired,' she says.

Her kindness is too much. I break down.

The kindness of strangers is harder to resist than that of friends and family. It opens a fissure in my rock-hard, angry façade; the pressure gives and the explosion comes. I am a great roiling river, ready to burst its banks at the most inopportune moment.

John calls to say he's afraid nothing will improve now.

'The best we can hope for is another spell of brightness like the one in August when she was on pregabalin. If the levels of medication are altered to good effect, we might see a small improvement for a short time, but I'm afraid she is likely to show a step-down decline with the spaces in between the steps becoming shorter and shorter.'

∾

By Easter 2014 Mum is allowed home again. The weather is once more doing its best to keep up with the madness. There has been a sand storm in the Sahara. A billowing mass of sand has found its way over to the UK. It leaves a coating of dust everywhere inside and out, including noses, ears and throats. Mum was right all along: the mess and the chaos cannot be kept away. Everything is falling apart, choked, dry, dying.

Occasionally we try to fool ourselves that Mum can get better. Occasionally she will sit still. She will turn and look at Dad as he holds her hand, and one of those breathtakingly beautiful smiles will break through the hysteria and the gloom. Or one of the kids will say something funny and she will look at them and smile and it's like a benediction. When this happens, I want to grab that smile and hold on to it and turn it around and show it to Mum and say, 'Look! You are happy! Look! You are beautiful!'

And then there is a clatter of plates from the kitchen or an ambulance goes past or Dad says, 'We should probably leave in about fifteen minutes,' and Mum is off, whooping and panting and panicking and repeating Dad's name over and over.

MARTINMARTINMARTIN.

Her clothes hang off her now, her hair is fluffy and unkempt all the time. She no longer stops to apply make-up, to check her appearance in the mirror, to tilt her head to see whether the hat she is wearing suits her.

Who are we kidding? John is right. She will never get better.

Twenty-five

'[People] with autistic spectrum disorder (ASD) can find it really hard to focus on things that don't interest them . . . but they can keep their attention on things they like.'[25]

'It's raining. Get your coats on. We're going to Grandma's.' Mum drives Carrie and me the short distance to our grandparents' house. When we get there, we run up the drive and open the back door. It's always unlocked. Sometimes neighbours just walk in when we are there. Just 'popping in', as they say. Mum hates it when they do that. She says it's rude. We are not staying today, though, so no one will be able to pop in. Grandma is waiting for us. She already has her gabardine mackintosh on, and she's clutching her handbag, which matches her shiny brown shoes.

'Let's go to the Wells,' she says, 'and take your mum shopping.'

The Wells is Grandma's name for Tunbridge Wells. It is where we go when Mum is sad, when she needs cheering up. We always do the same things when we go there. First we go to the big department store called Weekes. We go looking for sewing patterns and fabric and thread, and afterwards we always go for a treat in the café.

The fabric is in the section called the 'haberdashery department'. That is where we go now. It is Grandma's favourite place. Mum's too. Grandma loves to sew. She has been making clothes since she was fourteen and she's really old now, so she's had a lot of practice, which is why she's very good at it. She makes Mum's dresses and skirts and blouses. She makes me and Carrie dresses with long lines of lace sewn down the front. And she does something called 'smocking', which she says is very tricky. It looks tricky. Lots and lots of tiny pleats and stitches, which she does by hand. She even sews buttonholes by hand. She makes us coats and bonnets too. She makes Mum long, floaty gowns for parties and smart jackets and skirts for special dinners with Dad. Mum loves clothes. She likes to look nice. She always smiles when we go shopping. Even if she has been sad before we go.

The first thing we do in the haberdashery department is to look for a pattern. There is a sort of long white shelf that has all the pattern books on. Mum and Grandma spend ages poring over these. Mum concentrates hard on looking for the perfect skirt or the perfect shirt for Grandma to make. She turns over page after page. Grandma helps her.

Carrie and I start to get bored. We are not tall enough to look at the pattern books. I stare at the brown-stockinged legs of the other women standing around the table. The sharp, clean smell of new cloth hangs in the airless room and flecks of cut cotton spin in shafts of light like fairy dust. My legs begin to ache. I want to go to the café. Carrie twirls around and talks to her Yellow Ted and pretends to be a princess while Mum and Grandma choose some material. This takes almost as long as it did to choose the pattern.

I go over to the racks of Silko cotton reels. The rainbow colours are like jars of sweets. I stand in front of the reels of thread and run my fingers over them, sending them spinning.

I imagine the joy of owning them all. I would never use them
– just keep them in a box and count them, like Dad's story
about King Midas, greedily counting his gold.

Mum has spotted me. 'Don't touch!' she snaps.

'We're nearly done,' says Grandma quickly. She puts a hand
on Mum's arm. 'Let's get a coffee after this. I'll treat you,'
she says to her.

Mum's frown melts away into a smile.

The shop lady has heaved a huge, heavy bolt of dark-green
corduroy onto the long cutting table. Mum watches closely
as the lady pulls yards of the stuff out in long sweeps of her
arm. *One, two, three.* The lady draws her hand over the cloth,
pressing out any wrinkles or bumps like Mum does when
she's ironing. And then she picks up the scissors. Those scissors! How I dream of having a pair like that. So big, so shiny.
The lady makes a tiny nick in the fabric – a click, a snip – and
then she pushes the scissors along in a straight line to the
other side of the table. The other side of the cloth is called
the selvedge, Grandma says.

Haberdashery. Silko. Selvedge.

The magic of the words and the colours and the glorious
ripping sound of the scissors make me forget my boredom.

Soon we are in the café, drinking orange squash and eating
a Nice biscuit while Mum and Grandma drink weak, milky
Nescafé from light-green Woods Ware cups. Mum is chattering to Grandma about the new skirt she will soon be able
to wear. She has forgotten about being sad. She is excited
and smiling and happy. And so are we.

Twenty-six

'Stress is an important factor for families of autistic people and front line professionals working with them. Reports in the literature of "burn out" largely emphasise the difficulties and demands of living and working with autistic children and adults. The transactional nature of stress should therefore receive more attention. People forming the support network of the autistic person should be helped to understand their own stress and mindsets and how to manage these.'[26]

While Mum is in Dartford, Dad comes to stay. I have suggested it as a holiday for him since he can't go to Italy. He is reluctant as first as he doesn't want to leave Kent. He wants to be able to visit Mum every day. But as she sometimes doesn't seem to want to see him, he finally agrees to come for a couple of nights.

Carrie and I are worried that he is sinking under a tsunami of exhaustion. He arrives at ten at night, having spent the day going to Dartford to see Mum and then driving to me in Wiltshire. He is shattered, crumpled, full of a cold virus, lost and sad. I give him a hot toddy and pack him off to bed. Mothering Father now.

In spite of Dad's physical and emotional state, we have the kind of weekend I have long dreamed of having with my parents. Dad wakes full of smiles and ready to spend the day with Tom, who is eager to make an outdoor house for his newly acquired tortoise. Dad is thrilled that we have a tortoise and loves building things.

'Do you remember Moony?' he asks me, chuckling, as he sets to work planning the house with Tom.

How could I forget the tiny tortoise I had in 1978 whose existence was short, but whose name lives on in family legend? I talk about him every time I give a talk at a school visit; my own kids feel sure they must have met him at some point in the dim and distant past. The combination of my stories and a recent reading of Gerald Durrell's *My Family and Other Animals* had led to Tom getting his own tortoise, Hercules.

I watch as Dad relives happier days, pootling around with Tom as they choose lengths of wood and fetch chicken wire and set about making a run for the little tortoise so that he can be released from his box in Tom's room to enjoy the spring air.

Look at them: my father and my son. Laughing and chatting. Completely absorbed in one another and in what they are doing together. This is what the grandparent/child relationship is supposed to look like. And Mum is missing out.

Later that weekend we go kayaking. We drive two heavy sea kayaks down to the Avon near our house. Spring has arrived and it is loud and it is proud. The hedgerows are bursting with flashes of white mayflower. The fields are dotted with yellow kingcups. The river is green and clear and fresh and gives off its inviting earthy aroma. It is too cruel that Mum is incarcerated on an airless ward while spring is bursting into song around us. This is her favourite season. Yellow and green are her favourite colours. She should be here, watching us, strolling along the riverbank, turning her face to the sun, smiling. And yet, of course, I know that Mum, in her present state, can't behave like this. She wouldn't be able to enjoy this scene. She is better off where she is, I tell myself. Even if the tortoise is getting more fresh air than she is now.

The river has played an important part in Dad's life and, by extension, in the life of our family. Dad learnt to row on a tributary of the Thames when he was a boy. He has been messing about in boats ever since. He has brought me and Carrie up in this watery world, filling our heads with the adventures of Ratty and Mole and singing us songs about Michael rowing the boat ashore, long before we were strong enough to steer a boat ourselves.

He has a racing kayak and a Canadian canoe hanging from his garage ceiling. His Sunday mornings have been spent in a religious two-hour act of watery worship on the Medway, timing himself as he sprints around the island near the Rec, coasting along in silence watching kingfishers and water voles, letting his mind wander, allowing the race and pace of the week to be washed away on the current. Mum used to go out in the Canadian with him on lazy spring and summer evenings.

'I haven't been able to get on the river for months,' he tells me as we park the car and get out to unload the boats.

He doesn't have to elaborate on what this has cost him.

I reach up to untie the kayaks and Dad comes around to help. He winces and gasps as he helps me lift the first one down.

'What's up, Dad?'

'It's just my leg.'

It doesn't look like 'just' anything – he is in pain. I start to say something, but he brushes me aside. He lowers the double kayak into the water, gets in with Tom and paddles off.

Later that evening I do ask him about it. His leg.

'I've got a lump. Doctor says it's a strained muscle. From the stress.'

A lump.

It triggers a prickle of fear. No. Not that. Not Dad. Please, not Dad. Not now.

It's my turn to brush things aside. I ask no more questions. Now is not the time. Not when I have Dad to myself.

We talk instead about Mum. Our default setting.

'She was so bad last week I feared I had lost her for good,' Dad tells me. 'The staff say Mum relies too heavily on me.'

I bite back words of agreement. I swallow down comments about it being too late to be told this. I try distraction instead: good food, good wine, comedy on the telly, games with Tom. I am trying to hold on to him, to hold him up, to stop him from being engulfed, to get him to stay with us, to get him to forget his troubles – forget Mum.

Dad stays for two days only. I try to get him to stay longer, but he is keen – desperate – to get back to see Mum. When he leaves I argue with David. He needs me to listen to him, to focus on him, to be present for him. I can't. All I can do is talk about Mum and Dad. Mum and Dad. Mum and Dad.

MumandDadandMumandDadandMum.

'She's killing him!' I rage.

David doesn't need this. He has to leave at 4 a.m. the next day to get on a plane. He doesn't recognise this angry, broken woman, red from crying, stretched and raw from lack of sleep. He wants me, his wife, his best friend, back. He wants our life together back. He snaps and shouts. I wail and scream and storm out into the dark.

I pace around the village, crying, talking to myself, demented. I end up in the church, where I sit and listen to a Maundy Thursday service. I feel empty, disconnected, washed through and out with tears and grief and exhaustion. I want someone to notice me. To ask: are you OK? What's the matter? Do you need help? Then I don't want that at all. I want to be alone, to vanish into the night. I slink out and back home and sink into bed in the dark.

⁓

Mum is allowed home at the beginning of May 2014 'for a little while'. No one seems to know what this means. I ring her and she lashes out at me. She accuses me, among other things, of not being there for her. I wonder if she knows she is pushing just the right combination of buttons to send me spiralling down. Then I hear Grandma's voice, telling me, *You've just got to forgive her. She's always been like this.*

Yes. Yes, I know. She has always been difficult, moody, tricky to handle. So what? Why should we all tiptoe around it? Why does *she* get to have the monopoly on bad behaviour? What about me? What about Carrie? When do we get to scream and shout and still be cared for? 'I have feelings too,' as Mum used to say.

And suddenly I want to shout at her. To remind her of something; of her promises in that beautiful letter from the summer before. Of her vow to 'try and face the future more calmly'.

But then I think of my own promise. To not abandon her. Have I kept that?

I listen to Mum, who is still berating me. I try to keep breathing evenly, to not give in to the rage and the tears that are building up inside. I keep my voice light and chatter emptily instead. I give news of the grandchildren. Lucy is about to start her GCSEs. Tom will have to make his choices soon . . .

Mum is not listening. She switches abruptly from moaning at me to blurting out, 'I've got an abscess. On a molar.'

Dad comes on the line. I am pretty sure he has grabbed the phone from Mum. He barks that there is nothing wrong with Mum's tooth.

'I drove you to the emergency dentist in Rochester on Saturday night at nine p.m., didn't I?' he snaps.

I can hear Mum retreating, wounded, saying she is useless and sorry and that her tooth still hurts.

I should feel empathy. I should rush down there. I should help Dad out. I should take Mum off his hands so that he can have a break. I should ask him about his leg. I should not abandon them.

Instead I put down the phone, drink too much wine and write a text to Carrie.

You were right. The stress is going to kill Dad. Mum is going to kill him and I will never forgive her for that.

Twenty-seven

'There can be changes in sleep patterns and appetite, and a negative attitude that pervades all aspects of life and, in extreme cases, talk of suicide, or impulsive or planned suicide attempts.'[27]

On 23 May 2014 Mum and Dad come to stay for the Bank Holiday and Mum brings the rain with her again. We are stuck indoors playing board games, charades, watching telly. Toddler-minding. We suggest walks, using the dog as an excuse, thinking that fresh air would do Mum good.

Mum will not go out in even the mildest drizzle.

'Too much mud.'

Time drags and I can't help feeling relief when Dad says he would like to leave after lunch on the Monday.

'My leg is more painful after driving,' he says. 'I'd like to get home promptly so I can rest it before going to bed.'

I tell myself to ignore the nagging at the back of my mind. It's Mum I have to worry about. Dad is tired, yes, but Mum is the one who's sick.

A few hours after they have gone I notice Mum has left her umbrella behind. I will post it back as it's the only one she will use. I'll have to call to let them know I'll be doing this; an unexpected parcel can set off a cyclone of panic, as could the realisation that Mum has left her favourite umbrella at our house.

But I don't want to call. If I do, I'll be sucked into another whirlpool of misery. Mum will tell me every detail of the journey home and will moan about the fact that we live so far from Kent. I am tired and want a relaxing evening before we all go back to work and school. I decide to text Dad instead, thinking he'll pick it up the next day, by which time I will have posted the umbrella anyway. I have done my bit, having them to stay. I don't need to put myself through a phone call.

A couple of seconds after I have sent the text, my phone pings back in reply.

It's Dad: *Don't bother posting. She's in Pembury.*

Pembury? As in Pembury hospital? As in the hospital where I sat last May with Dad and gave Mum's medical history while she was tested for a urine infection and— what the hell is she doing in hospital?

The answer is already rushing to the forefront of my mind, but I push it away. I bring up my parents' landline number and listen to the ring tone.

My heart is hammering.

What's happened?

You know what's happened.

No. No. No.

'Tonbridge three-five-oh—'

'Dad, it's me. Why's Mum in Pembury?'

A sigh. Then, carefully, in a level, restrained voice, Dad says, 'Mum went up to the bathroom when we got home.'

I know what you're going to say. Don't say it. Don't.

'She took all her pills—'

No.

'She came down and told me what she'd done. I said I'd
call nine-nine-nine and she begged me not to. I ignored her.'
No. No. No.
He breathes. In. Out.
I breathe. In. Out. 'And?'
Dad's tone becomes suddenly careless. 'Apparently it's quite
difficult to kill yourself with these drugs. She won't have her
stomach pumped. They'll just monitor her while she becomes
woozier from the effect of taking so many. She is down to
have another psychiatric assessment later in the week.'
Apparently it's quite difficult to kill yourself.
So calm. So matter-of-fact.
As though it were a minor inconvenience.
What is wrong with Dad? Why isn't he angry? Upset, at
least? What is it with his carefree explanation about 'feeling
woozy', for fuck's sake? And those bloody drugs. They have
done Mum no good and now they have done this.
I want to reach down the phone, to shake Dad, to make
him listen to what he has just said, to make him cry. Anything
but this calm tone of voice, this level-headed attitude, chatting away to me as though trying to kill yourself with packets
and packets of pills is the most normal thing in the world for
a woman to do after she's spent a weekend with her daughter
and grandchildren.
Breathe. In. Out. In.
He's not calm. Of course he's not. He's not angry either,
though. He's not anything any more.
He's given up.
Family anecdotes run through my mind as Dad talks on
about Mum's depression. That story of the sea again. And
another one: how John and Mum would be walking along
the road together, mere children, and she would turn to him
and say, 'I can't see the point in carrying on.' Grandma, her

face creased with sadness, telling me how miserable Mum has always been.

Perhaps it's a miracle that Mum hasn't taken all her pills before now.

I remember my grandmother saying to me, her adult grand-daughter, 'I'm so worried about Gillian', using her name, no longer calling her 'your mum'. This is what Dad is doing increasingly now too. I didn't engage with Grandma's worries, just as I didn't engage with Dad that day outside the Albert Hall. I didn't say anything helpful. I didn't say, 'Don't worry, Grandma. You can rely on me. I'll look after Mum.' I heard what Grandma was saying, but I didn't listen. I didn't stop to think that Grandma had quite possibly also seen Mum try to end it all. And possibly more than once.

Has Dad seen this before? Is this what lends weight to his careless tone?

Been there, seen that.

His next comment makes me sure he must have. 'I should have known,' he says. He tells me about a night in 1963 when he and Mum were very much an item and had already talked of a future together, marriage, children.

'It was a beautiful June night. We had danced and laughed and had fun with our friends. As the evening ended and we walked out to go our separate ways back to our rooms, your mother became quite over-emotional. She was sobbing her heart out. I was worried that I had hurt her or offended her in some way. I asked her what the matter was and she said, "I am just so happy. Tonight was so wonderful. What if I am never this happy ever again?"'

I know the night he's talking about. I've seen the photo. I used to pore over it, transfixed by my mother, beautiful in a floor-length gown in damask fabric, which Grandma had made. Mum has a cream stole flung around her tiny shoulders and she's laughing into the camera, chinking champagne glasses with Dad. He is gazing on her with adoration. I have looked at that photo time and again as though it holds the key to understanding my parents, seeing them in the first flush of love. Look at them! They are both so happy. So young! This was before a time for mourning or weeping. This was their time to laugh; their time to dance.

The black and white, of course, lends the photo a certain glamour. But I imagine that even in harsh, unedited, high-definition colour, my mother would still look like a film star in that wonderful ballgown. Their eyes have the sheen of a couple of young people who have drunk more alcohol than they are perhaps used to. Dad's bow tie is askew and there is a slight tipsiness in his smile. Even so, there is much to be gleaned from this picture. Dad can't tear his gaze away from Mum, while Mum is looking out of the picture, towards the photographer or a group of onlookers, perhaps. I have often thought how this photo encapsulates their relationship: Dad ever the loving protector, unable to drag his eyes from Mum; Mum always looking away, never quite inhabiting the moment, looking for something else.

I am silent as I listen to Dad sigh. 'I should have known then, shouldn't I?' he says again.

But how could he – how could any of us – have predicted that things would end this way?

Twenty-eight

*'Many carers can all too easily get caught in a cycle of resent-
ment and guilt – resentful that their life is no longer their own,
and guilty for feeling like this.'*[28]

It is already July 2014. We are over halfway through a year
that I yearn to consign to history. I am wishing time away.
I need to pause, to escape.

I get the chance to do this for a few days because I am
promoting my latest children's book. The book is set in West
Penwith in Cornwall, so I go to the Penzance Literary Festival
to give talks, to stay with David's relatives and to walk and
swim and sleep and breathe. I try to focus on feeling my
limbs loosen, to revert to the version of me I am happiest
with: the writer, the nature-lover, the water baby. I slip into
my element and convince myself I have forgotten about that
other me: the daughter.

I can't keep her at bay for long, though. She is there,
nagging at the back of my mind all the time, prodding me to
call Mum and Dad, to do the right thing, to stop being selfish
in following my own pleasures while they are suffering. The
daughter's voice grows louder the longer I stay away.

One night an electric storm crackles over the sea. I sit in the kitchen at David's aunt's house and watch forked lightning split the ink-blue sky. Trains are struck by it. Huge chunks of ancient granite are knocked off balance and tumble into the water below. Sixty-foot waves crash up on to the coastline. Everyone is destabilised by this unseasonable weather; the chatter in the shops and cafés is about nothing else.

I am out of kilter too. I'm not entirely present when I'm talking to the girls from Cape Cornwall School about my ghost story. I can hear my voice as though listening to one of the tape recordings I used to make with my best friend and her brother when we were kids. It's a hollow, fake voice, reading from a script. There is no passion in my storytelling. I have been buffeted too hard by the storms of the past year. I don't care about my work any more. Can't care about it.

That's because I shouldn't be here. But seeing as I am, I should at least be phoning Dad every day. I should be asking him about his leg, which seems to have slipped off the agenda since Mum's suicide attempt. I should be asking after Mum, who, Carrie tells me, has recently made Dad cry in the street from stress.

I can't think about that. I am far away from it all, at the land's end. At the edge of the world. What use am I while I am here? I might as well try to enjoy it. Guilt pushes and pulls at me as I sit on the rocks every morning and watch the tide come in and go out.

∽

Two weeks later, on Friday 8 August 2014, I call Dad. He tells me he's going to have a scan on his leg today. I make sympathetic noises and wish him luck. I don't let myself dwell on this because we have to talk about Mum's birthday, which is coming up.

Mum's seventy-first birthday. She is not asking for any attention this year, which should be a relief. Instead it's worrying. I fear it's only the calm before the storm. It is too ingrained in me, the terror of being raged at for arriving late, of bringing the wrong present, of saying the wrong thing.

We will go, though. We will go and play our part because Dad wants us to.

When we get there, we find a woman who is no longer capable of the aggression she has displayed in the past. The happy, loving woman who was revealed by the wave of the pregabalin wand has also disappeared. Instead we find a woman consumed by fear. Mum's new drugs seem to have knocked all the stuffing from her. She is transformed. A ghost, far more terrifying than any I could conjure up for a story. It is too awful to hear her faint, quavering voice, to look at her haunted, white face, to see those once bright emerald eyes reduced even further to a milky jade, full of terror.

I take hold of her and hug her to me. She is small and her shoulders are bony.

She clings to me like my children used to.

'I am frightened of everything,' she says.

Dad refuses to talk about this subdued, shrunken figure in our midst. He is determined that we should make the day fun. That is what we are here for: to distract and entertain. He plays the over-exuberant host, cooking an elaborate meal while drinking most of a bottle of red wine in the corner of the garden, his back to us while he tends his beloved barbecue. He leaves us to struggle along, making conversation with Mum, who is not interested in us being here and wants only to cling to Dad.

'Go and play with her,' he might as well be saying. 'Daddy needs a break.'

After lunch, in desperation, we play charades. Lucy and Tom are young adults now. They don't want to play games with their alarmingly crazy grandmother. Dad suggests we go swimming with Mum. We used to do this when the children were small. I would take us down to the town pool and Mum would swim lengths while I played mind-numbing games of water-tag until I was told it was time for us to get out. But this was almost ten years ago, when the children were content to splash around; when they wanted nothing more than an afternoon in the sun with ice creams and swimming and sand pits and mini golf. Now they want to stay inside, gawp at their phones and preferably be ignored by us boring old farts. And who can blame them on a day like this?

Except that today they don't complain. Even in their most inward-looking teen mode, they can tell when the mark has been presented and they are expected to step up to it. So we go to the pool.

I am hopeful when Mum brings her swimming bag – the same misshapen, striped, quilted bag she has used for as long as I can remember. Maybe she will swim some lengths in the outdoor pool? Maybe she is taking advice these days about doing exercise?

We arrive and Lucy and Tom go off to change.

Mum stands in silence, watching them go. What is she waiting for? She knows this place inside out.

I hesitate before asking, 'Do you want me to help you?'

Mum shakes her head. A sullen child. 'No.'

'OK. I think I'll get changed then. Shall I see you in the pool?'

'No,' she says, 'I can't.'

I try half-heartedly to persuade her. 'Dad said it would do you good.'

'No. I want to watch the kids.'

Tom and Lucy are hardly at an age where it's fun to watch them splash about. They have long since ceased to chase each other and play tag.

It doesn't much matter. In the end Mum sits on the patio beside the outdoor pool and stares at the sky. She doesn't even watch Lucy and Tom. It is as though she is not aware of where she is. She is seventy-one. She's my mum, but she looks like a lost child.

'I can't' and 'No' have become her default position. It's as though she's shutting down all possible options before she has to deal with them. As though the labyrinth of choice she sees before her is too terrifying to contemplate. Easier and more effective to just say no.

～

We get through the day and collapse into the car in silence. I can't wait to be far away from my parents, tucked up on my own sofa in my own house with my own family and my dog, who is never welcome at Mum's.

The minute I step through the door my phone pings. An email from Dad. It is short. To the point. Its message so sharp, it stabs me in the gut. It is not something I can take in. Not something Dad can take in, either, I presume, as he was not able to say the words aloud earlier that day. Not in front of Mum. Probably not in front of the kids either. Another elephant, this time too big to be completely ignored.

'The lump in my leg is a "growth" according to the MRI. I have to have a biopsy and then an operation to get it removed.'

Lump.

Biopsy.

I re-read the email. I show it to David.

Lump.

Biopsy.

Everyone knows what this means.

But it can't mean that.

Not that.

Not—

There is no way I am saying the word that lurks behind this coded message. If I don't say it, it won't be true.

Dad can't have – that. He is Mum's other half. Her best friend. She is the sick one. He is the strong one.

'I love your dad,' she used to say, hugging and kissing him in front of us when Carrie and I were teenagers, making us squirm and hide our eyes and shout, 'Stop it!'

'If anything ever happened to your dad, I don't know what I'd do,' she would say, gazing at him lovingly.

And on days when the monster raged: 'If anyone ever tried to run off with your dad, I'd come after them with a KNIFE!'

We didn't doubt it – I don't think Dad did, either.

Dad and Mum. Mum and Dad. Two halves of the same being. There is no Mum without Dad.

I should be focusing on him now. I should have words of comfort to offer him. I should be telling him that he needn't worry, I will be there for him. And for Mum.

Instead, I am thinking and saying, over and over, to anyone who'll listen: 'Who the hell will look after Mum when Dad is in hospital?'

The storm is here now. I listen as the waves rear up and crash on to the shore. I am powerless against them. There is no way back from this. I will be dashed to pieces against the dark, hard, unforgiving granite.

Twenty-nine

'Unfortunately it is extremely common for people with Asperger's Syndrome to also have depression and anxiety challenges . . . I've also had some very dark thoughts about death.'[29]

C arrie and I spend the rest of the summer rushing about with our kids, packing in as much as we can before term begins again. We don't talk about Dad and the lump in his leg. It's as though we believe that if we don't talk about what's happening, if we keep busy enough, we will be able to prevent the inevitable.

On 30 August 2014 we can prevent it no longer. I go to see Dad. His face is twisted with the effort of finally saying the words aloud.

'It's most likely cancer.'

I keep my eyes on him. I stay completely still. I mustn't let a single sound escape from me. Otherwise I will fall apart.

'They have to do a CT scan, apparently, to see if it has spread before they do a biopsy,' Dad says. Always calm, always careful. Even now.

He looks almost embarrassed. What is he really thinking? Really feeling? I can't ask him. I have nothing to say that will not come out as hysteria. I nod and listen and eventually ask a few practical questions, and the conversation moves on, past the elephant. Nothing to see here.

∽

Over the next few days I tell myself, and Carrie, and Dad, that there's still a chance it's not cancer. I say it to Lucy when I take her aside to tell her the news. Her reaction – to collapse into my arms in tears – is too much for me. I can't respond to her emotions. I hold her firmly by the shoulders and say, 'It will be all right.' I have to say this repeatedly to myself, to everyone around me, because Mum is saying the opposite. She is panicking enough for everyone. She is saying what is ricocheting around my head every spare moment I have. She is saying what I am trying so hard to block out.

He's got cancer! Cancer! Cancer!

It is the end of her world. Mum needs Dad. She needs him to be well. He is the only one she trusts. The only one she can rely on. She needs him to be there every morning to make her porridge. She needs him to be there to count out her pills, to make sure she takes them, to pour her orange juice, to make her coffee. She needs him to sit with her, to hold her hand, to make lunch at one o'clock, to turn on the evening news at six. To tell her he loves her and he'll always be there for her. Always.

He can't go and have scans. He can't have biopsies. He can't have cancer. He can't . . . not be there.

Carrie and I tell Mum that we don't even know what kind of cancer it is yet. We tell her that people don't necessarily die from cancer any more. We tell her these things to try to calm her. We are not sure we believe them. It's all fairy tales. Myths and legends and bedtime stories.

Mum sees right through us. Of course she does. The word 'cancer' strikes fear into anyone who hears it, but most of us manage to get through life without assuming it is stalking us at every turn. For Mum, cancer has been waiting in the wings for as long as she can remember. And cancer has always equated to death in Mum's mind. There are no grey areas; there is no hope. Cancer is the end of the line. This possible diagnosis for Dad is simply proof to Mum that she has been right all along, and nothing we can say will help her to think about it differently.

When Mum had respiratory problems in her thirties and insisted on seeing an ear, nose and throat specialist who told her she had polyps in her sinuses, she was convinced it was cancer. When she had gastric problems in her forties and fifties, it had to be bowel cancer. When she went through the menopause she wouldn't even consider taking HRT because it would cause cancer. When she suspected prolapse in her late sixties, that was surely uterine cancer. When I had CIN2 or 'pre-cancerous cells' on my cervix in my thirties, I didn't tell her. I knew that it would lead to a level of catastrophising that I could not cope with.

Mum's health obsessions dominated family life. She would follow the latest advice on diet and nutrition religiously, in the hope that a new regime would contain her health-related anxieties. She would read out the shocking headlines over breakfast. She was the one in charge of shopping for, planning and preparing the family meals, so her latest fads would affect us all. One month we were eating beans in enormous quantities because someone had decreed they were the answer to long life and happiness; the next she was insisting on wholegrain pasta with everything. In later life she would regularly grab the butter from Dad before he could take a second helping.

'Don't spread it so thick, Martin! Think of your cholesterol! You might get stomach cancer!'

She would slather us in sun cream and get cross with Dad for wandering around without a shirt on in the summer.

'Skin cancer!'

She would not let us eat an apple before washing it with forensic attention.

'Pesticides – cancer!'

We didn't think anything of it, other than to occasionally get bored or annoyed. Mostly we ignored her pleas and lectures. We were used to it. It didn't mean anything. No one ever got sick, and yet still she still persisted in crying, 'Wolf!'

And now the wolf was at the door.

⌁

It's in my brain too, howling at me, hunting me through the night. I regularly wake at 3 a.m., gasping as though someone has chucked cold water in my face. I am assaulted by a taunting voice; a stream of panic that I spend the hours of daylight trying to keep at bay.

He has cancer.

But he might not have.

He is going to die.

Or he might not.

It might be one of those curable ones.

If they cut the lump out it will be fine.

But what if they have to cut his whole leg off?

Mum can't cope.

Mum is mentally ill.

Mum doesn't understand what's happening.

Or she does, which is worse.

She will never cope with him losing a leg.

Don't think about that don't think about that.
How will I look after her?
I can't look after her.
He might be dying.
He might not.
He has cancer.
But he might not have . . .

∽

On 9 September 2014 Dad has the scan and biopsy. He must wait a further two weeks to find out the results. On 17 September he is told he must start weekly radiotherapy from the following Monday. He has to travel from Tonbridge to Stanmore, north of London, for this: a round trip of 130 miles. He will be in too much pain – sorry, 'discomfort' – to drive, so he has to go by train, underground and train again.

He wants Mum to go with him. Mum will not go.

'I can't! I can't!'

Over the past year and a half, Dad has just about managed to continue taking her to Italian classes, to bridge games with friends, even out to meals. She has begun to protest more and more, however, making it harder for Dad to do anything with his own life.

'I can't! No!' is Mum's answer to everything.

Dad has persisted because otherwise what would he do? He can't stay in with Mum all the time. And he can't go out and leave Mum on her own.

But this time he will have to. She refuses point-blank to go to Stanmore with him.

John tells me, 'The radiotherapy treatment is not nice. It will leave Martin feeling awful. I'm afraid the outlook is not good. He has the sword of Damocles hanging over him.'

Dad is not the only one with a sword poised above his head. We are all waiting for the crash, although we don't talk about it. Instead we want to believe Dad's stoicism, his constant insistence that 'everything will be fine'.

∽

On 23 September 2014 Dad tells me, 'The biopsy shows that the lump is in my thigh muscle.' He pauses.

I want him to tell me. I don't want him to tell me. 'And—?'

'It's malignant. I'm probably going to have to have an operation, possibly before Christmas, which will mean Mum will be left home alone for a couple of days.'

I know what he wants me to say. He wants me to jump in, to reassure him that I will look after Mum. My answer is the same as hers would be: I can't. I can't. I can't. She is mad and I have two children and I live a hundred and forty miles away and she is mad and the last time I came to help I nearly went mad myself. I can't.

My throat is very dry. I say quietly, 'You'll need to rest when you're discharged, Dad.'

'No, no.' He brushes this aside. 'I'll be fine. I have Mum.'

Carrie and I have no idea what to do, what to feel, what to say. We try to allow ourselves to be carried along on Dad's wave of optimism. He is convinced that they will manage without professional help, but we know that Mum will not cope alone and that she will not let Dad rest after the operation. She is not letting him rest now. She pulls at his sleeve, follows him around the house, talks at him incessantly as though to reassure herself that he is still there. She is a child who is afraid of being left alone in the dark. A child who is afraid of being left alone for ever.

Thirty

'Many autistic people experience social isolation.'[30]

O nce again it is John who tips me over into action. He writes to me after spending a weekend in Cambridge with Mum and Dad.

Cambridge? What is Dad doing, taking Mum all the way to Cambridge?

More to the point, how has he managed it when days before she was refusing to walk to the corner shop with him?

I should have known Dad would move mountains to get to the annual Alumni Festival; this yearly reunion has been a highlight of Mum and Dad's calendar for the past twenty years – since Carrie and I left home. They would start planning the weekend as soon as the programme of events came out in the spring. They would chatter excitedly about the talks on Classics that they wanted to go to. They would meet up with old friends and with John (and, not so long ago, my Aunt Euphan too), and go for lunch in one of the cafés or pubs that have hardly changed, almost fifty years since they first met. They would go punting on the Backs, and laugh and reminisce, reliving the golden days of their youth for a weekend.

This time, however, those golden days are harder to conjure up. John writes that it was distressing to see his sister unable to engage with anyone or anything. He was worried that Dad had withdrawn further into 'his denial state'.

'There were tears in my eyes when we walked round the Newnham College gardens,' he writes. 'I remember happier days in 1965 when they were celebrating their engagement on the same spot.'

He goes on to say that he can't see how Mum can be left alone in the house while Dad is in hospital. 'The consequences are too awful to imagine.' He says that Mum will need caring for either in her own home or in a care home. 'I'm sure someone from the psychiatric team will be able to advise you,' he says.

But it's not me that needs this advice. It's Dad. He's Mum's first port of call and I can't do anything without his permission. Yet when I call Dad to try to put John's concerns to him, he tells me that he has it 'all under control'.

'Mum didn't cope well with going to Cambridge,' I say. 'How is she going to react to an even bigger change in routine when you go into hospital?' I can't keep the nagging tone from my voice.

Dad is used to nagging. 'Don't worry, love,' he says. His voice is warm, mollifying, as it has had to be so many times over the years. I picture one of his reassuring smiles as he goes on. His calmness breaks my heart and enrages me all at once. 'We've got some wonderful friends and neighbours,' he says. 'They've said they'll look in on Mum while I have my treatment. People have been very kind already. R and A have been around to sit with Mum. Sometimes they've even succeeded in getting her out of the house for short walks and meals. And they've played bridge with her! That kept her quiet for almost two hours!' He sounds exultant at this. As though Mum is a small child who's slept through the night for the first time.

'That's good,' I reply. I don't know what else to say. His, to me, obstinate optimism is an impenetrable wall.

Is this the way to keep Mum stable? By organising a series of bridge deals for her with friends while Dad has his operation? I try to tell myself that the bridge games are a good sign. It is true that the card game seems to have the same effect on Mum as ironing does. All her frenetic energy is reduced down into an intense concentration. It is a game that she takes very seriously and can talk about at great length – another obsession. I should be thankful that a card game with caring friends has come to Dad's rescue in this way.

Any feelings of gratitude are short-lived. When I get in touch with these friends and neighbours to thank them for their support, they give me a different picture from the one Dad has painted. They report back along the same lines as John: that Mum is very distressed – permanently panic-stricken, even – that she does not want to be left alone, but that, unless she is absorbed in playing bridge, she does not want to engage with anyone either. These people are clearly disturbed by Mum's behaviour and, in some cases, it seems that they are trying to tell me that they don't want to have to deal with it. I can hardly blame them.

One friend tells me, 'She wants people to sit with her and talk to her all the time, but she doesn't want to talk back. I brought her back to my house the other day because she begged me not to leave her alone. Once she was in my home she simply sat in the corner. She wanted the lights off and didn't want to do anything. I offered her a newspaper, but she didn't even want that. She just wanted to sit in the same room as me.'

I call Carrie.

'Mum is getting worse. She's lucky to have had the support of friends, but we can't rely on other people like this,' I tell her. 'We have to try to talk to Dad again about getting care for Mum. She needs professional support.'

My phone calls to my parents' friends have already elicited a string of emails and calls in response. It is clear that everyone is concerned that Dad is in denial. I am torn between feeling thankful for their input and frustrated that I am now having to answer all their messages on top of dealing with Dad and Mum.

∽

On 23 October 2014 I drive to Kent to see for myself how bad things have become. I plan to tackle the question of care for Mum in a face-to-face conversation. Dad is on his way back from another radiology appointment, so I agree to go straight to the station to fetch him. I plan to talk to him in the car before taking him back to Mum. I have practised the conversation over and over. I practise it again as I drive up the A4 from home. I have it all worked out.

'Dad,' I will say, 'I know you don't like me interfering, but I am so worried about you and Mum. You are already very tired and you will be even more exhausted after your operation. It's perfectly normal for people to have some help when they come out of hospital. Mum will be even more distressed when you come home and are not able to look after her.'

I will remind him how it was when Grandma had operations in the past. She had gone into respite care for a week to recuperate and Mum had been as glad of this as Grandma, as by then the balance of their relationship was beginning to tip. Grandma was needing Mum more than Mum needed her.

Even as I remember this, I realise that Mum and I reached that tipping point a long time ago.

I leave the M25 and pick up speed on the A21. This time I will get through to Dad. This will be a productive visit. I will achieve what needs to be done. I am almost smiling when I take the slip-road to Tonbridge when—

CLACK-CLACK-CLACK

The car makes an alarming noise, shudders and veers to the left. I slow down and pull in as soon as I am able.

A flat tyre. Five miles from the station. Two miles from the nearest garage. I call the AA and then call Dad and tell him what's happened.

'I'm sorry, I'm going to be late. The AA will be an hour, they think.'

'OK, love.' He sounds weary, as though he knew something like this would happen. 'Can you call your mother?'

I have made things worse already. Mum was expecting one thing to happen – for me to fetch Dad and then come and see her – and now another thing has happened. She will be upset that I have had a flat tyre. She will catastrophise the situation – probably equate it to a car accident. I will be responsible for making her more upset than she already is.

I call her.

'Hello?' I haven't said anything yet and she already sounds terrified.

I explain, calmly and carefully what has happened and that everything will be all right. Mum holds her breath, then gasps as though choking, then breathes fast and loudly, then whoops.

'Just sit tight, Mum,' I say. 'I'll be there as soon as I can. Dad will probably get to you before I do now.'

She replaces the receiver with a loud clatter and no goodbye.

As I sit waiting for the AA, I catch sight of a man dressed entirely in white walking down the middle of the road. I lean towards my wing mirror. I turn around to get a proper look. No, I'm not hallucinating. There is a young man, walking on crutches, following the dotted lines, ignoring the hoots from cars as they pass him at speed.

I sit there thinking, 'Someone will slow down. Someone will ask him if he's OK.'

No one does. I watch as he draws parallel with me. He doesn't look up. He stares with a dark, furious expression at the dotted line ahead of him. He doesn't attempt to leave the centre of the road. I can't even catch his eye. I think about calling out to him, but if I startle him he might get knocked by the next car that comes haring along.

I call the police instead. They say they will come and get him.

Where has he come from? Where does he think he's going? What will happen to him? Does anyone care? I think of my cousin Gemma's words about how lucky Mum has been, about how many people with mental illness don't have a loving partner, a family and friends who care for them.

I shake the thoughts away. I can't do any more for that poor man. I can't take him on too.

∽

I make it to my parents an hour later. Dad is there. I hug him. He smiles weakly. My dad, my once glowing, happy, jovial father. He is shrunken now. His face is thin, hollowed out. The light has gone from his eyes. He is sapped, his skin lined, his hair wispy-white.

Mum won't let me hold her. She greets me with, 'I'm ugly, aren't I?', then stares at the wall and whispers, 'Ugly, ugly, ugly.'

She sits down, leaps up, paces, wails and moans.

It's not surprising that her friends are uncomfortable in her presence.

'It's like looking after a child,' Dad says quietly.

I cannot bear to meet his eyes. How long will this last? Will even Dad find it too much in the end?

I stay for three hours and do not find a single opportunity to bring up the subject of respite care. I go and get a new tyre before driving the five-hour journey back home, my heart as heavy as the rain and the traffic.

Thirty-one

*'Whenever someone tries to change my plans I'll feel upset
because it feels I've been thrown into a new situation without
any chance for preparation. I need to plan and organise everything. I can't just spontaneously do something, my brain doesn't
function in that manner.'*[31]

Two days after my visit, Carrie gets in touch with Dad by
email. She says she doesn't like resorting to writing, but
that we are finding it hard to have a conversation with him.
Mum listens in on all phone calls now, or follows him around
the house if we try to call his mobile. Carrie's words are full
of love and concern. She makes it clear that all we want to
do is help; that we both care deeply for him and Mum.

There is radio silence after this email. Carrie and I call each
other frantically. Have we upset Dad? Is he going to cut us
out of the picture? Should we have gone down together to
try one last time to talk to him, face to face?

Two agonising days later, Dad responds by saying that my
last visit had upset Mum. He says that Mum had dreaded me
coming 'because she could not work out what she needed to
do or how to behave'. He explains that while I was there,

Mum became depressed, 'probably realising that she had not made the best of it'. He says he was upset too.

What has happened during those two days of silence? What does 'upset' mean? What has he had to deal with?

He doesn't elaborate. He says he understands our concern and frustration but he doesn't think that we can come up with a solution on our own, so he is going to ask the psychiatrist's advice. 'We are due to see him in November and tomorrow I shall ask him to ring me.'

He says that Mum will be 'upset by any new faces, so bringing in a contract care firm, who may provide different staff every day, could do more harm than good'. He says that he appreciates the 'strains and conflicting loyalties' this involves but he is 'sure that some family support is the best way of bolstering Mum's confidence'.

He sounds reasonable. He sounds calm and reassuring. That's because Dad is all those things. He always talks in a quiet and sensible way, smoothing ruffled edges, brushing away irritations. He has had a lifetime of dealing with drama and tension, both at work and at home. And he knows Mum better than we do – so goes the party line, at any rate.

I can handle your mother.

Except you can't, Dad, can you? You're sick now too and you can't care for Mum at the moment.

I call Dad to discuss his email, only to find that he has already retreated from any idea of setting up professional care for Mum.

'What would be lovely, would be if you could put the old girl up for a day or two,' he says.

The lightness and warmth of his tone does nothing to melt my stony heart. I have to refuse.

I am a horrible, horrible person. A terrible daughter. But I can't do this. Not even for Dad.

I tell him – tell myself – that it's because we have too many stairs, too many animals, too many tripping hazards and too much coming and going.

The real reason is simply that I can't have Mum in my house. I can't have her following me around, calling out for Dad, pawing at me, asking me to help her, to stop this, to make it all go away, to fix her, to cure her, to cure Dad. I can't have her to stay when I have teenage children to look after, when I am on my own all week just about managing to keep my head above water as it is. I can't have her. After everything that has been said and done. After the shouting and the recriminations and the nagging. After the shaking and the clenched fists and the bared teeth. I can't.

Dad knows this, but his silent acceptance and lack of resistance are more painful than any full-blown argument would be.

'Let me get you professional help,' I say again. 'I'm happy to ring around. I'll come to the psychiatrist with you to discuss plans.'

Dad finally agrees, but he is reluctant. He knows that any change to Mum's routine is going to upset her. But he must also know, deep down, that change has already come in its most terrifying form for Mum. There is no way that any of us now can continue to pretend otherwise.

Thirty-two

'A person lacks capacity in relation to a matter if at the material time he is unable to make a decision for himself in relation to the matter because of an impairment of, or a disturbance in the functioning of, the mind or brain.'[32]

Carrie and I ring family friends for recommendations and read online reviews and ring respite homes to talk about the care Mum and Dad might need. We call each other with updates many times a day. We make calls while driving, while walking our dogs, while sitting waiting for our kids to come out of school. We shoehorn in these calls, and emails too, darting between caring for kids and going to meetings and working to deadlines. Carrie is trying to hold down a job in a hotel while juggling responsibility for animals and small children. I am dealing with the trials and tribulations of family life and writing another children's book, which is due to be delivered in the spring.

Everything I do seems fruitless. My writing is refusing to come together, as I don't seem to have the energy to create funny characters in between writing letters and emails on behalf of Mum and Dad. The letters and emails aren't having any effect, and nor are the phone calls. No respite homes will take Mum and Dad together because of Mum's medical history. They are very wary of taking a mental health patient, particularly one with no clear diagnosis.

'We don't lock our patients in,' one woman tells me, by way of explanation.

Lock them in? I don't want anyone to lock Mum in! She doesn't need locking in. It's the outside world that terrifies her. She would stay in of her own free will.

No one is interested in my point of view. They have rules. They have policies.

I call Mum's psychiatrist, Dr M.

From what Dad says, this man does not seem to be engaging with the reality of Mum being left home alone while Dad is in hospital. Dad says that when Dr M asks Mum what she wants to do when Dad is not there, she says she will be fine on her own.

'He doesn't push her to explain how she's going to cope,' he tells me. 'I think the problem is, Mum is a bit frightened of him. She behaves herself in front of Dr M, but has a meltdown in the car park immediately afterwards.'

'But it's appalling if she's frightened of him!' I say. 'And he must know that she says one thing in front of him and another once she's left the room – that's why he suggested that Mum go to Dartford over a year ago! *And* he knows that she took all her pills!'

My voice is rising. I know I should get a grip. Dad doesn't like it when I get 'het up'. It just makes him repeat himself.

'Dr M doesn't think it's a problem for Mum to be left at home, as long as the crisis team are checking in every day.'

Both he and I know this isn't sufficient. The crisis team

consists of one over-worked nurse who comes when she can. I have tried to ring and speak to her but she is always unavailable.

I am going to have to call Dr M myself.

I write a list of questions and prepare myself for the call. I am going to ask his advice on how to find appropriate care. I want to ask what mental health provision there is for an older patient left home alone. I want to point out that Mum has already taken all her pills in an attempt to kill herself and cannot be left alone with all her medication. I want to ask him to let me come and see him with Mum. I want to emphasise that she will behave one way when she is in front of him and another when she is at home.

Dr M will not even come to the phone. He will not speak to me as he says, via his secretary, that it would be breaching patient confidentiality.

'But I don't want to discuss Mum's medication or even anything she's said to Dr M,' I tell the secretary. 'I just want to explain what she is like at home and ask advice.'

'He can't speak to you about any details of your mum's care,' she replies. Her Kentish vowels grate on me – they act as another reminder of everything that I hate about my home right now. I am hot with frustration. There is no point in me speaking to this woman, it is Dr M I need to speak to.

'I understand that – I am not asking to discuss her current care,' I say, trying to remain controlled. 'I am calling to explain that Mum is not in a fit state to be left home alone while my father is in hospital.'

'Your mum is the only one who can say how she wishes to be cared for,' the secretary says. 'It is your mum's choice.'

I feel bubbles of incredulous laughter mounting.

Her WHAT?

'She can't make a *choice* over what to eat or wear!' I spit. I am unable to keep my anger at bay any longer. 'How can she make a *choice* over whether to have care or not?'

'Your mother has capacity,' the secretary states. She is reading from a crib sheet. She is hiding behind words. She sounds like a robot.

I wish I could drive down there, march into her office, grab her and shake her and shout in her face: MY MOTHER IS MAD! WHY WON'T YOU DO ANYTHING TO HELP?

∽

'Your mother has capacity.'

This expression is repeated over and over in the next few weeks as Carrie and I continue to ring and write and to try to find our way through the labyrinth of mental healthcare provision. The phrase is never fully defined. Capacity to do what? 'Capacity' to me means 'being capable'; being capable of making decisions and choices and being capable of looking after yourself.

Mum is not capable of anything other than sitting in a chair in the dark and staring at the wall. She can't decide whether to wear a jumper or a cardigan. She can't decide whether to have porridge or toast. She has shut down her choices so that they no longer overwhelm her. She wears the same clothes every day, eats the same food every day, sits in the same place every day. How does this demonstrate 'capacity'?

One day, I make a discovery that is at once like a light being turned on and a dead-end presenting itself. I discover that 'capacity' is a trap for anyone trying to care for someone with mental health problems.

It is a neighbour who explains it to me. She runs a local care agency and offers to talk to me about what the possible options are for Mum. She is a nurse and her husband is a GP. She will be able to help me, I am sure of it. She listens intently, leaning forward in her chair as I explain the whole situation, and I finish by mentioning this baffling phrase, this bit of code: capacity.

'We keep being told that Mum doesn't have to accept professional help because "she has capacity".'

At this point, my neighbour sits back with a sigh, her expression telling me all I need to know: capacity is a brick wall.

'Has anyone told you know about the Mental Capacity Act?' she says.

'No.'

No one has told me anything useful, anything that gives me any knowledge or power.

'I suggest you read it. It's what the doctors and nurses are referring to,' my neighbour says. 'It's an act that protects the patient's rights to be cared for how they wish – which is admirable, if you think about how people used to be treated in the past.'

I nod. I know how people were treated: locked away and forgotten about. And I don't want to imagine the treatments I've read about. Of course I don't want that for Mum.

'But it does make things tricky for carers,' the neighbour goes on. 'Read it and let me know if there is anything else I can do to help. I can ring the Tonbridge branch of our agency to see if they can go and see your mum. They will need to assess her before agreeing to come and look after her anyway. That's assuming your mum will agree to be assessed – or cared for.'

If I knew this woman better, I would break down in front of her. She is being so kind. I know what she is saying, gently but firmly: Dr M's secretary was right. Mum's choice is final.

I swallow back tears. I thank her for her time. I go home and pull up the act online. I read it and weep. It slams a door in my face. Ties my hands fast behind me. Gives me a strait-jacket.

The Mental Capacity Act states that, 'a person lacks capacity in relation to a matter if at the material time he is unable to make a decision for himself in relation to the matter'.

In other words, Mum can take all her pills as she did last May in what seems clearly to be at best a cry for help or at worst an attempt to end it all, but when questioned about it afterwards, if she shows signs of understanding the consequences of her actions, promises never to do it again and makes it clear to a medical professional that she is clear in her mind at the point of being questioned – 'at the material time' – then she 'has capacity'. She will be judged fit and well enough to be left in charge of all her medication.

I am furious.

Mum is a vulnerable, confused, tortured woman.

She has tried to kill herself.

She cannot be left alone.

And she is Dr M's patient.

He has all the power. Why isn't he using it? He did before. Why not now?

I am knotted with emotion. I am locked in a soundproof box. I am screaming into the abyss. I may as well have been shut away in an asylum myself. Maybe I am the madwoman in this situation? Right now, it sure as hell feels like it.

Carrie offers to try speaking to him. She is more charming than me, more persuasive, more patient. She tries using other, softer words to get through to the psychiatrist. We need help. We can't do this alone.

Even Carrie can't get through. Even she begins to lose her patience.

'Can't you see that Mum behaves one way with the doctors and another way with everyone else?' she says to the secretary. 'It's a cliché, isn't it – that mental health patients behave in this way? Why are you pretending it is anything other than manipulative behaviour?'

The secretary tells Carrie that she has already explained all this to me. She cannot discuss Mum with us.

'Your mother has capacity.'

Carrie says that we understand this, but that the capacity has only been judged when Mum is 'behaving' in front of Dr M and that Mum doesn't 'behave' at home with friends and relatives.

We are sick of the sound of our own voices. Repeating and repeating and repeating. On a loop. Loopy. Loopy-loopy-loo.

The secretary becomes impatient and rude, telling Carrie that she has nothing further to add than what she has already said to me.

Carrie finally cracks. She gets angry. 'So, you're not going to help us then? Just so you know, I am recording this conversation as I don't appreciate your tone.'

The secretary immediately tries to sound mollifying, but will still not allow Carrie to speak to Dr M.

What is the man doing? He has written her off. He doesn't care. He is sending her home with a dangerous amount of drugs, knowing that she will be alone soon and could take them all in one go just like she did last time. He is leaving her to rot.

I don't think I have ever hated someone so much. And I haven't even met him.

I want to kick his door down. I want to grab this man by the scruff of his white-collared neck and spit in his face: 'You are our only hope. If you won't help her, then who will?'

I am desperate, raging, beside myself.

I cry and I shout and I take it all out on David.

I go for long runs down to the river and I howl where no one can hear me.

I talk to everyone I can think of who might be able to advise me. Friends in the medical profession gently explain that the secretary is right; I have to listen to Mum's choices, even if her choices change one hundred times an hour.

I want you to help me.

I don't want you to help me.

I want someone to come to the house.

I don't want anyone.

I want to be left alone.

I am terrified of being left alone.

Don't abandon me!

Go away!

Of course I know that a mental health patient needs protection. I know that the act has been constructed with the best interests of the patient in mind. However, one medic friend tells me that 'it is doubtful the act has room to consider the best interests of the carer.'

When I was a young parent, there were places I could go for advice, books I could read. There were toddler groups and health visitors and midwives and people who were on hand to help and reassure.

There are no guidelines for this situation, no manuals on 'how to care for your frightened, anxious mother'.

I am exhausted. I am broken. I have nowhere left to turn. I have absolutely no idea how to work out what to do next.

Thirty-three

'I have terrible worries about abandonment and I've had them for a long time.'[33]

D ad's operation is scheduled for Monday 5 January 2015. Carrie and I have agreed to cover the first week between us. Somehow Dad has persuaded Mum to accept a carer who will come at night during the time we can't cover. Friends and neighbours will come in during the day, as well as someone from the mental healthcare team. Carrie has to take unpaid time off work and sort out childcare. I have only my kids and the dog to sort out as my work is my own affair. In any case, it's just not happening at the moment. I can't write at all now. I can't even read. All I can do is obsess over Mum. Even so, I can't stay away from home for more than a few days as David is still working in Amsterdam. I can't farm the kids and dog out for long.

Dad's life, Mum's life, Carrie's life, my life – all built on a house of cards, all reliant on the kindness of friends, all so fragile that a puff of wind could make everything come tumbling down in a heartbeat.

On 18 December 2014 Dad has an oncology appointment and is told the worst-case scenario.

'They say if the whole tumour can't be removed, I'll have to have my leg amputated,' he tells us over the phone.

No. No, I can't let myself hear these words for what they are.

'But the tumour is self-contained, right? That's what they said?' I ask.

Dad murmurs a quiet, 'They think so.'

'You'll be fine, Dad. They deal with things like this a hundred times a week.' I have no idea if this is true, but I am clinging to a vague cloud of 'facts': that tumours can be removed and cancer can be cut out and people can be saved.

'Don't worry about amputation,' I say. 'It won't come to that. It'll be all right, Dad.' As soon as the words are out of my mouth I know I have just been echoing Dad's behaviour around Mum. *It's fine. We're fine. It'll all be fine.* Wallpaper words that barely conceal the horror-story cracks beneath.

∽

Carrie and I avoid discussing this possible amputation. We have no way of talking about this. It doesn't make any sense. Our mentally ill mother cannot be about to be left in the care of a one-legged man. It is the punchline to a bad joke. *Did you hear the one about the man who complained that he was too sick to be his wife's carer? The doctor said he didn't have a leg to stand on.*

We have a tacit agreement that we will do what our family has always done: sweep unsightly things under the carpet and stagger on regardless. Mum is not computing what's happening to Dad. Carrie and I can't be sure that she has clocked any of this. Does she really understand that Dad is too sick to look after her now? She never says anything specific about her fears for him or what it will mean for her to be left at home without him. I am too frightened of her reaction to ask her outright.

The day after Dad's announcement, Mum finally gets to see Dr M, who still refuses to talk to me or Carrie. He admits that the pregabalin is no longer working. Instead he prescribes a new drug, reboxetine. This will be introduced gradually and reviewed in six weeks' time, with a view to taking Mum off the pregabalin altogether.

I no longer have any faith in these drugs. They are sticking plasters. They are doomed experiments. They are mere tinkerings with the finely tuned and little-understood chemicals in Mum's brain. We are whistling into the wind, now. And we have Christmas to get through.

We don't talk about Dad's leg. We don't talk about Mum's drugs. We *limp* through the next few weeks. We keep *stumbling* into using expressions like this, *kicking* ourselves for our insensitivity. Putting our *foot* in it. We rage about Mum digging her *heels* in over her care. Dad won't push the issue as he doesn't want to upset her; Mum is his *Achilles heel*. I am sick of the mental health team dragging their *feet* over what to do with Mum while her husband hovers between life and death. One *foot* in the grave. And the other? By then it will be chopped off and thrown down a sluice into an incinerator with hundreds of other useless body parts.

But we won't talk about that.

∽

On 5 January, Dad goes to Stanmore alone. He is prepped for his operation with no one he knows – no family, no friends

– to hold his hand, to reassure him. Everyone is focused on Mum.

Carrie takes the first shift.

'It's awful,' she says, calling me one evening once Mum has gone to bed. 'She follows me around the house, she won't let me look in cupboards or do any cooking or cleaning. The house is already looking shabby and Mum is wearing the same clothes day in, day out. I'm not even sure that she's washing. I've tried to get her to go out for some fresh air but she will not leave the house at all, not even to go into the garden.'

I am dreading going down for my shift. I am dreading how time will drag. I am dreading the claustrophobia, the alarming behaviour. I remember those days in May 2013 too well – and then I had Dad by my side. What will I do if Mum has another psychotic episode?

'I brought some food with me because she told me she didn't have any,' Carrie is saying, 'but the fridge was stuffed full of salmon and ham and lettuce. Most of it going off.' She sounds angry. 'And then this afternoon Mum wouldn't let me turn on the lights. I've been sitting in the dark with her since three o'clock.'

I look at my watch. It's half past eight.

'Oh God, Carrie. I don't know what to say. Can you watch TV with her? Do a puzzle?'

'We watched a bit of TV just now but she had the sound turned up so loud I couldn't bear it. There's no way I can do a puzzle or anything like that because she won't sit still for longer than a few minutes, and when she does she will only sit in the green chair in the corner. She's been restless all day, getting up and pacing the house and then begging me to sit with her. She doesn't want to have a conversation; she just wants *me* to talk to *her*. I'm exhausted. That's why she's in bed so early – I suggested it. I'm going to have to go to bed too now.'

A few days later I arrive in Kent to take my shift at the same time as the mental health nurse who has been checking in on Mum as often as she can. The nurse asks Mum how she is. Mum repeats over and over that she is 'in a state', but will not elaborate.

The nurse nods. 'What's upsetting you?' she asks.

Mum taps the arms of her chair repeatedly. I recognise this as a sign of high stress. Mum has always tapped surfaces or run her thumbnail back and forth over her bottom lip when she is very upset. She doesn't answer the nurse straight away. Just keeps tapping.

I have to hold myself back from jumping in. *Tell her the reason you're upset is that Dad's got cancer!* I am a tightly coiled spring and the slightest provocation will have me leaping across the room.

'Gillian?' says the nurse. 'Can you tell me why you feel upset?'

'There's no food,' Mum says.

The nurse nods and makes a mark on a notepad.

I can't stand this.

'There *is* food, Mum,' I say. 'Carrie brought you some.'

I am desperate to show that we are doing our best to care for Mum, but things are critical. We need more help. I need to make the nurse see how worried I am. I know I have only minutes. The nurse will be in a hurry to get to her next patient. And I can't mention Dad, or Mum will get more upset.

The nurse sits. Mum sits. We all sit, and not much more

is said. The nurse makes it clear she doesn't want to talk to me. She looks only to Mum. And Mum doesn't want to talk to the nurse. She looks only at me. I avoid looking at either of them in case I say something I will regret.

The nurse and I walk out into the hall and I lower my voice to try to get my point across in a snatched conversation.

'Can you talk to Dr M about Mum going back to Dartford for a while? She was easily this bad the last time—'

The nurse interrupts me. 'Your mum has capacity to make her own decisions about her care.'

Capacity.

This is it. The coil is unfurling.

I hold on to the shelf above the radiator to steady myself. It's no good, though; the more words I say, the more my anger builds.

'Mum doesn't even know what's in the fridge,' I say. 'She's filling it to the brim with the same stuff, over and over, and then leaving it to rot. I don't even know if she's eating. Do you? How is this normal behaviour?' I am aware that I am clenching my jaw, my fist, my spine, trying hard not to shout. 'How is this "capacity"?' I can't help it; I am spitting.

The nurse reaches for the door handle. 'It's her choice if she wants to keep buying food,' the nurse says. There is an edge to her voice.

The edge to mine is sharper. 'And let it rot? And not eat it? Anyway, it's not just about the food, is it? You know that.'

Mum comes out in to the hall. 'Anna? Anna – come and sit with me.'

The nurse excuses herself politely. She hasn't got time for an angry relative who lives over a hundred miles away and wants someone else to solve her family's problems. She is doing her job, coming to deal with Mum, and she is not

prepared to deal with me. She has other people to care for.
Other people who may be in a worse state than Mum and
who have no relatives whatsoever.

I know all this, yet still I want to scream obscenities. I allow
myself the short-lived satisfaction of slamming the door
instead.

'Anna! Anna, don't slam the door!'

Mum is trotting on the spot, treading water. Her face is
sweaty and she looks completely terrified, as though I am an
attacker who has her cornered. I have to stop, breathe. I take
her in my arms to make her stop moving. She clings to me
like Tom used to do when I had to drop him off at nursery.
Her feet are still moving and she is moaning.

I am furious – with Dr M, with the nurse, with anyone I
can think of who should be able to fix this. What is the point
of them if they can't fix this?

As my anger builds, Mum calms. She stops wriggling in
my arms and her breathing returns to something like normal.
I take her by the hand and settle her back in her chair and
put on a DVD as the weak January light fades and the room
darkens.

I watch Mum's face in the flicker from the TV screen. Her
eyelids are dropping; she is nodding off. Her face is smooth
and innocent in the warm light. I am flooded with grief; for
Mum, for Dad, for me. I feel it weighing me down, pulling
at my shoulders, washing through my chest. I wish I could
scoop Mum up in my arms and carry her to bed and tuck
her in and wish her 'sweet dreams' as she used to do me. I
wish I could kiss it all better.

I can't. I can't do any of these things. I can't protect her.
I can't make her happy. I can't fix her. I sit in the dark and
stare at the screen.

What is the point of me if I can't fix her?

Thirty-four

'Carpet, dirt, germs, clutter, blemishes, lips, breath . . . Yuck!'[34]

At the beginning of January 2015 I go to Istanbul on a book tour. This is a trip I have been looking forward to for a long time. I had been worried I would not be able to go, but Dad is discharged from Stanmore with some wonderful news.

'It's been successful!' he announces. 'They've removed all the tumour.'

He's home! No more talk about amputation. No more conversations about what could go wrong. Dad was right – it's all turned out fine.

'It's so good to be home,' he tells me. 'And Mum is glad to see me.'

I let myself share in his happiness, although the gratitude I feel for the success of the operation is tinged with guilt. Guilt for not having visited Dad. Guilt for continuing with my plans to go away. Guilt at the relief I feel about Dad being back so that the responsibility for caring for Mum is his again.

When I talk to Dad about my trip, he says I must go. 'And

come and see us when you get back. I'd like to hear all about it.'

Dad used to travel to Istanbul for business himself. He loves the language, the food, the people. Once I am there I can see why: I am welcomed with smiles and open arms everywhere I go. I am given fantastic food, taught delicious phrases that roll around my mouth like the sweet pomegranates and oranges I have for breakfast. I am taken to lovely places to stay, driven around from pillar to post, looked after, cosseted. I don't have to think about anything other than the talks and workshops I am giving. Nothing is a problem. Nothing is too much trouble. I can't access email easily, but this is a blessing; my phone doesn't ring or ping the whole time I am there, so I am free to concentrate on one of the best parts of my job – working with children. I spend three days living in one school where I am looked after as though I am royalty. A play is put on for me, I am taken on a trip to Hagia Sophia and the Blue Mosque. I have raucous suppers with the teachers and we laugh and laugh and laugh. I have not felt like this – my true self – for years.

The last day comes and I almost weep when I say goodbye to the bookseller who has organised the trip. I want to stay here where everything is like a dream.

⌒

As soon as I get home, I call Dad. I can't wait to tell him about my trip, to share with him the excitement of having spent a week immersed in another culture. I haven't allowed myself to think about what has happened to him while I've been away. I knew that the district nurse was visiting regularly to change his dressing and the mental health nurse was still checking in on Mum. They were getting the care they needed, so there was nothing for me to worry about – right?

When Dad picks up, he sounds a lot less chirpy than before I left for the trip. It occurs to me for the first time that I had not asked about his set-up at home on being discharged. I had been so worried about Mum that I hadn't put any thought into his after-care. I had let myself be convinced by his euphoria on being allowed back home.

'How are you feeling, Dad? You sound tired.'

'Yes, well, I am a bit. My leg's quite sore still. I suppose it's a big wound. It'll take time. I haven't made it upstairs yet.'

'Oh – so where are you sleeping?' The question slips out before I have had time to formulate a thought about the answer. There is nowhere to put a bed downstairs. And anyway, how would they have managed to move one downstairs without help?

'On the sofa,' Dad says.

A familiar feeling of dread creeps through me: he is hiding something. 'The sofa? That doesn't sound good. Do you want me to talk to the district nurse about getting you a bed downstairs?'

'It's fine. I'm fine.'

No, you're not. You're not fine at all.

'I'll come and see you tomorrow,' I reply.

He doesn't try to put me off.

I walk in to my parents' sitting room on 1 February 2015 to find Dad lying on the old green sofa. The room is dark, save for a wash of watery winter sunlight. Dad looks up when I walk in and gives a weak smile.

'Hello, love. It's nice of you to come.'

He means it as he says it, but I hear my conscience over-laying Dad's words with sarcasm. *Nice of you to finally bother. Nice to know you care.*

Mum trots behind me, panting, wringing her hands.

'You shouldn't have come,' she says.

Oh, but I should. I should have come a lot earlier. What was I expecting? A neat white bed made up with hospital corners? Dad in clean pyjamas, smiling as Mum hands him a cup of tea?

Whatever I was expecting, I wasn't expecting this. Dad looks dirty. His glasses are smeary, his pale, sallow face is sheened with sweat. He is wearing his dressing gown, which has a stain down the front. It is loosely tied around him so I can see he is wearing only pants underneath. His legs are bare and a huge bandage is visible on his right thigh. It is very tight: the skin is red and bulging over the sides of the cloth. The sofa doesn't convert into anything resembling a bed, and someone (I assume Mum) has covered it with a sheet of plastic. Dad is lying directly on this plastic. It looks old and sticky and it makes a crackling noise whenever Dad shifts to try to get comfy. I worry that it has come straight from the garden shed. There is a sickly-sweet smell in the air.

'That's not the plastic you use to cover the garden furniture?' I ask.

'Yes,' Mum says, sullen.

'It must be filthy!'

'I don't want his leg dripping on the sofa,' Mum says.

'It's not dripping,' says Dad. He is trying to sound patient but there is an edge to his voice, as though he is countering a complaint he has heard many times before today.

'It's oozing,' Mum says.

That is what the plastic is for. Like the rug on the pink sofa whenever the grandchildren came to stay. And the J-cloth to wipe up drips of water on the work tops. No mess allowed. Nothing out of place. Even when you have cancer. Especially when you have cancer.

I step in front of Mum, forcing her to look at me. 'Dad is unwell. He needs to be in a proper bed. A clean bed. When was the last time the nurse came?'

'She changed the dressing yesterday,' Dad says. 'She's coming again later today.'

He pushes himself upright and grimaces with the effort. He heaves himself to standing with the aid of a walking stick. He staggers more than once. I lurch towards him as he topples forward.

He waves me away. 'I'm all right.'

He is not. He is not. He is not. Nothing is all right. Everything is all very, very wrong. Dad went into hospital looking tired but not unwell – not next to Mum, anyhow. Now he looks worse than she does: ghoulish, yellow. Terrifyingly un-Dad.

Mum will not sit still. She totters into the kitchen to make lunch. She won't let me help her and she makes Dad furious when she dishes up yet another plate of ham and lettuce.

'I can't eat that!' he shouts. 'It hurts my mouth.'

She pants and paces and whoops and says 'Martin!' over and over again but doesn't seem to know what she is asking him for.

'I think we should call the doctor,' I say, over lunch.

The sickly-sweet aroma is powerful. I have never smelt anything like it before, but something about it tells me I need to give it my full attention. And then there's the obvious pain that Dad is in. It takes all his effort to sit at the table to eat. Mum won't let him eat on the sofa. Crumbs. Stains. Drips.

'I think you should be back in hospital, Dad,' I say.

Or in respite or having twenty-four-hour care at home, as Carrie and I had suggested over and over. But there's no point in saying that again now.

'No!' Mum says. 'Don't call the doctor.'

'Mum, I have to – Dad needs help!'

'No!'

'Anna, just leave it,' Dad says. His mouth stretches as though he might burst into tears.

We go back to our places in the living room after lunch – Dad on the sofa, me in one armchair, Mum in hers in the corner. I try to chat about things – anything – the kids, Turkey, the weather. Mum calms for a bit while I am talking. As long as I keep up a steady stream of empty words, we will all be fine. Sweeping it all away. Piling it up under the carpet. Neat and tidy. Out of sight.

Then Dad pushes himself up off the sofa again. 'Need a pee,' he says.

He is so unsteady, so feeble, I feel I should offer to help. But what would I do? Images of helping my father to untie his dressing gown, to— No. I push that idea away.

He stumbles to the bathroom alone. I take the chance to try again with Mum.

'Dad's not well. He needs care. I really think I should call the doctor. He's had a major operation. It's not hygienic for him to be lying on that plastic.'

'No, no, no!'

The same words, the same responses, over and over.

There is no point. All I do is make things worse. I give up.

Dad staggers out of the downstairs loo. I look up to see him making his way back into the sitting room. He is shivering fiercely.

I rush towards him. 'Dad! What's the matter?'

'I – don't – feel good.' His teeth clatter against every word. He is slick with sweat.

I touch him. He is freezing cold. I help him back on to the sofa, pull a blanket over him.

'That's it. I'm ringing nine-nine-nine.' I hear myself – angry. Scared. Is he going to die? He looks as though he might. His face is waxy. His breathing is harsh. The shivering is horrifying.

Mum leaps up and grabs my arm. 'No!' She whoops and begs me repeatedly not to call an ambulance. 'Don't! Don't! No, no, no!'

I do what I should have done a long time ago: I ignore her.

I pick up the receiver and dial. She is still shouting at me. Dad is still chattering. Shaking.

I have not called 999 since I was a child and a friend called to tell me the kitchen was on fire; the dog was trapped and she didn't know what to do. I called on all my Brownie Guide knowledge and told her that she should shut the kitchen door and that I would call the fire brigade and come down to be with her. I knew, aged ten, that was what you did. I was a good girl. I had got my Safety in the Home badge. I knew that when you called 999 you told the operator which service you required and then that service would come directly to your aid. I had called once before for Mum when she had fallen down the stairs and Grandma had not answered the phone.

The ambulance will come. The paramedics will take over. Dad will be all right. It will be all right. I focus on the wallpaper. The small flowers. The layers of white gloss paint on the wooden shelf the phone rests on. The address book that has sat here for nearly forty years. I can't look at Dad. I can't listen to Mum, who is pacing and panting and repeating, 'No!'

'Emergency. Which service?'

'Ambulance.'

I am put through to the relevant Kent station and immediately start to describe the situation.

'My dad has recently been discharged from hospital after
an operation to remove a cancerous tumour from his leg.'

'NO!' Mum is moaning, she is saying, 'Martin! Martin!'
She is not going over to sit with him, though. She is not
holding him or reassuring him.

Dad is saying nothing. I glance at him as I talk to the
operator. 'He is now shivering violently, has gone grey and is
freezing cold. His leg also smells. I think he has an infection
and I am worried he has gone into toxic shock.'

I don't actually know what toxic shock is, but the words
just come to me and they sound like the sort of description
that might make the emergency services listen. The smell is
toxic and Dad's condition looks like shock. They will come
quickly now. They will ask for the address and they will be
on their way, sirens blazing.

'Is your father breathing?'

'Yes, but it's loud and rasping – it's not right.'

'Is his forehead hot?'

'No, I just told you – he's freezing cold. He said he was
hot before, but he feels freezing.'

'Is his chest hot?'

I hesitate before sliding my hand through the fabric of
Dad's dressing gown and placing my hand on his chest. He
doesn't react. I am shocked by how bony he feels. He's not
hot, though.

'No.'

'Have you taken his temperature?'

Why all these questions? The questions are panicking me,
confusing me. Why aren't they sending an ambulance immediately?

'No, I haven't taken his temperature. Listen – he's really unwell! He's nearly seventy-one and has been in hospital for a serious operation. I don't think he should be at home he—'

'Is he able to walk?'

'Only with a stick – he's had a tumour cut from his leg. He's struggling to walk. It's painful for him. He's got *cancer.*' I'm babbling now. Grabbing at words. I need them to hear how serious this is.

Mum groans loudly. I don't even look at her. She can fuck off. She is useless to me.

'Can he speak?'

'Yes.'

I'm being worn down here, aren't I? That's what they want. That's what these questions are for. To wear me out and make me back down and admit that I don't need an ambulance after all. I made a mistake. Dad's fine. All this is just a minor setback.

'Can he understand what you're saying to him? When did he last eat?'

The questions go on and on and on and whenever I try to interrupt – 'His wound is oozing. His skin is bright red and swollen. It stinks!' – I am over-ridden with more questions. Questions that do not allow me to answer in such a way that the operator will see what I see: a desperately sick man, lying on a filthy sheet of plastic while his mentally ill wife whoops and totters around him.

I am no good at this. I can't make this person listen. Just as I couldn't make the mental health nurse listen and I can't get through to the psychiatrist. I have never been any good at standing up to authority. I do what I am told. I'm the one who's fucking useless.

I put the phone down, defeated.

'An on-call doctor will be with us soon,' I say.

Mum stops pacing. She sinks into her chair and is still. Dad has stopped shivering. He falls asleep.

I collapse into the other armchair. I sit and look at my parents. My poor, sick, diminished parents.

I can do nothing for them. Nothing. I am screaming through glass. I am opening my mouth and no words are coming out. I am trying to shout underwater. I am not waving, but drowning.

'The ambulance isn't coming, is it?' Mum asks.

I look at her haunted face, her wide, wild eyes. I realise I have been too frightened to look at her properly today, because I knew what I would see when I did: a woman who is terrified that her husband is dying and that she will be left alone.

She was not asking me to stop calling for the ambulance. She was asking me to keep Dad with her. And to let him live.

Thirty-five

'Safeguarding adults is about the safety and well-being of all patients but providing additional measures for those least able to protect themselves from harm.'[35]

The next day I am about to give a radio interview when my mobile rings. It's Mum.

'Dad's got an infection—' She gasps, whoops.

So I was right.

She gulps out her words with a lot of panting in between. 'The doctor didn't come until the middle of the night. He said Dad should go back to hospital. He's just left for Stanmore.'

I have five minutes before I have to turn off my phone. I talk as calmly as I can while my mind whirls. I reassure her that this is the right thing for Dad. Even as I say the words, I have no idea if this is true. He must have picked up the infection in hospital in the first place.

I go into the interview feeling sick to my stomach. Mum is home alone again and I will have to find someone to go around to check on her. And Dad? As usual, I can't think about him. I am tied to my mother by an invisible, muscular, umbilical cord. How can I concentrate on anything when Mum is home alone and Dad is in hospital again?

The interviewer asks if I am ready.

I nod and smile, switching to friendly children's author mode.

⌒

The next two months are spent repeating the actions of the months before Dad's operation. I phone everyone I can think of who is supposed to be caring for Mum. I can never get past the gatekeepers: receptionists and secretaries who are employed to filibuster relatives like me. They use slippery language, throwing phrases at me that I fail to grasp.

'Your mother can only be accepted into respite care if she agrees to be assessed.'

'Assessed by whom?'

Turns out it doesn't much matter as: 'Your mum can't be assessed unless she agrees to it because she alone has sufficient capacity to decide whether or not she wishes to see a doctor.'

'But she won't agree – that's part of the problem. She tells me she doesn't want to be left alone and then tells the mental health nurse that she wants to stay at home. She keeps changing her mind – how is this capacity?'

'If she wishes to change her mind, that is her wish. If she understands what is being said to her at any given time and she understands the implications of being left at home alone, then she has the capacity to decide that this is what she wants. You must respect her wishes as long as she is harming no one and is safe.'

Aha! A loophole at last.

'But she's not "safe",' I say, triumphant. 'She tried to kill herself with an overdose last May.'

'According to your mother's notes, and following an assessment at the time, she was not deemed to be a risk to herself or others.'

'Trying to kill yourself seems like a pretty high risk to me,' I snap.

The robot on the other end of the phone repeats itself: 'Your mother is not a risk to herself or others at this time.'

I try a different tack. 'Listen, Mum just can't look after Dad once he comes out of hospital. He has cancer. There's also a possibility that he may have to have his leg amputated,' I add, more for effect than because I have actually come around to believing this. The tumour was removed. He will not have to have his leg cut off.

'Your mother has said that she is your father's carer and that she wants to be at home to look after him when he is discharged.'

Nonononono. A carer doesn't put a sick man on a filthy plastic sheet. A carer doesn't leave a sick man unwashed for days. A carer doesn't give a sick man ham and lettuce for every meal when he has told her that it hurts his mouth to eat it. A carer CARES. Isn't that the whole bloody point?

I tackle Dad's end of things instead. I phone the hospital and ask to speak to the social services team.

'I am worried that my father is going to be discharged home to an insanitary and unsafe situation.'

'Your father has told us that he wants to be discharged home as soon as possible and that his wife is his carer.'

Dad's story about Theseus navigating his way in the Minotaur's labyrinth could not be more terrifying than this. As I remember the story, Theseus was given a golden thread to help him find his way back. I have no such luxury. I grope forward, feeling my way along the walls, listening out for monsters, shouting into the dark: 'Is there anyone there? Anyone who can help me? HELP ME!'

The monsters swiftly build another wall in front of me. I need a golden thread. I need a guide. I need someone to shine a light in the darkness, to show me the way.

At last, thank God, I get one.

I do something I have never done before: I post details about our family's situation on Facebook. As I type I think what a futile gesture this is. All I can hope for is a thread of sympathetic comments below the post. But maybe that is what I need – validation in the form of sympathy. I don't really know what I'm expecting, but I'm so desperate now, I type and post anyway.

Within minutes a friend has put me in touch with someone who works for Age UK and was once a social worker. It's a miracle. This man not only understands why I'm not getting through to the powers that be, he gives me the tools – the language – to make people sit up and listen. He shows me the way through the tangle of departments and paperwork and gives me the words to help me find my way out.

I am overwhelmed with gratitude. I keep telling the man how thankful I am. 'I am only doing my job,' he tells me. YES, but everyone else so far has 'only been doing their job' too, and look where it has got me – round and round in ever decreasing circles. Whereas now I have the tools. I have the words. I have the power.

Ever since I was small I have suspected that language has magical properties. As a child Dad would teach me new words in as many languages as he knew. If we went abroad for a holiday, he would make sure we knew the words for 'please', 'thank you', 'hello', 'goodbye' and the numbers up to ten. I went on to study languages and have never grown tired of the effect of trying out a new phrase and making the intended connection with someone in their own tongue. I am good at learning vocabulary. When we lived in France, Tom had a kidney infection at two months old and was diagnosed with reflux. I learnt all the words – *échographie, pyélonéphrite, cystogramme* – this got him the care he needed.

It's no different now. I'm learning all the words, drinking them in, repeating them to myself as though I will be tested. Hell, I *am* being tested. I start to dream in this new language – always a good sign that your brain has assimilated a new way of communicating.

The phrases are now at the tip of my tongue: Continuing Care Assessment, Section 2, Section 5, Lasting Power of Attorney vs Enduring Power of Attorney, Community Care Assessment, Mental Capacity Act 2005, Care Act 2014, Safeguarding, and finally, and most effective: Vulnerable Adults. And slowly but surely, I begin to make myself understood, to make myself heard.

'Put everything in writing,' the man from Age UK tells me. 'And ask for a discharge meeting at Stanmore as soon as possible. Ideally this meeting should involve you and your sister and parents alongside a hospital social worker, consultant, occupational therapist, representative of the mental health team and possibly a social worker from the county council. In a perfect world your parents' GP might be involved too, but this rarely happens in practice. The health and social care team should be assessing both your parents' health and social care needs as well as their needs as carers. Ask the hospital if they are putting a Section 2 in place or whether it needs to be a Section 5. Phone calls will help, but do put it all in writing; if you have everything written down people have to act because you start a paper trail.'

He is right. The paper trail soon becomes my golden thread. And laying this trail stabilises me. It is something I can do.

The jargon is dizzying, but once I start to pin it down on paper, I begin to feel an element of control. I know the power of using the right words in the right context and I know that the pen is mightier than the sword.

Armed to the teeth I write letter after letter, cutting my path through the labyrinth. Mum used to say I wrote a good letter. 'You sound so much better on paper,' she said once. 'I understand you better on the page.'

No amount of writing is any good, however, if you're trying to communicate in the wrong language. I needed the right words. When I call the hospital to follow up my letters, the response I get from using the correct phraseology is breathtaking.

'I have written to you to ask for a meeting to discuss my father's continuing care needs after discharge. As I have explained in my letters, he can't go home unless a continuing care package is put in place because both he and my mother are vulnerable adults.'

'Right. OK.' I am pretty sure I can hear a shuffle of papers on the other end of the line. I have the woman's attention. 'Martin Hankey . . . He never told us about his home situation.'

No, but I did. AND YOU DIDN'T LISTEN. She's listening now.

'I will issue a Section Two to Kent County Council and put in a request for a care package. Immediate care is free for a maximum of six weeks after discharge.'

FREE? Six weeks? Why does no one tell you?

It's a good thing this is a phone call and not a face-to-face meeting. If we were face-to-face I would not know whether to throttle the woman or kiss her.

⌘

It wasn't enough to tell our story. I had to tell it in words that the people in power would understand. I had to tell it in a way that left no room for doubt, no room for wriggling out of responsibilities. In saying that Mum and Dad were 'vulnerable adults', I was saying what I had already said: that both of them were in danger unless the medical profession stepped in to help. What on earth do you do if you are never taught this vocabulary? If you haven't the contacts or the education or if English is not your first language? You can describe how helpless a married couple is, both sick, both suffering, both incapable of caring for each other – you can lay it on as thick as you like – but unless you say, 'They are vulnerable adults who need safeguarding,' you may as well be pointing and miming and making it all up. You may as well be speaking Ancient Greek.

Thirty-six

'Going out doesn't feel healthy to us,
because it doesn't feel safe.'[36]

Tom is doing the Duke of Edinburgh Award. For the skills section he has chosen to help ring birds on the Marlborough Downs. He has to meet the others in the group before dawn in order to string up nets to the catch birds while it's still dark. One morning I drop him off at 4 a.m., then drive on up the motorway to Stanmore to see Dad. Dawn breaks and the sky above me is a beautiful, late-spring pinky-mauve.

I arrive at Stanmore at 5.45 a.m. The ward is flooded with sunlight. All the patients are asleep. Even Dad. It's almost beautiful, this peaceful, sunlit scene. I sit down next to Dad and watch him sleeping, his eyes twitching slightly under their paper-thin lids. I look at the lines on his forehead. Each line tells a tale. And I have not bothered to listen to most of them. My dad. My daddy. I want to smooth those lines away, to stroke his hair, to kiss him and tell him everything will be all right, the way Tom and Lucy used to let me not so long ago. I want to sit and watch him like this and for him not to be disturbed. I also want him to wake up because I have to leave in an hour to fetch Tom and I don't want this long drive to have been wasted.

His eyes flicker open. He sees me and smiles. 'Hello, love.'

We talk quietly so as not to disturb the other patients. When the ward round begins, the noise level can be unbearably intrusive. Best to let sleeping patients lie. I tell Dad Tom has gone ringing again. I know he will like to hear about this. My dad who loves the great outdoors, nature, wildlife. And his grandson. He would prefer to see Tom and have this conversation with him, I know. But there just isn't time enough at the weekends to fit in the activities and sports matches and trips and dates with friends and time as a family on top of driving the kids such a distance to see Dad.

Or this is what I tell myself. Is it more that I don't want them to see their grandfather like this? Because if they did – what? I would have to confess that things are a lot worse than I have admitted to them. Or myself. I would have to confess that there might not be enough time left, full stop.

I laughingly say that I can't imagine my son ever becoming a typical slug-a-bed teen. 'He's always been up with the lark – and now he is, literally!'

'Good for Tom,' Dad says. 'I wake up early here too.' He glances at the curtain-less window. He can't see much of the red-tinged sky from his hospital bed, although he tells me he can hear the birds. 'I lie back and listen to the robins. They start off the dawn chorus,' he tells me. 'The blackbirds are quick to join in. Then the wood pigeons.'

My throat tightens as I think of the wood pigeons back in Kent that would nest in the trees around Mum and Dad's garden. And the blackbirds. Dad is missing his garden. His home.

'Do you remember the blackbird that used to come into

the garden when I was little?' I ask him. 'The one with the white tail feather?'

'Punk.' Dad beams as the nickname comes back to him. 'He was a character.' Then, fixing me with eyes that are watery with pain and sickness, he says, 'My dad would have loved Tom, you know. He would have been so moved by his love of nature. They would have had a lot in common.'

As you do, I want to say, but my throat has seized shut. I try to change the subject, to avoid painful and emotional topics. 'I was thinking it might be nice for Mum to have a bird table outside the conservatory – she doesn't want to go outside any more, but at least she could watch the birds. It might help to calm her.'

Dad's brow furrows, his mouth twists. 'I've tried that,' he says. 'She said no.'

'For God's sake – why?' I blurt out.

'Rats,' Dad says. 'She's convinced we'll be overrun by them.'

The prospect of the outside coming in. She can't keep everything at bay! Is there no end to her anxieties? It would seem not.

∽

Later, back home, I call Dad to tell him that Tom has had a wonderful morning.

'He held a kingfisher in his hand! He was glowing. He couldn't stop talking about it.'

Dad makes a sound, which I think is appreciative. Then I put down the phone and think, did I make him sad? Giving Dad this image of his grandson with the bird that means so much to him? A kingfisher. A martin. A bird he loves and would love to watch with Tom.

Martin is Dad's only given name. It is also the old name

for a kingfisher: St Martin's bird. The French, Italians and Spanish still call it 'the fisher-martin': *le martin-pêcheur, il martin pescadore, el martín pescador*. Maybe because of the link with his name, or maybe because of his love of the river, Dad has always had a thing about kingfishers. Just like Ratty in *The Wind in the Willows*, he loved nothing more than 'messing about in boats', and he would often take me and Carrie to mess about with him to give Mum a break at the weekends.

'There!' he would shout, as the current took us around a bend.

'What?'

'A kingfisher – you missed it!'

We always missed it.

∽

Tom never misses a kingfisher. He sits on the riverbank, quietly, patiently and waits until one zips along its surface. He instinctively knows the calming, soothing power of being out in nature. Just like his grandfather.

Meanwhile, Mum sits in the dark in her green chair and refuses to let me set up a bird table. Refuses to let me open the window to let in the fresh spring air. Refuses the very thing that, as far as I can see, has the power to soothe – even to heal.

Thirty-seven

'Staying close to my family – who know everything about me,
my idiosyncrasies, quirks, and who love me unconditionally –
combined with staying away from other people, makes me
happiest day to day.'[37]

I visit Dad once a week throughout February and March. I
do not visit Mum, and nor does Carrie. Are we making
up for the time we lost in January when Dad first went into
hospital and we didn't go and see him? Am I pushing Mum
out because I haven't got the strength to give my all to both
of them?

I don't really have to ask myself these questions. The reason
Carrie and I look forward to seeing Dad is that – even though
he is stuck in bed and in pain, with no solution in sight for
the raw, weeping agony of his wound – he is relentlessly positive. He is convinced that he will get better, even though all
the evidence points to the contrary. His skin won't heal. His
wound is getting bigger and bigger. His leg is being eaten
away. We are told it's *E. coli*. Then we are told it's not, that
it's something else, that they are not sure.

Dad smiles it all away, writing chirpy emails to friends and relatives, telling them that he is sure he'll be home soon. He tells me and Carrie that he has had 'something of a spiritual enlightenment' on the ward, meeting men who have been through events that he sees as being much worse than his own predicament. He is particularly taken with a man who is a head teacher, has recently had both legs amputated to the knee and is working hard at his rehabilitation in a bid to return to work as soon as possible.

'He has written poems about his cancer,' Dad says, his eyes shining.

Dad in his optimism is the polar opposite of Mum, who, in her own words, can see 'nothing but misery' and has lost all the vocabulary of hope.

Meanwhile I am adding to my arsenal of medical vocabulary. 'Tissue Viability Service' becomes an important and repeated phrase. The TVS comes regularly to 'debride' Dad's leg. It sounds so efficient. Language is used yet again to keep the patient and the family at arm's length; to avoid panicking us, they hide behind 'debride' when really they mean 'slice' and 'saw' and 'cut' and 'hack'.

Still, Dad smiles whenever he sees me, and he is the chattiest I have ever known him.

'I can't seem to stop talking,' he says during one visit. 'It's like a cork has been pulled from a bottle. I'm sorry.'

I'm not. It is wonderful to hear him talk. He has his iPad with him and is up-to-date on current affairs. He is also reading a novel in Swedish and has his dictionary next to him to help him navigate the trickier words and phrases, which he enjoys telling me about. The best conversations we have are when he talks about his childhood, particularly about his parents, whose names have always been mud in our house.

Mum had fallen out big time with her mother-in-law very early on in her relationship with Dad. Carrie and I have long since given up trying to find out how or why this happened. But now that I listen to Dad telling me about his mother and her funny habits with food and her insistence on her boys learning their spellings and tables and not being allowed out to play until everything had been done to her satisfaction, I think, possibly, the problem lay in the similarities between the two women. Is this why Dad has always been so much more forgiving of and relaxed with Mum's idiosyncrasies too? He had learnt how to live with a 'difficult' woman from a young age.

'Sometimes I think I would have liked to have stayed in Australia,' he says at one point in his reminiscences.

We went to live in Mosman, just outside Sydney, when Carrie was eighteen months and I was three years old. Dad had been relocated by his bank for a short stay and the timing seemed perfect, as both my sister and I were pre-school age.

For Dad, Australia was everything he loved: the outdoor life, the sun, the incredible wildlife, open and friendly people, beer, barbecues and beaches. Living by the sea was a particular draw. Dad was able to keep up with his rowing and I learnt to swim in a shark-proof pool on the beach near our house. For Dad, Australia was freedom.

'Why didn't we stay?' I ask, knowing the second the words have left my mouth what the answer will be.

'Mum missed the UK.'

Of course she did. For her, Australia was everything she hated: terrifying spiders you had to check the loo seat for, scorching sun you had to protect your kids from, over-friendly neighbours who didn't seem to operate under the same social code Mum was used to, and most upsetting of all, it was just too far away from everyone and everything she had ever known.

This was 1974. People didn't pack up their lives to spend

years abroad with the ease they do now. There was no
internet, no video conferencing, no cheap phone calls, no
emails, no mobile phones, no easy way to get flights for
family and friends over to visit – or to go back home for
a short stay. Even the simple act of phoning home meant
booking in a time and keeping it short to avoid over-
spending. Mum was used to picking up the phone and
chatting to her mum whenever she wanted to – needed to.
She was used to popping down the road for moral support,
for instant love and understanding, for help with her two
small girls. In Australia she had to muddle through while
Dad was at work. The days must have seemed insufferably
long and lonely.

I remember Mum talking about that time with regret.
Grandma and Grandpa were only able to come over once to
visit and Mum had no help with childcare – she always resisted
nannies, au pairs, even cleaners, talking of them as an indul-
gence, but in reality just not wanting anyone else to come
into her home unless they were family.

When I was a young mum myself, living in France, I had
more than my fair share of long, empty days. I would look
at the clock, expecting it to be lunchtime and see it was only
half past nine. I would take Lucy out for a walk, struggling
up the hill, my swollen pregnant belly leading the way, and
would pray I could make the trip last for longer than the
twenty minutes it took to walk the length of the little shopping street. Some days I would cry from the loneliness. So
I'd empathised with Mum when, in the past, she had talked
about her time in Oz.

'That winter when we all had flu,' I remember her saying.
'It was the worst winter of my life.'

It must have been: no Grandma for support, no family GP
who had known her since she was a girl, no idea where to

go for help and advice, and feeling rotten herself while caring for two screaming, sick kids.

Later I find a diary Mum wrote during our eighteen months in Mosman and some letters that she sent home to Grandma. She tries to write about what it's like raising two small children on the other side of the world where she doesn't know anyone. She struggles to express what it's really like and how she's feeling. The letters are repetitive and talk about how much she wishes her parents could see me and Carrie growing up. 'They change so fast.' Her diary entries soon give up any personal commentary and descend into lists: lists of the meals she prepared and the shopping needed to prepare more meals, lists of clothes that need mending, lists of household jobs that need finishing. The diary stops altogether after a couple of months.

The lists make me think, and I wonder about her mental state back then. It seems as though she was trying to control a situation she found alarming. It seems as though she is doing this now with her insistence on the same clothes, same food, same chair in the corner of the room. But this time it's all to no avail. Mum can stick to a pattern as much as she wants, but she can't change the fact that life is no longer agreeing to fit into a rigid, controlled and calming routine. And she can't change the fact that Dad is not coming home tonight.

Thirty-eight

'The best time to figure out what to do in a crisis is NOT in the middle of the crisis. It is important to plan ahead and know what to do in these situations before it actually occurs. Developing a crisis plan with your team or behaviour specialist is a critical first step to effectively managing a crisis situation.'[38]

C onversations with Dad invariably turn to how much he is missing Mum. He seems to have forgotten how often he lost his temper with her, how tired he was when he was looking after her, how distracted he was all the time.

'I can't wait to get back to her,' he tells me.

Stay here, I think. *You're better off here. You can't go back to the madness at home.*

Friends and neighbours are now calling and emailing me and Carrie regularly, telling us how worried they are about Mum, who is still on her own, asking if there is nothing more we can do for her, insisting that she needs professional care.

A friend of Mum's rings me one day as I am leaving for an appointment of my own and tells me, 'You must come now! I've just been round to see your mother and she is very distressed!'

As if I didn't know. But rushing to Mum's side achieves nothing. I know this because Carrie has recently rushed down to Kent from her home in Norfolk, leaving her small children with a friend. After more anxious phone calls from friends and neighbours she pushed for an emergency psychiatric appointment for Mum, calling the psychiatrist's office from her mobile on the train down.

'It was hopeless,' Carrie tells me afterwards. 'Mum wouldn't get into the taxi, then once she was in she wouldn't get out. Then when I got her in to see the doctor, she suddenly snapped out of panic mode and into sullen and sane mode. Dr M told me there was nothing he could do as Mum clearly knew her own mind. And then she was panicky and out of control on the way home,' Carrie says. Her words run into and over one another. 'I can't keep bundling the kids off and I can't keep walking out of work either. Especially as once I get to Mum it's clear she doesn't want my help.' She pauses, then says with feeling, 'There is no way I am *ever* rushing down there like that again.'

There is no way I am either. Friends and neighbours continue to message us, pleading with us to do something. We explain how much we have done, have tried to do. They continue to phone and email anyway, not wanting to hear that things are just the way they are: hopeless, as Carrie says. It's hard not to get frustrated – angry even. People are only trying to help. We know they feel helpless too. After a while they give up calling and messaging. They give up on Mum too. Just as Gemma had warned us they would.

There are people who talk less and act more. These are the people who just get it: they get how difficult things are. They go out of their way to support Mum and us. They quietly pop round and check on her. They try to persuade Mum to play bridge, they sit and encourage her to talk. They are patient and willing and kind, but after a while even these people start to withdraw, to visit less. It's very hard, trying to help someone who refuses help. Who turns you away. Who says, categorically, 'I don't want you to come.'

Carrie and I continue to harangue every medical contact we have on Mum's behalf, in spite of knowing it will probably do no good. We call the GP's surgery, the psychiatrist's office, and the mental health team and social services. We ring them while we are driving to and from school, while we are watching our kids play sport, while we are cooking our kids' tea.

A GP calls me back one day while I am in Primark waiting for my daughter to try on clothes. Lucy comes out of the changing room, asking for my opinion, but I wave her away. It is almost impossible to get a GP to return a call and I am not going to miss this one. Lucy retreats meekly into the changing cubicle, already well versed in leaving me well alone while I am talking to, or about, Grandma.

The GP is so polite, so patient. Yet as the conversation goes on, it's clear he's as weary as I am at the failures in the system. No, he can't help me find a place for my mother in a home. No, he can't go and visit her unless she requests it. No, he can't discuss the details of my mother's care needs with me. No, he can't help me to get through to Dr M, who won't speak to me. All because of Data Protection and patient choice and safeguarding and rules, rules, rules.

The GP finally tells me, in a voice edged with irritation, 'I can't do any more – we are going to have to wait until we have reached the point of no return.'

Later I tell Carrie about this. She calls the doctor herself and asks, 'What exactly is the point of no return? Can I call you in a couple of months' time when Dad is dead and Mum has thrown herself down the stairs?'

If she thinks this is going to shock the GP into action, she is mistaken. He simply sighs and answers, 'Yes. This is exactly what I am expecting – things will only get worse.'

'So you're saying we have to wait until a crisis happens?'

'Yes, we do.'

Carrie says he sounds as though he has had this conversation with a hundred other families already that week. We start openly talking about our wish for that 'crisis' to come, sooner rather than later.

Thirty-nine

'The symptoms of stress can be both mental and physical, and can vary from person to person. Mental symptoms can include anxiety, anger, depression, lack of appetite, sleeplessness, crying often, tiredness and difficulty concentrating.'[39]

On 12 March 2015 Dad celebrates his seventy-first birthday in hospital. He says it's the best birthday he has ever had. He is overwhelmed with love, cards, presents and cake from friends, family, doctors and nurses.

Mum does not call or even send him a card.

I am 45 the following day. It's not the best birthday I have ever had. Mum doesn't send me a card either.

I am officially middle-aged. My mother is officially mad. My father is officially rotting from cancer. We are all officially dying, so what is the point in celebrating a birthday? What is the point of cards, which will be thrown in the recycling? Of presents that you can't take with you when you go? What is the point of any of it?

On 2 April 2015 Dad calls to say he's not allowed home as the hospital are not satisfied he'll be able to get his dressings seen to by the district nurse over Easter. I'm relieved for Dad and panicked for Mum. And me.

The panic increases when Kent Social Services call to say that they can't get into Mum and Dad's house and wonder if they should call the police.

Is this it? Is this the crisis Carrie and I have wished for? Have we brought it upon her?

I ring around the numbers I have for Mum's nearest neighbours and discover that she has been sitting alone in the dark and refused to answer the door.

I immediately call her. 'What do you think you were doing?' I shout. 'We were worried sick about you!'

But are we? Really? Not so worried that I want to swoop down and scoop Mum up to take her to be with me. I know this is wrong. I know I should be doing more, being the good daughter, helping, being there, having Mum at my house. BUT I CAN'T. I can't do this any more. I want it all to stop.

I am crying all the time at the slightest thing.

I have pains in my chest.

I can't eat.

I can't sleep.

I tell Carrie, 'I just want Mum to vanish. When will we ever be free of her?'

When I do sleep, the nightmares come back. I dream my parents are told at birth that I will die in a car crash. The dream plays out like a fully realised fairy tale of doom and disaster. Mum and Dad decide that the only way to prevent the prophecy from coming true is to prevent me from going

in any cars. When I am eighteen I am not allowed to learn
to drive. I get sick of being controlled like this, of being
treated differently from my friends, and decide one night to
run away. I climb out of my bedroom window, slide down
the drainpipe and slip away to the house of a school friend
who has a car. 'Teach me to drive!' the dream-me demands.

I'm smiling as I put my hands on the smooth leather steering
wheel; I'm laughing as my friend shows me how to turn the
key. I'm giggling as I hear the engine spring to life. I'm singing
along to the radio as I speed along the empty streets. The
windows are down, the music is on full volume, the wind is
in my hair.

I don't see the truck come bolting through the red light. I
don't hear the screech of brakes. I don't feel the impact as
the truck hits the car. All I know is that I am flying, soaring
into the clear night sky, up towards the stars.

The curse has been lifted. I have survived. I am flying. I
am free.

❧

I dream that David and I are renewing our wedding vows
during someone else's wedding. The other bride wants rid of
me and tries to kill me. I run and hide in a room in the hotel,
tripping on my long wedding gown. I wake, convinced I have
been screaming aloud, and I am confronted with a trolley full
of dead children wrapped in see-through body bags. When
I properly wake, all I can think of is Dad's leg, his diminished
figure in a hospital gown.

I dream I find a baby, which is all head and no body.

I dream that Mum has left an answer machine message, asking,
'How do you turn the lights on?', in a calm, haunting voice.

And then there are the nights when I don't dream because

I don't sleep at all. I pace the house, moving from room to room, making herbal tea, trying to read, crying, muttering angrily to myself, writing scrawled notes in my diary.

All I want to do is sleep. Very, very deeply. I want the nightmares to go away.

⌇

On 7 April 2015 Dad calls from hospital. The nightmares have leaked into real life.

'They think the cancer is back,' he tells me. 'A junior doctor did the ward rounds this morning and saw a bump protruding from the scar area, which is still not healing properly. He said, "I don't like the look of that."' Dad hesitates. 'I don't know how to tell Mum.'

I don't know how to tell her either. The mental health team still think Mum is 'fine' at home alone with no carer. And now Dad's cancer is back. As if we really believed the story that it had ever gone away.

I stop my ears to the menacing voice that whispers, 'You know what it means when a cancer comes back, don't you? You wished for this. You wished for a crisis. You wished for everything to be over.'

⌇

The next day I drive to Stanmore at 6 a.m. through a dawn that could be heralding midsummer. Red kites wheel overhead as a crimson beach-ball sun rises slowly over the motorway. The sky is so alarmingly beautiful it's as though it's taunting me. Look how good life is. Look how vibrant and warm. See how it calls out to be lived? See what your father will be leaving behind him when he goes?

He's not going, though. He's not. He's not. He'd better bloody not.

Dad is having an MRI when I arrive. I sit and wait for him. He shuffles out of the scanner room, an old man in a shabby green towelling dressing gown, matchstick-thin legs sticking out from under the frayed hem. His face is closed with pain and the effort of walking. He sees me and smiles. The smile does not eclipse the pain and effort.

I think of my father-in-law, three years older than my own dear dad, who over Easter was striding across the garden with armfuls of logs, digging his veg patch, marching up the hill to the village to get his daily newspaper. It's not possible that he and Dad are almost the same age. It's not fair, either.

Dad tells me that he has been shown his wound and that it looks 'dreadful – like lots of meaty lumps'. He says, 'I feel as though I'm back to square one.'

I worry it's worse than that. I worry that we are at the final square on the board. At checkmate. Game over.

Forty

'Death terror . . . the all-encompassing dread of death that bypasses the subconscious and just haunts me pretty much twenty-four seven.'[40]

It is worse. On Monday 27 April 2015 I'm sitting at my desk, hurtling towards a deadline. I'm wrestling dialogue into shape, honing descriptive passages, cutting, hacking, sawing. Debriding.

The phone rings and Dad's number comes up. I answer.

'It's me.'

His voice. Something about it.

But of course, I know.

I know why he's calling.

I turn away from my computer. I bend over, my head between my knees. Stare, stare, stare at the carpet.

'Hi, Dad.'

Silence.

'Dad? What did the doctor say?'

Silence.

Then

a whimper.

The noise is alarming, childlike.

A year on, two years, three years, four years on . . . I will hear that whimper for ever.

Dad starts to babble. 'I'm so sorry. I'm sorry to disturb you. I know you're working. I know you have a lot to do. But I wanted you to know. I wanted to tell you.'

No, don't tell me. Don't—

'I'm afraid I don't have much time left—' His voice catches.

I must. Listen. I must. Take this in. Understand. Feel this. Moment.

I must.

I can't.

Thisisrealthisisitthisisitthisisit.

Shit.

I manage two words. 'Not . . . much?'

'I'm so sorry,' he says again.

Why apologise? For this seeping, oozing, black evil that has entered you uninvited? That is taking you from me? From Carrie. From Mum. Why do you apologise for this fucking shitting bastard of a disease that is set on having its way with you? Sorry? I'll show it sorry. Just give me five minutes alone in a room with it. Just five minutes.

But we don't have five minutes. Time is suddenly something that is in very short supply.

'The cancer has gone to my spine, my lungs and my collar bone,' Dad says, his voice gathering momentum as he tells me what 'they' have said. 'They think I have got three months. It's between me and my maker, I suppose. It's so upsetting for everybody.'

Upsetting.

Sorry.

As though death were a poor choice, a wrong turning, a bad decision on your part. Whoops. Silly you. Should have set the

Italian satnav. Good old Giovanni would never have let you down.

What do I say next? I can't remember now. I hope I tell him to stop apologising. I hope I say I can't believe it. I hope I say how much I love him. I suspect I say none of these things. I am too worried about how Mum will take the news.

Words fail me. Always irritating, to say the least, when you are a writer. They have failed me a lot in the past few years. In my conversations with Dad, with the doctors, with the social services. On paper and on screen.

I put down the phone and close the document on my computer.

What next? Crying seems the right response.

I try to cry. I need to cry. I want to cry. I have spent so much time over the past two years crying, but now, when it really matters, when I really need to feel those tears, to feel anything, I can't.

I curl up in a ball on the landing floor and try to force the sobs out. Nothing comes. I squeeze out what little air there is in my lungs. I open my mouth wide; I close my eyes.

Nothing.

Not even the tiniest trickle.

I am dry with fury and terror.

I shout instead. A wordless, animal yelp that grows and grows until it is a full-throated roar. It's a sound I have never heard myself make, or anyone else for that matter. I hear myself and I think, *I am being ridiculous. What kind of a noise is that?* But I can't stop it.

I stay curled up in a ball on the floor and I roar and I roar and I roar.

Forty-one

'Sticking to time accurately is also essential for me to live as secure a life as possible. I feel anxious if things are not on time.'[41]

Time is running out.
  Three months. It's nothing.
A school term.
A trimester of pregnancy.
A paragraph of a life.

∽

Time. Always time. Too early. Too late. Bad timing. You're late. Don't be late! Hurry up, we'll miss the train/the bus/the boat. The traffic will build up and we'll be late! Why are you early? I'm not ready for you.

∽

We are not ready for you, Death.

∽

The clocks in my parents' house tick the time away. There's a carriage clock on the bookcase in the sitting room, a grand-father clock in the hall, a clock on the wall in the kitchen, Mum's watch that she checks over and over and over. And she paces in time. Back and forth. Back and forth. Her heels clip-clopping on the parquet floor. Tick tock, tick tock. Like Alice's White Rabbit, bustling back and forth.

∽

All that time wasted, worrying about Mum, trying to help Mum, when I should have been trying to help Dad.

∽

Make the ticking stop, someone. *Stop all the clocks, cut off the telephone*, as the poem goes. Make time stand still so that I can rush around and fix things like a character in a time-travel story while everyone stands frozen. I could turn back time. Make Mum well again. And Dad. And Dad.

Forty-two

'If you wish, you can appoint someone you trust to make deci-sions for you. This is called making a Lasting Power of Attorney (LPA) and enables you to give another person the right to make decisions about your care and welfare.'[42]

D ad is now home. 'They have said there is no point in my staying in hospital and that I should make the most of the time I have left.'

Part of this involves 'putting his affairs in order'. A ridicu-lous phrase. A sick innuendo. Why can't we just say what we mean? *Mum is mad. Dad is dying. This is the end. You now have permission to scream.*

'Can you come and stay the night? I need to go through things with you,' he says. 'Money and things,' he adds. He is subdued and vague. 'And I think we should make legal copies of our LPAs.'

It's no good asking Dad to speak plainly when he is dealing with the unspeakable: *Mum is mad. I am dying. This is the end. It's all up to you and Carrie now.*

Carrie can't come with me this time. She can't get away from work and has no one to mind the children. So for the moment, it's all up to me. I don't want it to be. I'm not fit for purpose. I know nothing about the mysteries of money. That is Dad's world. The vocabulary of banking and finance is one that I will never master.

Dad takes me into his study and resolutely clicks through files on his computer, mumbling about investments and savings, using that lawyer's voice again.

Mum doesn't try to stop him, or me. After a breathless, panting, 'Hello,' she has gone to sit in her green chair in the corner. I don't go to sit with her. I'm here for Dad today.

Not that I can grasp what he's saying. I can't catch hold of the words and pin them down. They float away from me. I am underwater again.

Dad has taken out a folder from his filing cabinet. He opens it and passes me two pieces of paper stapled together.

'This is my will. Mum's is in there too.'

I nod. 'OK.' *Thy will be done.*

We don't allow our eyes to meet. Least said, soonest mended. More stuff for that pile under the Axminster.

I glance at the neat rows of type. They blur and ebb and flow as I catch sight of Dad's name and Mum's name and then find I can't read on. It's unreal, anyway. I'm not actually sitting here with my dying father talking about his last will and testament. Talking about what I'll have to do when he's dead. It's ludicrous.

I pass the document back. Dad returns the pieces of paper to the folder and tucks them away in the filing cabinet drawer in the bottom right-hand side of his desk. I do at least take note of this. I will have to remember it, after all. The next person to lift it out again will be me. In three months' time.

A place for everything and everything in its place.

In three months' time I will lift it out, knowing that the

last person to touch it before me is no longer here. Like I said: ludicrous.

'Let's do the LPAs next,' Dad says. He is keeping up the pretence of sticking to a planned agenda, an organised meeting. He calls for Mum, and I follow him as he hobbles painfully into the bleak, sparse dining room.

How I have always hated this room. This cold, dark cave that was sliced off from the open-plan living area nearly forty years ago. This uninviting, formal space in which we have been forced to have stiff, awkward meals since we became adults; this room in which we have argued, fussed and fought with Mum.

I needn't worry; Mum won't put up a fight today. She is not enraged. She is deadened. By drugs. She sits at the table, doing as she is told. Like a good girl.

I look from my pain-wracked father with his useless leg to my slumped, sweaty, dead-eyed mother. Suddenly I have to fight the urge to push back the chair and run. I can't do this. I can't take all this responsibility. When I signed the LPAs a couple of years ago they were just bits of admin; pieces of paperwork that needed a signature and an address and a witness. Like applying for a passport or signing a new book contract. I've not given them a second thought. Did I read them properly at the time? Did I understand what I was doing when I put my name to them? I remember Dad saying, 'I thought it was a good idea to do these now as I'm worried about Mum.'

I didn't really consider what this meant. With a few strokes of the pen I had taken on the responsibility of caring for Mum. Now I realise that Dad was not only worried about her: he was worried about himself too. Worried that he wouldn't always be here to look after Mum.

The thought that I have tied myself to Mum for ever chokes

me. I have to focus on breathing. I have to hold on tight to the edge of the table and instruct myself not to think.

I breathe. I watch as Dad passes Mum page after page of the Lasting Power of Attorney for Property and Financial Affairs, and the Lasting Power of Attorney for Health and Welfare. I know, thanks to Age UK, that it is important to have Lasting Power and not Enduring Power as this will give me and Carrie another set of golden keys to make sure that Mum and Dad get what they need when they are no longer able to fend for themselves.

We sit at the dining room table in the fading light for over an hour while Mum and Dad both write and sign a declaration at the bottom of each page of the copied document: *'I certify that this is a true and complete copy of the corresponding page of the original Lasting Power of Attorney.'*

Mum's hand moves shakily. It is like looking at a child copying out lines for punishment. Watching her, I wonder what her psychiatrist would make of this. Has she 'got capacity' at this moment in time? Does she realise what she is doing? Signing away life and hope? Signing away responsibility ultimately to me and Carrie? Does this count as coercion, making her sit here and write this? It both looks and feels that way to me.

And I should know, because once it was me sitting with Carrie at the kitchen table next door, being made to do our homework before we were allowed outside to play. I didn't mind the spellings, but I still got some wrong. I hated getting things wrong. Mum would get upset and I didn't like that. She would bang her fist on the table and I was never completely sure that fists wouldn't fly in other directions too.

'Se-PAR-ate, not se-PER-ate,' Mum would bark. 'From the Latin, "se-PARARE", to pull a-PAR-t.'

I would bend my head over the page and copy it out. Three times for each word spelled incorrectly, that was the rule.

Mum would often invoke Latin as a way of teaching us our spellings and grammar and usage. 'You in-FER meaning from what someone has said – from the Latin, in-FER-re, to bring or carry or bear. You can't infer something *to* someone – that is im-PLY-ing. I *imply* something to you and you *infer* my meaning.'

As for 'less than' and 'fewer than' or when to use 'I' and not 'me' . . . You had to have your wits about you at all times in case you invoked the wrath of the grammar gods. Mum's mnemonics were helpful to me, but they were always delivered with such impatience and often anger when I couldn't get what she was saying straight away.

'You are CARE-LESS!' she would shout, each syllable enunciated like a hammer driving a nail into my skull.

❧

Now Mum is the one being careless. Her handwriting is shaky, and I have to point out omissions and spelling mistakes that would render the copy redundant. In a way the LPA doesn't change much; I am already making decisions for her. Mothering Mother again.

Forty-three

'Death is a complicated concept to grasp,
especially for people that have difficulty
understanding abstract ideas.'[43]

J ohn calls to say that he went to visit Mum and Dad after
I did.

'It was the saddest day of my life,' he says. 'Gillian needs
the right diagnosis so that we can get her the best care possible
at home. Then I think the next stage has to be to move her
to a residential care home.'

He is right, as he has been all along. But I can't think about
Mum's care now. The thought of having to look after her
once Dad is gone is just—

I want someone else to take over, if I'm honest. But I don't
ask John to. It wouldn't be fair. He has his own life. And he
has been through enough of his own grief.

I'm refusing to face this, I know. I haven't yet spoken to
any doctors or nurses about Dad since he came home. I've
been given the name and number of Dad's designated
Macmillan nurse, but I can't bring myself to talk to her. Carrie
and I have been told we can call this nurse whenever we like

and ask any questions at all. Carrie has done this already.
Dad has urged me to speak to her as well.

'She is there for you too – I think you will need her,' he
tells me.

The difference in care provision for Dad now that he is
dying is overwhelming. The GP was right: now that we are
in crisis mode, the system steps up. It's just that this wasn't
the crisis Carrie and I had had in mind when we'd started
wishing for it. Back then, it was Mum's care that needed
cranking up a gear, not Dad's. And now that Dad is dying,
that need for Mum is even greater. But Operation Mental
Health is not on a par with Operation Cancer.

∽

On 6 May 2015 Mum's mental health nurse rings to tell me
that Mum has said she doesn't want her to come any more.

'I'm sorry?' I say. I'm not . . . I'm livid. 'You're not going
to visit my mentally ill mother any more, just at the point
when her husband is about to die and leave her alone?'

'Your mother has requested that I no longer visit,' says the
nurse, backing away behind pompous phraseology.

'So you're washing your hands of her?' I know I'm pushing
my luck. I'm getting close to being rude, abusive even. But
SERIOUSLY?

Apparently so. As I have been told multiple times already,
if Mum 'doesn't want' something, then there is nothing
anyone can do. Even if the alternative is for Mum to sit in
the dark and wait for Dad's death, closely followed by her
own. I have been brought up to be polite, to respect authority,
to accept what I am told – to do what I am told. But I am
finding it harder and harder to keep more animal instincts
at bay; shouting, screaming and punching seem to be more

appropriate responses to the brick walls that are being constantly thrown up around me.

∽

Mum phones. 'I can't think of what to eat. And I can't use the computer.'

'Don't worry, Mum,' I say. 'You don't have to use the computer.'

She is silent. Does she is even realise that Dad is dying?

Then Mum reads my mind. 'He's going to die, isn't he?' she says, in a monotone.

And because I am stupid and insensitive and because I don't know how to end the conversation, I say, 'Yes. But we're all going to die one day.'

∽

One weekend David drives me and the kids to Kent. Mum doesn't smile when she sees Lucy and Tom. She has shut down. She makes no effort to speak to us other than to chunter about food as she trots back and forth from the kitchen. The kids chat to Dad. He loves this, sitting surrounded by his family. But we wear him out.

He falls asleep on the sofa and Mum starts to nod off too in her chair. I whisper to David that we should probably leave.

We start to quietly gather our things and I go over to Mum to tell her we'll be going. She opens her eyes and immediately glances across to Dad, who is fast asleep now, his head tilted back, his mouth slightly open.

Alarm flashes across Mum's face and she leaps up and rushes over to him.

'Martin! Martin!' she cries, prodding him awake.

Poor Dad comes to in shock and shouts, 'What?'

Mum backs off and retreats to her chair, looking closed and empty again.

'What on earth did you do that for?' I ask. 'He was asleep!'

It's not until we're in the car on our way home that David turns to me and says, 'You know she thought he was dead.'

∞

It is 14 January 1983 and I am twelve and I would like to talk to someone about death. Mum never wants to, and she definitely doesn't want to right now because her dad – my grandpa – has just died. We never talk about death in this family.

I would like to talk about it because Carrie and I aren't allowed to go to Grandpa's funeral. But I *am* twelve. Nearly thirteen. And Carrie is ten, so I would say we are definitely old enough. My friend Sarah went to her gran's funeral. When I asked Mum if I could go to Grandpa's she got angry and said I was 'morbid'. I had to look that up in the dictionary. I don't agree that I am 'morbid'. I don't have an 'abnormal or unhealthy interest in death'. I just want someone to answer my questions. Like, what happens when we die? Where do we go? What happens in a funeral? Will Grandpa's body literally be in the coffin for everyone to see? In which case I would like to see it because I haven't seen him for weeks. Months, actually.

He went into hospital because of his emphysema. I had to look that up in the dictionary too. I knew he had problems with his breathing because whenever we had to walk up Mount Pleasant in Tunbridge Wells, he would have to stop and hold on to something. He would say he had to 'catch his breath', as though he could see it floating away from him. On cold days you could actually see it floating away in great puffs of white. He had emphysema because he had smoked cigarettes for years and years. He said once that, in the war, people were told that smoking was good for you. How crazy is that?

Adults are always getting things wrong. They were wrong about the smoking and I think they are wrong about the funeral. I want to go. I want to say goodbye to Grandpa. I miss him. I miss him sitting in his chair in the corner of the room while Carrie and I tell him stories about what we have been doing at school. I miss him watching the rugby and swearing when Wales are losing. I wasn't allowed to visit him when he was in hospital. I never saw him get really sick, so part of me doesn't believe that he did. Part of me doesn't believe he is dead and that I will never see him again.

Mum won't talk about it. I haven't even seen her cry. She is just angry. As though it is my fault that Grandpa has died. I don't understand.

∽

It is 26 September 2008. Grandma died last night. At 11.15 p.m. last night our phone rang in Wiltshire, waking me out of a deep sleep. I answered, but all I got in response were distant voices, as though coming from underwater. I thought it was Mum and John. I called out to them, but they didn't reply. I went back to bed and was woken next at 7.45 a.m. by Mum calling to say Grandma had died at 11.15 p.m. yesterday. I told Mum about the call and she laughed. She has always scoffed if ever I say I think I have had a sign or if I tell her I believe there is something more to us that this brief existence. 'Always thinking of the sublime,' she teases.

I told her that a few months back I woke in the middle of the night and sat bolt upright in bed, a gasp catching in the back of my throat. I could smell Grandma in the room: her musky 'old lady' smell; her favourite flowery talc mixed with the sadder aromas of urine and sweat that had become her signature scent in recent months. The next day Mum had told me that Grandma had suffered another stroke in the night. I knew it was her calling out. She's done it again. For the last time.

Mum said she had to hold on to Grandma while she was dying. 'She kept rearing up, trying to get out of bed, I think.'

No. I don't think it was that. I think she was holding on to life, not wanting to leave. Not wanting to leave Mum. She knew what would happen once she went.

Forty-four

'There is growing evidence to suggest that people with ASC may show greater difficulties with cognitive empathy (the ability to correctly identify other people's feelings or beliefs) and understand the reasons for these.'[44]

It is 2015 and Mum is falling apart. She wants her mum and I want mine because Dad is dying, dying, dying.

I don't know how to talk about death. Luckily some of my friends do because, unluckily, they have already looked it in the eye. One friend who has recently lost her step-father tells me that her neighbour is a wonderful person to talk to. That she has always found him wise and helpful. He is a retired nurse. He has seen a thing or two. It turns out I know him. He is a reader at our local church. I am no longer sure of what I believe, but faith in something – anything – seems to have a place at a time like this. I have heard this man speak before and I feel that I can trust him, that he won't try to put a gloss on things, but will listen and offer words of comfort. Possibly practical ideas too.

I email him and he invites me around for a cup of tea. We sit in his living room while his wife stays discreetly out of the way. We end up talking more about Mum than we do about Dad dying. All paths lead to Mum, as they always have done.

'I don't know how to talk to her,' I tell him. 'I don't know how to deal with her. I am terrified of what will happen when Dad dies. She can't cope now. She won't be able to cope at all once he's gone. I—' I break off, ashamed of what I am going to say next, but needing so desperately to say it out loud to someone who will not judge me. 'I wish she were the one dying instead of Dad.' I let my face fall into my hands and try, try, try to hold back the welling-up of grief.

The reader waits. His face is so kind. He sits and lets me cry. Then he says, 'I visit my sister regularly. She has dementia. She doesn't recognise me. She is always angry. The visits are awful and I pray for her death. It's not wrong to want someone to stop suffering, you know. There's no shame in this,' his own eyes filling with tears. 'It would be so much better if we could talk openly and honestly about these feelings.'

I am grateful to him. But your own *mother*? You can't wish for the death of your own mother and still be a good person, can you?

When I can speak again, he asks me about my relationship with Mum. He guesses at Mum's violent nature in the past without me having to be explicit.

'This anger – something must have happened to your mum to make her angry. Maybe it's to do with her mental illness, which has been there all along. Maybe it's something else, but the point is that even though she's displaced that anger on to you, *you* have broken the cycle with your own kids. And that is something to be proud of.'

Proud? What have I got to be proud of? I'm sitting in this man's house telling him that at this point in time I hate my own mother and I want her to die in place of my dad. Not much to be proud of there. I have broken all my promises.

I have abandoned Mum, I cannot save Dad, I am useless, useless, useless.

The reader can see pain written all over me. He sits forward. 'The only person you are ultimately responsible for is yourself,' he says quietly. 'You'll never make your mum well. You'll never make her happy.'

The permission to let go, to be me and not to hold on to Mum, is like a long, tall glass of iced water on a hot day. It's like the warmest blanket placed over shivering shoulders. It's complete and absolving and pure. But it's too much. I can't take it in. I can't truly believe it. I'm not ready to believe it.

Through more tears, I start to talk about washing Mum's hair. I don't know why; maybe because the memory is so bittersweet, maybe because in saying it aloud I am reminding myself of Mum as she could be, or maybe because I need to paint myself in a better light. I tell the reader about the intensity of the love I felt for Mum as I rubbed the shampoo into her scalp and gently rinsed it clean.

'You should take that as a gift. A reminder of who your mum really is, underneath her illness and the drugs,' he says. Then he adds, 'But don't worry if you can't hold on to that image of her. She is who she is when you are dealing with her in any given moment too. And you can't be a saint.'

More absolution. More kindness. I can't process it right now. I just have to keep talking. We talk about suicide. About Mum's attempt to end it all with pills last year.

'I need to get her to accept some professional care. I can't allow her to remain home alone if she's going to try to take her life again,' I tell him.

'I'm afraid the doctors are right: if your mum ultimately chooses to hurt herself, that is her choice; it is not your responsibility.'

I wasn't expecting this. Not from a man of faith; a nurse,

someone who exudes love in the talks I have heard him give. I was expecting to be told to step up to the mark. I was expecting an admonishment that was in line with the voices in my head, telling me what a terrible daughter I am.

'You can't make your mum live, any more than you can make her well – or happy,' he says. 'I'm afraid that things might get worse before they can be dealt with,' he adds. 'Just try to remember that everything you're doing is out of love. Because you are, you know. I can see that.'

We have talked for two hours. I could sit here forever, talking to this man, listening to his kind, gentle voice. My friend is right: he is wise and he is helpful. But more than that – he has looked into my frightened soul and given me something I desperately needed, something I would not get from doctors or nurses or family friends or neighbours. He has given me understanding.

Forty-five

'The rate in mortality goes up among mourning spouses after their loved one dies. Researchers at the University of Glasgow followed 4,000 couples and found that widows and widowers were at least 30% more likely to die of any cause during the first six months following a spouse's death, compared to those who did not lose a partner.'[45]

It's 11 May 2015 and I am staying in Kent again because I'm going to the Macmillan Cancer Centre in UCLH with Dad. He has an appointment to discuss his options, namely: to be eaten alive by cancer – or not to be, but to lose a limb instead and end the heartache.

The surgeon who removed the tumour in Dad's leg wants to amputate because the cancer is devouring Dad from the inside out.

'He says if I have the leg off then I will be more comfortable,' Dad explains.

Comfortable? With a wound going into his pelvis? What they mean is 'in marginally less agony', but they are never going to say that.

'The oncologist is not so sure, apparently,' Dad says.

Nor am I. It feels mediaeval. And if Mum can't stand Dad's
oozing thigh, how is she going to respond to having a one-
legged husband? Plus, yet again, what will we do with Mum
if Dad has to go back into hospital?

And what will happen to Dad with one leg? He will be in
a wheelchair. This house is not adapted for a wheelchair. And
where will he sleep? He has the sofa bed in his study now,
but a wheelchair will not get over the step down into that
room. He can't go back to the narrow green sofa in the sitting
room. And what about going to the loo? And what about
when the cancer progresses? And what about if he dies at
home with Mum and there's no one there with them?

Questions, questions, questions.

Every time I close my eyes I see horrific things. Images of
chainsaws and dismembered limbs.

I am not going to be able to sleep. I turn on the light and
try to read, but the book I've brought with me is not holding
my attention. I need to find something comforting.

I go to the shelves on the landing outside the room my
kids used to sleep in. I run my fingers over the crumbling
spines of the *Mr Buffin*s, the *Little Grey Rabbit*s, the Beatrix
Potters, the *Rupert the Bear*s. The *Orlando*s – I pull out these
beloved volumes, old picture books with pencil-soft images
of the 'Marmalade Cat', which Dad has kept since his childhood. I flick through them, remembering Dad reading them
to me as his mother did to him.

On the bottom shelf, stuffed in between an illustrated
children's Bible and an atlas, I find a large picture book with
cardboard covers entitled *Martin: the Kingfisher*. I don't
remember seeing this story before. It is a natural history book
by a French writer with the nom de plume, Père Castor. I
open the worn-edged cardboard covers and find an inscrip-
tion: 'to darling Martin, love Mamma'.

I leaf through the book. It tells the story of the little king-fisher, Martin, who defends his territory on the river with pride. One day Martin meets Martine and they mate for life, as kingfishers do. I read that Martine 'fidgets about, never very far away from him' and 'talks to Martin in a very deter-mined way, without ever stopping to close her beak'. I smile as I think that Dad has chosen just such a mate for himself. I read on: the two birds 'never leave one another. Never.'

I close the book with tears rolling down my face; the story seems so apt, so revealing of Dad's nature.

A story about a martin for Martin.

It reminds me of one of Dad's bedtime stories too: of Ceyx and Alcyone.

'When Ceyx died,' Dad told us, 'Alcyone was so sad that she threw herself into the sea.'

'Why?' we cried. It seemed so brutal.

Dad would smile. 'Don't worry – there's a happy ending,' he said. 'The gods transformed them both into kingfishers, or what the Greeks called "Halcyon birds". They lived together as kingfishers forever.'

Dad and Mum. Ceyx and Alcyone. Martin and Martine. Will they find peace at last? And together? Who knows? The peace is the important bit.

There I go again, using stories to try to make sense of it all.

I am decided. I can't allow Dad to have his leg amputated. He and Mum must be kept together now, for the remainder of his days. It is the way things should be. The way I see them, at any rate.

Forty-six

'"Respite" is a short break, anything from a couple of hours to several weeks, away from caring to give you time to recharge your batteries. You may find that it helps you stay well and feel better able to cope with caring.'[46]

D ad and I take a taxi up to UCLH, leaving Mum home alone with the promise of a visit from a friend. I am no longer torn between staying with her and going with Dad. It's obvious where I need to be today. Carrie is going to meet us at the hospital too.

We take the route via Docklands that Dad used to drive when his office relocated there from the City in the Nineties. I catch him looking wistful as we pass familiar landmarks. He sighs, still looking out at the scene, and I think he's going to relay a memory, a story from the time when he was a vital younger man, whizzing about, working hard, travelling, going to the pub after work, nipping down to the river for a row on summer evenings.

'You know,' he says, without turning to face me, 'Mum has said she will commit suicide once I've gone.'

His tone is so conversational that it takes a beat for me to marry his words with their true meaning. How can he say this out loud? So casually? In front of a stranger, the taxi driver? I glance in the rear-view mirror to see if the driver is listening, but he shows no sign of having heard anything. He has the radio on low and Dad's voice is very subdued.

What do I say now? I stare out of the window, my mind scrabbling for something – anything. I find nothing to say in response.

When I look back to Dad, he is still staring out of his window. I try to hold his hand, but he pulls it away.

The rest of the journey passes in silence. I never do think of the right thing to say to Dad's pronouncement. My mind veers off instead, and I find I am thinking again of the anecdotes, dropped casually into family conversations, of Mum's impulsive and at times suicidal behaviour as a younger woman – not that it was ever explicitly referred to as such. I think of the story I told the mental health nurse when giving Mum's medical history in A&E two years ago, of Mum throwing herself into the sea.

If this had been the only occasion of such drama, perhaps I would not be dwelling on it now. However, there were also the stories that Grandma told me later in life when I would phone her in tears because Mum had taken out her rage on me again.

'Anna, she's always been like this,' she would say.

I know what she meant was, 'It's not your fault.' She was trying to tell me what the reader had said: 'You can't make your mum live, any more than you can make her well – or happy.'

I want to reach back into the past and make Grandma look me in the eyes as I ask her, 'Why didn't you explain all this better? Why didn't you do something to help Mum? To help us?'

Of course, I do know that she couldn't have. As she said to me and Carrie, so many times, her face collapsed with pain, her voice full of sadness: 'I just don't know what to do with her.'

John and Grandma had told me more than once of the time Mum had marched off up Snowdon by herself after an outburst. Then there were the disappearing acts, taking herself off on long walks, leaving no details, leaving her family worried sick. And she used to shout that she would 'end it all' more than once.

'She would literally – and I mean literally – take leave of her senses,' John told me recently. 'She would do things that any rational person would consider ridiculous and to many would appear attention-seeking.'

∽

Glancing at Dad, still staring out of the window, I think of Mum waving the carving knife at him. Of falling down the stairs at my house. Of taking all her pills last year. I think of all the things in their house that are the potential weapons of suicide: plastic bags for suffocation, bottles of bleach to burn the stomach and gut, packets of pills to send you into a coma, razor blades to hack, slash and slice, bottles of spirits to send you into oblivion . . .

Has she thought of all these things? Has she really thought of doing this all her life? Has she regularly woken up, wishing that she hadn't?

∽

Carrie is waiting for us in the hospital foyer. I am alarmed by how thin she is. I am also ashamed by how much effort she has taken with her appearance: perfect make-up, smart jacket. I must look like a bag lady in comparison, having slept badly and not given myself enough time for a shower this morning.

My beautiful sister beams her trademark dazzling smile and we fall on one another in tight embrace. I want to tell her what Dad said in the taxi, but she whispers, 'Let's not talk about Mum today, OK?'

When I release my sister, I see Dad staring at a food stand. He looks like a small child with his nose pressed up against a sweetshop window.

'Do you want a cup of coffee, Dad?' I ask.

'I'd like something to eat,' he says, looking embarrassed.

We take him over to the counter and he orders some gluey macaroni cheese, the sight of which does nothing to unknot my nervous insides. I carry it over to a small table and Carrie brings three coffees.

Dad wolfs his food down. It's a cliché, but it fits the bill; he attacks the food with canine ferocity, eating it as my Labrador would, almost inhaling it in his hurry to get it down. *He is starving.* I take in his bony hands and sunken cheeks. *No doubt Mum has allowed nothing but fucking ham and lettuce.* Heat rises in me as I think of how wicked it is to allow this dying man to be 'cared for' by his mentally ill wife.

Carrie and I exchange glances. She looks pale and upset, so I keep my promise not to mention Mum and I don't speak my mind.

Dad sits back and wipes his mouth on an inadequate paper napkin. He lets out a small burp of satisfaction. He must have been desperate for something hot and filling if he has enjoyed that disgusting congealed mess. It has served to whet his appetite, in any case, as he smiles and sits back in his chair.

'Maybe we could go out for lunch later,' he says.

⌒

We take Dad to his appointment. The oncologist looks up as we walk in. Her eyes flicker between me, Carrie, Dad. She looks stricken. My stomach falls as I watch the doctor avoid our gaze by looking at the floor, the ceiling, her computer screen as she tries and fails to hide her obvious mortification behind words. A lot of words.

The only ones I hear are: 'I am alarmed at how fast the nodules have spread in two weeks.'

She must have had only seconds to see the scan images before we walked in the door. This is why she is talking and talking: so that we don't have time to ask any questions. She has had no time to compose herself or to think of what to say to this man who is dying right before her eyes.

We already know that coming here today was never a question of finding a solution. There is no solution to death. There is no avoiding the end of the sentence. The best we can hope for is a semi-colon. A brief hiatus before the inevitable full stop.

'I'm afraid the drugs no longer appear to be having any effect,' the oncologist says. 'All I can offer is ways to make you more comfortable.'

That phrase again! I could scream!

We're told we're looking at more and more morphine and Dad having more and more care from the hospice nurses.

Added to this is the fear of Mum's safety and welfare.

It is unreal. It is monstrous. It is impossible. And yet it is the truth. Stark. Bare. Laid before us.

We are subdued as we leave the oncologist's room. There is a tangible sense of us fighting not to cave in.

∽

Once we leave the building, however, a strange elation takes hold. We are kids let out of school early. We are demob happy. We are on holiday from death and have left it behind in the airless chrome and glass of the hospital. And we don't have to rush Dad back home – back to Mum. We can enjoy a couple of hours' brief respite.

'Please let's go out to lunch!' Dad says, his eyes shining. 'I remember there was a Turkish restaurant near here. If it's as near as I remember then we could walk there. Can you google it?'

Carrie looks on her phone. 'Taš . . . Found it! . . . It's nearby.' She glances at me with a tiny shake of her head.

He's not going to be able to walk even as far as the end of the road after the morning he's had.

'We'll get a taxi,' Carrie says firmly.

She knows Dad doesn't like taking London cabs – too expensive. But the rulebook has been ripped up today. And Dad is clearly so keen to make the most of his hard-won freedom that, for once, he doesn't protest.

∽

We are giggly and giddy as we speed down backstreets in the cab, Dad reminiscing about his working life in the Square Mile, laughing about raucous drinking games and long boozy dinners.

We arrive at the restaurant to find we are the only ones in there. I glance at my watch: it's early for lunch, and it's

Tuesday, so of course the place is empty. I am losing track of time often these days, what with all the broken nights, early mornings, late evening phone calls.

Dad picks up the menu and is already trying out his Turkish, reading out the names of the various *meze*, attempting to remember the bits of vocab he has picked up over the years. It feels like a celebration as we work our way through plate after plate of meatballs and aubergines and yoghurt and cheese and olives and stuffed vine leaves and marinated red peppers. We share a bottle of wine, acknowledging how 'naughty' this is for a Tuesday lunchtime.

Dad regales us with more memories. 'When I went to Japan with the bank, we used to work late, then go back to the hotel for a kip. We'd set our alarms for two or three a.m. and then meet in a karaoke bar and drink *sake* 'til sunrise.'

This is a side of Dad we have only ever had glimpses of. We knew he liked a drink and we knew he liked to sing. But this level of partying is hilarious. And not a little bit outrageous. It is glorious to hear him talk like this. To see him as a person rather than a dad.

It feels, too, as though we are running away. Playing truant. Cheating – on what, or whom, we're not sure. We almost forget what it is that has brought us, Dad and his two daughters, out for a meal. We have never done this. Never gone out, just the three of us. Never heard the stories he is telling us today. Mum has always been there, taking centre stage, fussing over whether we will be too early or too late, scrutinising what Dad is eating, complaining about what she is eating, draining all the joy and energy from any time we have ever had together as adults. Maybe that's the real reason we feel naughty – because we are cheating on Mum?

We admit ourselves defeated by the food. Dad insists on paying and then he gets up to go to the bathroom. He labours down the stairs, dragging his useless leg behind him, refusing all offers of help. The laughter and smiles fade as we watch him go.

'He looks awful,' I say to Carrie.

She nods. 'He's in more pain than he will admit.'

For a few hours, we have escaped the inescapable. And I realise as I watch my Dad's agonising progress back up the stairs that it's not Mum we've been cheating on.

We've been cheating on death.

Forty-seven

'Some people think people with Asperger's Syndrome have no emotion, but actually a lot of us are too sensitive and too emotional. I'm so emotionally sensitive that it's easy for me to become totally consumed in my worries about anxieties, fears, guilt, depression, suicidal moods, loneliness, feeling different and any other intense emotions. Inside I am full of intense chaos.'[47]

On 13 May 2015, almost exactly two years to the day that Dad and I took Mum to A&E, Dad's Macmillan nurse rings Carrie to say that Dad has about two months left.

Tick tock. Time and tide. The sand in the hourglass slipping through. Water coursing through our fingers.

I try to keep normal life going, floating along on the surface. But the undercurrent is Dad's looming amputation. It's becoming more and more likely, and has become the new obsessive topic of conversation. Carrie and I are worried that it's a bad idea – the oncologist is too. There's not enough flesh left on Dad's leg to be able to close the wound.

It doesn't matter what we think; Dad wants the operation. His leg is no longer part of him as far as he's concerned.

'I just want it off,' he says, screwing up his face in disgust. 'The horrible, rotting thing.'

Carrie and I should be more involved in this decision. We will be Mum's sole carers once Dad is back in hospital. And he might die there. We won't be able to rely on the kindness of friends who have rallied around for so long to keep an eye on Mum. They were only doing it for Dad, we see that now. Dad is the lovable one. Dad is the charming, easy-going, fun one. Mum is a burden, a worry, difficult, a pain. Who is going to want to drop in on her 'for a chat' once Dad has gone?

WhataboutMumwhataboutMumwhataboutMum?

The question goes around my head on a loop. It interrupts every conversation, every thought, every family meal.

One night David snaps. He shouts, 'I wish you'd shut up about your fucking mother! Your father. Has. Cancer.'

He doesn't understand. My mum is my biggest concern. She always has been. She always will be. I can't leave her to fend for herself, and yet that is what is going to happen. Mum is going to be left behind, stuck on her island of green velvet in the middle of an ocean of anxiety, clinging to her chair the same way she clung to the rocks when she was twelve. The sirens call, and the tide is too strong for her this time. This time, she is not holding out her hand and allowing herself to be pulled ashore. She will kill herself and end it all. Or worse, she will call out to me but then refuse to let me help, and we will both be caught in a never-ending whirlpool of madness and panic and anger and remorse.

I'm sitting in the car one evening, waiting for David. A woman in her sixties is walking from door to door, collecting Christian Aid envelopes. She is not getting very far with her task, as doors remained resolutely closed. Another woman, older, knocks on my car window and crossly asks me if I have just rung her bell.

'You ran away before I could get to the door,' she says. Her eyes are pale and milky with glaucoma.

I explain that it wasn't me, but the Christian Aid woman. I point to her. It occurs to me that the older woman can't see where I am pointing, and then I see that she is clutching a red and white envelope. I offer to run and give it to the charity volunteer. Both women are astonished.

The Christian Aid woman laughs and says, 'No one has ever run after me to give me money before!'

The older woman seems genuinely touched that I have done this little thing for her.

I want to say, *You might be someone's mum. Maybe someone's wife. You are alone. That's all.*

I don't. She would think I was mad.

My mum, Dad's wife, is going to be alone soon. She already acts as though she is. She sits in her green chair in the dark and tries not to breathe. She tries not to look at Dad. At his leg. She tries not to look at chaos and death, sitting across the room from her. She tries not to look at life either. Both are equally terrifying.

Forty-eight

'Empathy means sensing what another person is feeling. It's an important way of showing love and concern for another person.'[48]

Life consists of a series of episodes where, in each, you sit in a room, being told things by people who know more than you. First you sit in a classroom and listen to people telling you things you may never need to know, then you get a job and listen to your superiors telling you how to do what they do, then you buy a flat and get a mortgage and listen to the bank manager, the estate agent, the solicitor, then you get pregnant and listen to people telling you what to expect when you are expecting.

Now it seems that dying is the same. We have meetings about the operation, about the rehabilitation after the operation. Everyone is so calm. They talk as though having your leg cut off is routine; an inevitable stage of life, like going to university or getting married.

We are sitting with a team from occupational health. They are explaining what Dad will be able and not be able to do once his leg has been cut off from the hip. Sorry, not 'cut' – 'disarticulated'.

'We'll need to get your home assessed,' says the physio-
therapist. 'You'll need access for a wheelchair. Do you have
a room downstairs where we can put a hospital bed? And
then there are grab-rails that can be fitted . . .'

I can't bear this. The kind young woman's calm manner
serves only to stoke my anger.

Assess his home? And how will they do that when Mum
won't let them in? Move a bed in? Fit rails? Make the doors
wider for a wheelchair? You're off your rocker, you are. Mum
will have a fit! And anyway, what's the point? HE'S DYING!
Why isn't anyone addressing the blindingly obvious?

Dad goes out for a wee and I lean across the table. My jaw
is tight, my teeth are clenched, my hands are balled fists of
fury.

'Listen,' I hiss, 'there's no point in any of this. My mother
is mentally ill. She won't let you change her dining room
into a hospital room. She won't let any carers into the house,
even to bring her food. She won't let anyone open cupboards
or go upstairs or move a pile of unopened post from one
table to another. She will not let anyone move the furniture
around! She won't be able to cope with hospital equipment!'

They look briefly alarmed, but quickly smile and nod and
talk on about what Dad needs.

It's no good. I can't get them to listen. I can't get them to
see. If you haven't seen Mum's panic attacks, you can't understand. Dad needs to stay in hospital if he's going to have this
bloody hideous operation. He can't go home to the madhouse!

I do know I sound insane myself; telling these professionals
that Dad can't have what he needs, that he will just have to
grin and bear it, this rotting leg of his. But I have to get them
to understand.

'Why the hell,' I spit, as the physios sit very still and very quiet, 'are we talking about rehabilitation for a man who will be dead in two months?'

Dad comes back from the loo. I sit up, pretending I have not been talking about him behind his back. The physios shuffle in their seats, clear their throats and turn their attention to Dad. They explain that he'll have to learn how to sit again once part of his pelvis has been removed.

The bald facts. Delivered as though they are instructions on how to make a cheese sandwich. Dad nods and smiles and accepts it all and doesn't say a flipping single word about Mum.

∽

Later, in one final, desperate attempt to get him to change his mind, to go home, take morphine, to allow me and Carrie to nurse him, to not put him – and Mum – through this, I look him in the eye and say, 'Dad, have you really thought about the difference between dying at home, with me and Carrie beside you, and dying in hospital?'

He gives a small smile, reaches across, takes my hand and squeezes it. 'Yes.'

My throat tightens. I can't falter now. 'And—' I swallow. 'When you think about having your leg cut off, do you feel peaceful?'

'Yes.' He leans forward then and looks at the floor and says, 'I don't want to offend anyone.' He pauses. 'I mean, I don't mind what you do on the day.'

The day. He's talking about his funeral.

'I do have one request.' He clears his throat, embarrassed, then says, '*Hic timor, hoc votum est: mea membra frigore terra ne celes; leviter surgat ad astra cinis.*'

What the—?

'I'm sorry, Dad. My Latin's rubbish these days. Something about the earth – and . . . stars?' I say. Pitiful. I am pitiful. He doesn't want to say what he wants, but I am making him.

'"This is my fear,"' he replies, translating quietly, '"that my body will be confined to the cold, dark earth. This is my wish: that you will scatter my ashes to the stars."'

OK. I can't hold back any more. That's it. Grief has got its way. I am defeated. My dear, dear Dad. He just wants me to listen to him. He just wants me to take over now. And he has to ask me his most personal wish in Latin and even that I can't understand. I can't even do that for him.

I throw my head down and take huge, gulping breaths, but I can't stop the sobbing. 'I – I just want—' I gasp and sob. 'I just want you – to have a good death.'

'I know.'

He's so calm. So much calmer than I have seen him in years. He is facing this. And I must listen. Mum always said he was stubborn, but that's not it; he is determined and resilient and brave.

∽

Later still, once Dad is back home, he texts me to say that he thinks Mum will have to go into care. He also tells me that he has completed his tax return.

Tidy and efficient to the last. Tying up the loose ends, even parcelling Mum off. It feels like the end of their marriage. The end of everything. But if Mum is allowed her choices, he must be allowed his. This is his decision. His death.

I must listen. He is telling me, firmly but kindly: *I can't go home and wait for death, because that would be giving up. I have to stand up to it, even if that is on one leg.*

Forty-nine

'It's a good idea to deal with any feelings of guilt. Feeling guilty makes you feel bad, and also makes it hard to care for someone else, and makes it difficult to function in other parts of your life.'[49]

It is late May 2015. Just at the point when I feel we have hit a wall with regards to Mum's care, Carrie rings to tell me she has found someone who can help.

'She's called Marina,' Carrie says. 'I found her on an agency website. I've been in touch and she says she is very experienced in dealing with older people who are refusing care. She has looked after people with Alzheimer's. She says she could move in while Dad is in hospital. She lives near Mum and Dad so I said we'd meet her the next time we're down. Will you come?'

Carrie sounds elated. She believes she has found a solution at last. I am not so sure; we have been here before. We have come up with ideas, so many ideas, and Mum has kiboshed the lot of them. But I will go and meet Marina. I will try anything.

Carrie and I meet her in a café in our home town. She is

waiting outside. A tall, blonde, well-dressed woman in her fifties who beams at us in recognition from the photos we have sent.

'Like two peas in a pod, you two!' she cries, her face shining.

I want to hug her. I want to hold on to her in case she is a chimera. In case she disappears in a puff of smoke.

We sit, talking over our cappuccinos, as nervous as if this were a blind date, giving out intimate details about Mum's mental health and Dad's personal requirements. It's a meeting of minds. Marina immediately understands what we're saying about Mum. After months of trying to explain to professionals and friends and neighbours alike that Mum isn't simply 'depressed and anxious' but that she is in fact very ill herself, we have finally found someone who gets it.

In the years to come I will discover that it is always the carers who 'get it'. Time and again I meet women – for they are more often than not women – often not paid, and when they are, always underpaid anyway. Women who have given up vast swathes of their own time to care for others; who know what it is to sit with someone hour after hour; who have been told more than once to go away, and yet who keep coming back. To wash and dress and clean and cook, yes. But more than this, to sit. To hold a hand, to stroke a cheek, to wipe a tear, to give a hug. These people are priceless.

Marina is one such woman. She has cared for and helped other people all her life. Her own kids. Other people's. She tells us of the years and years she has spent in caring for people. Old people, sick people, angry people, people feeling guilty, people feeling broken-hearted, people at the end of their tether. She gets it.

'I'll come and meet your parents,' she says, 'but I'll act as though I am there for your dad and I won't talk to your mum unless she wants me to.'

'You can do that?' we ask. 'But what about mental capacity? What about Mum having to choose whether or not she wants you to care for her?'

'It's no longer just about her though, is it?' Marina points out.

Is it possible? That we have at last found someone who speaks our language?

We have. Marina comes to see Mum and Dad at our insistence. Mum doesn't want her to come, but Dad knows that he has to agree on her behalf. Marina gets the measure of Mum immediately. She says hello to Mum, introduces herself and then focuses entirely on Dad. She talks about what he is going through, what he needs, what he thinks Mum needs. She talks about getting panic buttons, key safes so that she can access the house at all times. She agrees to help with getting the hospital equipment into the house for Dad's 'recovery'. She uses all the right words in all the right combinations. Dad falls under the spell and agrees to let Marina step in and help so readily that I feel I must be dreaming. This is too good to be true, surely? It can't be this easy, after years of struggling?

But it is.

'I am going to see this through,' Marina tells us, whenever we protest that she has done too much for us already.

Marina is employed as a carer, but she will become so much more, and willingly, often at her own suggestion. A furniture remover, a healthcare liaison official, an agony aunt, a cleaner, a taxi driver, a housekeeper. Above all, a friend.

In the midst of all the pain and loss, Marina is a shining beacon of hope and succour and love. She is a bridge over troubled waters, a lighthouse on the rocky shores of grief. We bless the day she walked into our lives, from the parched, golden land of South Africa to a cold, grey, crowded high street in a small town in Kent. We could not have survived without her.

'No guilt, girls!' she says. 'You've done everything you can.'

∽

'No guilt, girls!'

How can I not feel guilty? Dad is not going to survive. Mum is not going to survive. I have lost all the chances I had to save them.

I go down to Cornwall at half-term and I stand on the rocks and stare at the waves and I wish, I wish, I wish that I had braved Mum's rages and panic attacks and hatred of mud and rocks and damp and cold water and wild animals and that I had brought them both here. To the sea. While I still had the time. I wish I had held Mum and told her it would be OK. I wish I had turned her face to the sun and pleaded with her to drink in the warmth and the salty air. I wish I had pleaded with her to live so that Dad wasn't now facing death.

Dad is dying, but he's still living. He talks of his rehabilitation as though it is the answer to everything. He doesn't talk about death any more. No more talk of funeral plans or finances, no more embarrassed requests in Latin. He talks of getting back into his kayak.

'If I can figure out a way of getting it down to the river, I'm sure I'll be able to get in it for a paddle. I do miss the water,' he says wistfully.

He will never see the river again.

He will never see the sea.

He will never swim, kayak, paddle or dangle his feet in fresh, cold, blue-green water.

He will never see a kingfisher.

And Mum? She is living, but she may as well be dying. She does not go out. She does not leave her chair, unless compelled to. She keeps the house dark and cold as a tomb.

He will never.

She will never.

Never. Ever. Ever again.

∽

Is this grief already? This tiredness? This frustration? This burning desire to be able to fix it all?

No one tells you. No one tells you that you can be grieving someone who is terminally ill while also fervently hoping they will live. No one tells you that grief can feel like anger, like hatred, like murder. You assume that grief comes after death and that it is a straightforward sort of sadness. With lots of crying. No one tells you that there is nothing straight-forward about grief at all. That it doesn't follow a neat pattern. It doesn't have a clear starting point, a once upon a time, a line in the sand. No one tells you that it can make you feel like breaking glass, like smashing rocks, like cracking open skulls.

For me, right now, it's an angry sea, held back by fragile defences. The grief is there, in the background all the time. If you allow yourself to listen, you will hear it churning. It is best not to listen. So you do what you can to keep the defences well maintained.

Every day you do an inspection. You do it as soon as you wake, tentatively feeling along the surface of the wall for cracks. You tell yourself that this way you will be in control. As the day goes on, you feel the sea pushing, surging, hurling itself against the rickety materials you have used to keep it at bay. Sometimes you have to stop what you are doing to rush and fill in any small holes that threaten to let through even a trickle of grief.

Other days, the sea is calm; the sun comes out and the water glistens. You stand on the wall and look out at the horizon and feel the warmth coming back into your limbs. You spot a boat coming into the bay, and you tell yourself: I will survive this. I will be rescued. I will tame this sea of grief.

Fifty

'All the fun is in the planning. The party itself is terrifying.'[50]

' I would like to have a party.'

Now that the operation date is set and Marina is in place to look after Mum, Dad is full of joy and hope. It's hard not to be carried along with his new-found enthusiasm for life. But still, a party?

I tell Carrie I am worried Mum won't be able to handle it.

'A house full of people? After months of solitude? And we'll need to move the furniture around. She won't let us.'

'Then we'll have to find a way to get her out of the house while we set things up,' says Carrie.

She is determined. She is also excellent at organising events. It's her job. It's what she knows. She gets on the case immediately. She understands that Dad needs this, and that Mum is going to have to come second to his needs for once.

Carrie calls caterers, talks to Dad about wine. I draw up a guest list for Dad's approval. As I do so, I think: *in less than three months we will be doing the same but without his approval.* He won't be at that party, so he deserves to have this one.

But Mum? I can't let myself get as carried away as my sister.

❧

Mum has always 'got into a state', as she would say, about hosting social events. The smallest lunch with family could throw her into a rage or panic. She was initially all right, so long as she was left to get on with the organisation. So long as no one got in her way or did anything to disrupt her plans. So long as the children were seen and not heard and did not interfere.

And she wanted to be the hostess. She knew it was part of her role as a housewife, and as the wife of a man who worked in the City. They did a lot of entertaining, my parents. Dad would be in charge of the wine, Mum in charge of everything else.

She would make endless lists and then drag Carrie and me around Sainsbury's, ticking items off. We knew better than to behave as my own kids did when they were small – running off, pulling treats off the shelves and trying to hide them in the trolley. We followed meekly behind her as she took her carefully pre-planned route around the store. We were not allowed to help put things in the trolley or on the conveyor belt and we certainly were not allowed to pack any bags. There was a system for that and only Mum knew how that system worked. I remember the floor of that Sainsbury's very clearly. Orange and white tiles. I used to count the orange ones to pass the time.

Mum's anxiety would build as any planned event drew closer.

'Don't eat that!' she would shout, if Dad went to help himself to something in the fridge. 'It's for tomorrow night.'

'Who's been at the cheese?' she would roar. 'I needed that for Wednesday's Ladies' Circle.'

'Don't sit on the sofa! I've just plumped the cushions.'

'Don't leave your shoes there!'

'Don't hang your coat on the banister!'

'Don't leave your bag in the hall!'

Then the people would come and she would drink one glass of wine too many and say something offensive about someone's clothes or hair or husband or child.

'She could be a bit brusque,' one friend said to me shyly, as though confessing to a long-held view that she'd felt she had to keep to herself. As though it wasn't common knowledge.

And yet Mum put herself through so much entertaining over the years. Cooking elaborate lunches for Dad's business contacts, hosting evenings for Tupperware parties, Ladies' Circle, the French Society, her book group. Why did she do it if she hated it so much? Because she saw other people doing it and thought she should too?

In any case, she hasn't done any entertaining for a few years now. So if she found it stressful when she was well, how is she going to cope now that she is not? With caterers crawling all over the Formica and us moving the pink sofa to make room for guests and then the guests themselves, milling around, potentially spilling drink and crumbs and walking mud in from the garden . . .

⌢

'I think we'll have to keep it a surprise,' Dad says. 'Otherwise Mum will fret about it.'

'Fret'. The master of understatement does it again.

Yes, she will 'fret'.

She will say, over and over, 'I can't do this, Martin. I can't. I can't. I can't.'

She will beg him to cancel.

She will shout, 'Martin? Martin! Where are you, Martin? I need you, Martin!'

She will whoop and scream and follow Dad around, repeating herself over and over.

She will say that the house is filthy, that they do not have any food, that she does not have anything to wear, that people will make a mess, that she wants everyone to leave now. *Leave now!*

She will say all this, forgetting that her husband is dying.

Or rather, she will say all this so that she can forget.

⟋⟍

Dad pours us a glass of wine the night before the party. It's from a bottle he quietly places before us, without comment. We notice only afterwards that it is a Shiraz Cabernet called 'Optimist'.

You'd have to be an optimist to hold a party when you've got a rotting leg and an insane wife. But maybe Dad's attitude is the right one. At least he enjoys himself on the day. Carrie and her husband manage to get Mum out of the house for a pizza, containing her panic by constant distraction and the promise of seeing her two younger grandchildren. David and I move the furniture around and let the caterers in and remind them to ignore Mum if she harangues them. Dad goes with my brother-in-law to get the wine. And then people arrive.

And it is 'fine' while everyone is there. Mum is shell-shocked, yes, but not hysterical. She drifts through the party like a ghost while people talk to her with manufactured smiles and carefully formed comments.

It is only afterwards that she has a complete meltdown. As soon as everyone leaves she begins to pace around. She cries, 'I need to fill the car with petrol!' Her demand is repeated and her voice rises. It is as though holding it all together for her friends for a couple of hours was more than her system could bear.

We try to mollify her. To get her to sit. She won't.

'Petrol! I need to go and get petrol!' she insists.

'But Mum, you can't drive in the state you're in,' we tell her.

'But I need to! I need to fill the car with petrol!' She is almost screaming now.

She trots, she whimpers, she moans, she whoops. Carrie videos her to show Dr M just how bad she can be when she is not making an effort in front of him. It is further proof, surely, of the need for the psychiatrist to take some responsibility and stop being so bloody passive. Why have we had to take matters into our own hands, to find Marina, when Mum is like this?

Eventually David takes the car and fills the tank. He comes back and tells her what he's done.

She slumps into her chair, sullen and with no word of thanks. She has exhausted herself, like a toddler after a tantrum, like the Gillian of John's stories of old. She is out of fuel herself now: dull, empty and lifeless.

Fifty-one

'As the patient ages and the environment becomes more demanding, social communication impairment may underline the development of social anxiety, especially if the patient is high functioning and aware of his/her social incompetence.'[51]

On 2 June 2015 I go to see Dad at Stanmore. He is on the high dependency unit. HDU. Another abbreviation to add to my collection.

Dad is asleep. It's immediately clear that his right leg is missing. The blanket falls away from his torso leaving the bed neat and flat on his right side. Everything around him is neat. Neat and tidy. Clean and perfect. The sheets have sharp hospital corners. The beeping machines are lined up nicely. Ordered and professional and reassuring. A place for everything and— oh, fuck it.

I wasn't prepared for this, which I now realise was stupid. I suppose I thought that with blankets drawn up over his body it wouldn't be obvious that he had lost a limb; that he would still look whole. Poor, poor Dad. Lying there. Thin, white, reduced, his cheeks sunken, his mouth open, his face already a death mask. Two people have to turn him every

two hours to prevent him getting bed sores. He is hooked
up to the machines. Wires and equipment and flashing lights
surround him.

I sit and drink in his face, his hands. I brush a wayward
eyebrow hair out of his eye. I touch his warm, gentle hand.
I stroke the white-blond hairs on his arm. It is criminal that
his wife is not here to do this for him.

He mumbles some nonsense from his diving-bell slumber.
I hear him say something about cutlery. I chuckle through
my tears. What visions is he having? A picnic on the riverbank
with Ratty and Mole, I hope.

⌒

When I get home from seeing Dad, Mum's oldest friend calls.
A friend from primary school who knows Mum as well as
anyone in the family. She has been to see Mum and she is
alarmed by what she has witnessed.

'I don't think she has washed properly in a very long time.
Her sheets definitely hadn't been washed. She has completely
given up on her appearance.'

How did this friend manage to get upstairs? Mum has not
let anyone up there for months. Marina has not been allowed
upstairs. Should I tell the mental health team about the filth?
What's the point? Living in filth is probably also a 'personal
choice'. Carrie and I wanted Marina to be with Mum 24/7
but Dad persuaded us not to put this in place. 'Not yet,' he
said. He is worried about money. We know that we will need
her to be with Mum and Dad once he is discharged. And
after Dad dies . . . ? It's clear to me that he's anxious about
the care Mum will need once he has gone. Dad has always
been cautious with money, but even so; there is only a finite
amount available before we would have to think about selling

the house. We need to keep Mum at home. She is already losing her husband. She can't lose her home as well.

I go to see Mum. She sits in her chair and asks me to talk to her. I try. I start with the grandchildren. I soon run out of jolly anecdotes. She does not initiate any other conversation other than to say, 'Talk to me' again.

I try. I start talking about my visit to Dad.

'He's doing really well,' I tell her. Embroidering the truth with pretty words and empty phrases.

She tells me to stop.

We sit in silence. Listening to those clocks. Fucking tick, fucking tock.

My shoulders stiffen, my back aches. I am thirsty. I want to go home. It's going to take me a good four hours to drive back.

'Talk to me.'

'What do you want me to talk about, Mum?' I try not to sound impatient. I don't succeed.

'Anything,' she says.

Her voice is a monotone. She doesn't smile. Her face is blank. She sits, looks at me.

'Talk,' she says.

'But about what?'

'Anything.'

'I don't know what to say.'

It's like she has some script she wants me to follow, but I don't know the lines.

'Just talk to me.'

Fifty-two

*'Anything that occurs in an unpredictable way is likely to
throw the person into a panic and may trigger a withdrawal
or an avoidance.'*[52]

D ad's bed is shrouded by curtains when I next visit.
I hear him call out, 'Anna? It's all right, you can come
in.'

Before I have a chance to think about what is going on
behind the screen, I have walked in and am confronted by a
fleshy stump where Dad's right leg once met his hip.

I struggle to keep my expression straight and fix my eyes
on Dad's face. 'Hi.'

His face crumples. I have given myself away. 'It's not too
revolting, is it?' he asks.

I didn't want to see it. My imagination was bad enough. Now
I have seen it I cannot un-see it. But who am I to think I should
be protected from something that is Dad's reality? I have been
critical enough of Mum for not facing this. And it may be me
helping him at some later stage with getting dressed, going to
the loo, with bathing. Marina can't be there 24/7 even if Dad
has the funds. She needs a break at some point.

I need to grow up. I need to see this stump as part of Dad. I also need to cheer Dad up – he has become miserable again because Mum is being difficult.

'She told Dr M that she no longer wants you or Carrie to be consulted or listened to about medical matters,' he says. I open my mouth, but before I can protest, Dad goes on. 'Dr M is trying to do the right thing. He went to visit her with Mum's mental health nurse and tried to convince Mum to go into respite care. They said she needed a proper rest and that Marina's help wasn't enough. Mum refused.'

At least they visited. I wonder if the video of Mum at the party had some effect, although I know that Dr M responded to it by telling Carrie that, 'There is nothing there that will present as evidence to a board of psychiatrists.'

And now he won't talk to us again anyway. How is it that I can talk to Dad's medical team and his Macmillan nurses about anything, but I can't talk to this bloody psych?

Bloody psych, bloody psych, bloody, bloody, bloody psych.

Dad says, 'If Mum insists on playing silly buggers I don't want to go home.'

I have nothing to say to this. We have been here so many times before, there are no words left.

Dad decides to lighten the mood by showing me how he can get from his bed to a wheelchair and back again, relying entirely on upper body strength. He is excited. So am I. Watching him is like watching someone cross the finish line of a marathon and achieving their personal best. He used to do kayak marathons on the Medway. He would build up his strength by doing pull-ups on the door frame of his bedroom. He has always been proud of his strength. I am proud for him now too.

He says YES to everything and Mum says NO.

I say, 'Shall we go outside and get some fresh air?'

Mum says, 'No.'

I say, 'Shall I sit with you for a bit?'

She says, 'No.'

I ask her, 'Do you not want to do the right thing to get Dad home quickly and help him?'

She says, 'No.'

Dr M insists it's Mum exercising the right to make her own decisions.

Marina says it's Mum's defence mechanism to prevent the conversation going any further.

I think Marina knows more than Dr M when it comes to Mum, and she's known her for only a couple of weeks versus the psychiatrist's couple of years.

It makes perfect sense to me when Marina says, 'Gillian shuts down because then the things she is most worried about can't affect her – it's easier and simpler for her not to engage with unpredictable things that frighten her.'

Why would she want to engage with these things? Your husband losing his leg and then dying from an aggressive form of cancer that no one understands is pretty 'unpredict-able'. I can hardly blame Mum for her panic and withdrawal.

The hospital wants to discharge Dad in a week's time, 'silly buggers' or no. This means we have only seven days to turn the dining room into a bedroom. It has to be the dining room because the study doorway is too narrow for a wheelchair and has a small step down too. I think of all the other hazards that my childhood home contains. The step down from the porch. The narrow kitchen with its too-high breakfast bar. The bathroom with no shower. All as lethal to Dad as the potential suicide weapons are to Mum.

Everything will have to be adapted. Changed.

And Mum is – of course – hyperventilating.

Change is frightening. Change is scary.

'No! No! Nonononononono!'

Mum's panic feeds mine. The minute I hear her hyperventilating my chest tightens. I start to catastrophise too.

We can't do this. We can't do it in time. We'll have to take the furniture away and put it in storage. We'll have to hire a van. I might have to drive the van. I can't drive a van! I can't! Nonononono!

I am on the phone to Carrie every evening, planning, 'fretting', worrying. I find myself daydreaming of when I will be able to spend time with Carrie and her small kids, my young niece and nephew, without Mum and Dad being the focus. Maybe in some ways that will never happen. Mum and Dad will always be there, the Unexpected Guests.

I speak to Dad to reassure him that everything is being done to get the house ready for him. He hardly responds; he sounds so tired.

The Macmillan nurse told him he would get more and more tired, sleep more and more and then slip away.

I pray that he will last the summer. I am selfish in wanting this, I know. I am supposed to be going to Thailand on 18 July with David and the kids. The holiday of a lifetime while Dad's life ends.

I look in the mirror. I have deep lines etched around my eyes. White hair at my temples. I look wrecked.

∽

Carrie rings. She is livid.

'I can't handle her any more!'

'What now?'

'She wouldn't let the removal men in.'

Carrie has spent days finding out about removal firms who could go to Mum's house to prepare the dining room for Dad's return. Mum had agreed to it. Social services were all set to deliver the bed and other equipment.

'They arrived and Mum would not open the door. Instead she insisted that Marina help her move all the sitting room furniture into the conservatory – except her green chair, of course.'

'Sitting room furniture? What good is that? Dad needs the dining room for his bedroom.'

'I know. But as far as Mum's concerned, that's not going to happen because she's not going to let anyone in tomorrow to set up the hospital equipment. I had to tell Dad and he was so upset. He told me he doesn't think he can live with Mum any more.'

I can suddenly see how easy it would be to suffocate or strangle my own mother.

'Let me handle it,' Marina says. 'You need to go on holiday with your family and rest and relax. God knows you are going to need all your strength when you get back.'

I give in. I stop phoning Mum. Marina is in charge.

Fifty-three

'There may be times when you are unwell but don't realise it or don't want help. When this happens doctors may say you lack insight. The Mental Health Act 1983 means doctors can force people to go to hospital if their illness puts them or other people at risk.'[53]

It is Sunday 5 July 2015. I am going to Thailand in thirteen days. I don't want to go. I want to go. I don't want to. I want to so much. I am exhausted. The temptation of tropical sun and sea and vibrant colours is overwhelming. It is an unrelentingly cold summer here in the UK. I could also do with a break from driving up and down the A4. But I don't want to leave Dad. What if he dies while I am away? David and Carrie and I have talked it over and under and inside out and it's been decided.

'Go,' Carrie says. 'I'll call you if we need you.'

I have driven to Stanmore to see Dad. It's a cold, grey morning. Dad is due to leave hospital in the next couple of days. I can't wait to never have to see this place ever again. I hate it. I hate the dilapidated car park. I hate the building-site ugliness, the Victorian architecture no longer fit for purpose, patched together with shonky Seventies plastic-and-breeze-block nastiness. I hate it for its smells, for the state in which I invariably find the toilets, for the silence of the corridors. I hate it for the amount of time it has claimed from my father's life. If I'm honest, I also hate the place for keeping Dad from Mum and for giving me the pieces to pick up as a result.

I don't want to go into the building. Sundays are the worst. No café for a much-needed caffeine fix. Even the nearest visitor loos are shut and I have to walk down corridors to find some that are open. I pull into the car park, find a space, turn off the engine and sit for a moment. At least you don't have to pay to park here. Small mercies.

My mobile rings. It's Carrie. I think about not answering. I should go straight to Dad. Procrastination wins.

'Hi, Carrie!'

She talks over me in a panicked rush before I've finished asking how she is.

'Mum's had a fall.'

'No!' Adrenaline surges.

'It's OK. Marina found her. This is actually good,' Carrie is saying.

I think of Carrie's rant to the GP mere months ago. *'So you're saying we have to wait until a crisis happens?'*

We'd thought that social services calling the police was enough of a crisis, but it wasn't. Is *this* it?

Carrie clearly thinks it is. 'Mum's in Pembury. I called the GP and he sounded excited,' Carrie goes on. 'He said, "This is our chance." We can get her into a home from here.' She is smiling, I can hear it. 'We can take control. This is proof that she cannot be left alone. Proof that even Dr M will have to take notice of.'

She sounds so happy. I suppose I should be happy too.

But I am crying, sitting in the car park of the hospital where our Dad is lying waiting for me while his wife is in another hospital fifty miles away. Is this how it ends? How – when – will it fucking end?

'The GP says we need to get her assessed by another psychiatrist while she is in Pembury,' Carrie is saying. 'If someone independent from Dr M can say that Mum lacks capacity, then she can be admitted to Dartford. We need to push for this.'

Push. Push. Push. That is all we have done. For months, years. My shoulders ache from pushing. And for what? I am Sisyphus, a man in another of Dad's stories; a man who spent all day, every day, pushing the same boulder up a hill, only to lose hold of it the minute he reached the summit. I am as cursed as he was. Every day I push and every evening I watch my efforts disappear from sight.

⌒

Dad is asleep. He is sleeping more and more. Sleeping his life away. He is propped up, his mouth partly open, his face smooth with morphine. I look at where the sheets fall away flatly from where his right leg once was. I look at his hands; his gentle hands, resting on his lap.

I can't tell him. I can't tell him that his wife of nearly fifty years has fallen and is now in another hospital. I can't tell him what this means: that she will most probably not be at home when he is discharged. That she will most likely be sectioned for twenty-eight days. What if Dad hasn't got twenty-eight days left? I can't begin to think through the consequences of this.

Dad opens his eyes, sees me and smiles.

I smile too, take his hands and start to explain.

Fifty-four

'A Section 2 requires an NHS body to notify social services of a patient's likely need for community care services after discharge . . . A Section 5 notifies social services of the proposed date of the patient's discharge.'[54]

Carrie and I call Pembury many times a day. Push, push, push. Sometimes the phone rings and rings and rings and no one answers. Sometimes we get through to someone who tells us Mum is 'doing fine' and 'should be home soon'. We are not going to let that happen. We keep phoning. Pushing. Watching the boulder roll back down.

Finally, I get through to the ward sister.

Before I have had a chance to say much beyond who I am, the sister barks at me, 'Your mother needs a psychiatric assessment. She's driving me around the bend.'

I almost laugh. *You and me both.* She is brusque, but at least it sounds as though I can get this woman on side.

'So how do I go about this? She's already under a psychiatrist, but he says Mum has capacity.'

'Does he?' the ward sister scoffs. 'One moment she's got us all running after her, calling out and demanding three-course meals, the next she's sitting up in bed like the queen saying she's fine and she has to go home because her husband needs her—'

'No, no, no,' I butt in. 'She can't be his carer. He's just had his leg amputated and he's dying. They're both . . . Vulnerable Adults,' I say, reaching for the golden-key vernacular of social services.

'Oh, God.' I picture the sister holding her head in her hand. 'Look, I'll do what I can, but you're going to have to insist on the assessment too. Your mum's physically fit enough to be discharged and I want her off my ward.'

Push, push, push.

I tell Carrie about the conversation. 'I'm arranging for a care home to come and assess Mum,' she says. 'I've explained the situation and they think they could take her. But she has to agree.'

She doesn't agree. She tells the care home what she told the ward sister: 'My husband has cancer. He needs me at home to look after him.'

She has not uttered the C-word in front of us – not once since Dad's diagnosis.

'The care home won't take her,' Carrie tells me.

I get advice from a friend who works in psychiatry in another county.

'I think you'll have to make a formal complaint against your mum's psychiatrist so that you can get her case reviewed,' he tells me. 'I should say, in defence of the man, that he has acted within the bounds of what is reasonable up to now. But he should not have cut you and Carrie completely out of the loop. He can't discuss your mum's treatment without her consent, but he should be open to listening to the family's concerns. That is one of the ways that we judge what kind of care is needed.'

That decides it. Dr M has not listened, he is not prepared to act, and I need action FAST.

I make the complaint.

Even as I have the necessary conversation, I feel guilty. I am putting a mark against a man's name. I am asked if I want to take the complaint to the highest level. I say no. However much anger I feel, I can't do that to him.

∽

Two days later, on Tuesday 7 July, Dad calls.

'I'm coming home!' His voice is bursting with joy. 'The ambulance is booked for ten o'clock. I should be home by lunchtime.'

I hear the anticipation, the expectation of what 'home' looks like. How can I tell him that it doesn't look like that any more? That there is a hospital bed downstairs, a special stool and grab-rail in the bathroom. How can I explain that Mum is still in hospital and that it looks likely, if the assessment finds her lacking in capacity, that she will not come home before Dad dies? How can I tell him that I am pushing for this – to keep Mum away from him – so that he can have a peaceful death?

I can't.

'That's great,' I say. 'I will drive over and be there to make you lunch.'

The best-laid schemes o' daughters and men . . . The ambulance breaks down on the M25. I am caught in traffic. I hope that I might still make it to the house before Dad, to tidy up, fill the fridge. Even the second ambulance beats me to it.

Dad is already exhausted by the time I arrive. He is in his wheelchair in the sitting room. Pale and small. His stump covered by a neatly pinned-up trouser leg.

'It is so good to be home,' he says, tears in his eyes.

I know I should allow him to have this moment, to relax and enjoy the fact that he's back in the house where he has spent forty years of his life. But there's too much to do, too much to sort out and talk about before I have to get on the phone again to discuss Mum. And I have to leave tomorrow. It's nearly the end of the school year and there's so much I am needed for at home.

'Dad, do you know when social services are coming?' Dad looks shifty. 'They are coming, aren't they?' I say.

He looks like a child caught with his hand in the sweetie jar.

No. He hasn't—?

'I couldn't wait for them to sort out the care package,' he admits. 'I asked to be discharged early.'

I make myself wait a beat before replying, in case I lose it. *He did WHAT?*

'I didn't mean to be a nuisance,' he says.

He sounds like Tom does when he's apologising for something. I have to steel myself not to cry.

'It's OK,' I say. 'Carrie and I will sort it out.'

'I've learnt how to get around on my Zimmer and I can cook scrambled eggs standing on one leg!' Dad says, clearly trying to impress. 'The OTs taught me how.'

He'll wear himself out hopping around on his Zimmer. He'll get to the end of the day and he won't be able to get himself to the bathroom. I can't tell him that. He doesn't want to hear it. He wants to live, to live, to live.

I offer to do some jobs for him before getting on the phone again. The fridge is empty – Marina kindly cleaned it of its rotting detritus when Mum went into Pembury. Dad gives me a shopping list that is so pathetic, I feel tears rising again.

One large potato, one tin of tomatoes, two apples, two chicken breasts.

One leg. One wife in hospital. Zero chances of survival.

∾

When I come back with the shopping I decide to quietly get on with making sure Dad has what he needs. I make up the hospital bed, which stands in the dining room where only last month we hosted the party. It seems to sit in judgement, to announce the finality of his return. I fill the fridge, make tea, do some hoovering.

Dad insists on hopping back and forth on the Zimmer. He gets slower as the afternoon wears on. He eases himself on to the sofa and I make him comfortable so that he can have a snooze.

I take the opportunity to make some calls. First off, social services. They are as irritated as I am that Dad has been allowed to discharge himself without the care package.

'It's much harder to put in place now that he's left the hospital,' a woman tells me. As if I needed telling.

Next, the hospice. We've been given the number in case Dad deteriorates and needs more morphine. No one has said this is where Dad is expected to die, but we know that is what is meant. They promise to send a nurse around tomorrow.

Next, Marina.

'I've taken your letter of complaint about Dr M to Pembury. Carrie asked your parents' friends and neighbours to write down why they believe Gillian can't be discharged home. And they will have me to deal with too,' she says.

Thank God for Marina!

By the end of the day things are starting to fall into place.

I cook Dad some supper and we sit and eat in the dining room as the kitchen bar is too high for Dad when he's in his wheelchair.

'Mum is going to be assessed by a new psychiatrist tomorrow,' I tell him.

'Oh,' he says. His face crumples. 'I miss her.'

And I am taking her away from you.

As usual, I am powerless in the face of Dad's emotions when it comes to Mum. Besides, it's nine o'clock and I am so tired I could fall asleep in my chair.

'Come on, Dad. We're both exhausted. Let's get you ready for bed,' I say, thinking I'll get an early night.

∽

Two hours later I have managed to get Dad washed, dressed into clean pyjamas and into bed. Two hours. Two whole hours of painstaking steps and moves and adjustments. How did he think he could cope alone with no care package? There is no point in saying this, though. Dad is fully aware now of just how much was being done for him in hospital.

In any case, he looks so small, so sweet in his cotton pyjamas, beautifully ironed by his dear wife. How could I possibly get angry with him? I make a silly performance of 'tucking him in', push the hair out of his eyes and bend to kiss him on the forehead.

When I was small, Dad would do just this. He would kiss me goodnight and say, 'Night, night. Sweet dreams. God bless.' Did he ever imagine then that one day I might be doing the same to him?

My voice cracks as I say, 'Would you like a story?' more in jest than because I really mean it. It's what he'd say to me back then.

He doesn't smile at the joke. He looks as though he might
cry. 'Yes, please,' he says.

I am suddenly embarrassed by this role reversal. I become
brisk, telling him to sleep well, saying I'll be upstairs if he
needs me.

I hurry away, gulping back tears, and run to the spare room
to bury my head in a book.

Why don't I go back? Say, 'What about *The Wind in the
Willows*? *The Hobbit*? Or even *Martin: the Kingfisher*?' Why
don't I indulge him? Allow him to be the child for once?
Why am I so appalled by this?

I can only think it is because I am tired, so tired of being
the one who cares. The one who shines the taps and looks
after Mummy. The one to whom they all turn when they want
something fixed.

I am tired. I am also very afraid.

Fifty-five

'The nearest relative has some rights when someone is, or may be, detained under the Mental Health Act (this is sometimes called "being sectioned" or "being held under section").'[55]

I sleep fitfully, worried that Dad will fall out of bed, will not make it to the bathroom, will feel frightened or lonely. I lie awake, worried about how all these things could happen once I am no longer here.

I have to get home.

I should be staying here.

When I go downstairs the next morning to check on Dad, he tells me he is exhausted. He has realised, he says, that he needs more help than he had thought he would.

'I'm sorry.' He looks defeated. 'I didn't discharge myself early to be naughty.'

There is nothing I can say that will make either of us feel better.

The hospice nurse arrives mid-morning. She is another of those infinitely kind and caring people, a woman who dearly wishes she were able to give more than ten minutes to Dad before shooting off to visit someone else. She is patient where

I have only ever been impatient, listening to Dad as he answers her questions in a rambling, non-specific way.

In my head, I am screaming: *Tell her you need someone to help you wash! To cook for you! To get you up in the morning and to bed at night!*

Instead Dad says, 'My wife's in Pembury hospital.'

The nurse nods. 'I'm sorry,' she says.

Dad falls forward in his wheelchair. I jump, thinking he has had some kind of fit. Then I hear him whine. And I see that he is crying. Proper, full-on sobbing. Tears streaming down his sunken cheeks, his mouth drawn back into a mask of deep, deep sorrow. It is horrifying. He hasn't once cried about his cancer, about his leg. He hasn't ever cried about himself.

'I miss her more than I can say,' he weeps.

He is crying about Mum.

The phone rings and I leap to answer. Better to act than to sit there, stupid and useless.

It's a social worker. Called Martin. Seriously? Is this a good sign?

Depends what you mean by good.

'I'm ringing to advise you that your mother has been assessed by Dr P, the in-house psychiatrist at Pembury general hospital. The hospital wants to discharge her now because she is physically fit and she has expressed a desire to return home. She keeps saying she wants to get back to look after her husband,' Martin says.

Not this again!

I open my mouth to protest, but this man is one step ahead of me.

'The reason I'm calling is that I've read a lot of the letters and emails you have written about your mother over the past few months. I've also read testimonials from neighbours and

friends – your mother's carer passed them on to us via the
hospital's social services team.' He pauses. 'I'm ringing to say
that I doubt very much that your mother can go home.' He
is grave, as though worried I will protest; that I will say, 'No!
You can't take my mother away!'

My heart leaps painfully.

Martin is still speaking. 'If your mum refuses to be transferred to a mental health unit of her own accord we shall
have to detain her under the Mental Health Act 1983. Are
you prepared to be named as her "nearest relative", bearing
in mind your father's prognosis?'

'I . . .'

1983. In 1983 I was 13, reading Adrian Mole's secret diary,
having my first chaste kiss at the school disco, passing notes
in class and doing handstands up against the gym wall.
Giggling and gossiping. Speaking, understanding and thinking
as a child. I am now about to discover what it is to put away
childish things.

'I have to ask if you understand the term "nearest relative",'
Martin goes on. 'It is not the same as next of kin.'

'OK. I'm – not sure what it is.'

'"Nearest relative" is a legal term used in the Mental Health
Act,' Martin explains. He is reading from a script he must
have delivered countless times.

I don't want to think about how many other people have
sat on the edge of a bed and stared at the carpet while a
social worker has read these words out to them.

'As I say, it's not the same as the next of kin,' he goes on.
'The next of kin has no rights under the Mental Health Act.
The nearest relative has some rights when someone is, or may
be, detained under the Mental Health Act or "sectioned" or
"held under section".'

'Uh-huh.'

'The nearest relative can ask for an assessment to decide if their relative should be detained,' he continues. 'They can also request that their relative is discharged from hospital. An application can be made to the county court to have a nearest relative removed or changed if they do not feel that they are the right person for the role. It is also important you know that the nearest relative does not have the right to be told everything about the patient. This could include information about what treatment the patient is taking. This will depend on whether the patient is happy for information to be shared.'

Rights. Capacity. Choices.

I force myself to concentrate on what Martin is saying. It is as though my world has shrunk to this one spot, on this island of a double bed in which my parents have slept together for nearly fifty years. I am here, on this island, and Martin is talking to me from another world. Is this really happening? Am I, the eldest daughter, really about to give permission for my mother to be locked away in an asylum – because, let's not hide behind fancy words, that is where she is going – while my father dies? It feels like the worst betrayal a daughter could commit.

I stare down at the flowery bedspread. This was the bed onto which we bounced on Christmas morning. This was the room we came into to watch as Dad performed his 'Canadian Airforce' workout routine in front of the mirror, counting the squats and the press-ups and the sit-ups and the burpees in a bid to stay fit as middle-age encroached on his once rowing-fit body. He took it so seriously. Carrie and I wanted to giggle, but knew somehow that we shouldn't.

This was the bed into which we snuggled for early morning cuddles or after a bad dream. Mum may have been strict and orderly in most other things, but she loved having us in bed with her and never complained about having her sleep disturbed. We were always welcomed into the warm cave of sheets and blankets, no matter what time we tiptoed across the landing. This was the bed that anchored our family. With love and laughter and safety. Mum used to crave cuddles. She is not so keen on them any more. She hangs limp in my arms, her own arms by her side.

This is not Mum and Dad's bed any more. Mum and Dad will never sleep together ever again. I am about to make sure of that.

I listen to Martin the social worker go through the rights that Mum and I have under the Mental Health Act. It feels much as though he is reading an arrest warrant.

You do not have to say anything.

Anything I do say may be used against me in the court of public opinion.

You have put your mum in the loony bin, Anna. How do you feel about that?

How *do* I feel? This is what I want, isn't it? I should feel immense relief. Mum will not be coming home for at least twenty-eight days. She will have a solicitor assigned to her case and there will be a review after the twenty-eight days, so there is a chance that she might be detained longer under a Section 3, although that is unusual. I tot up the days. If Dad's prognosis is correct, he will be able to end his days peacefully, without his wife, the lunatic, raving and presenting with extreme morbidity and melancholia and pacing and crying out and 'driving us all around the bend'. This is it. This is 'our chance', as Carrie put it, to get Mum what she needs and to give Dad some calm and respite.

But then I think of Dad, sitting in front of the hospice nurse, crying because of how much he misses this broken, brittle, beloved wife of his, and I cannot allow myself to feel anything like relief.

'Yes, I understand,' I say, when Martin the social worker has finished his spiel. 'I will be named as Mum's "nearest relative",' I say.

I sign her warrant. And I know that in many ways I have signed Dad's as well.

Fifty-six

'I knew the end was coming, but I just couldn't face it.'[56]

I go home and Mum goes to the Dartford Mental Health wing the same day. I go back to my kids and their end-of-term excitement and our plans for the summer. Plans which will include flying to Bangkok and swimming in waterfalls and sipping fresh fruit cocktails. Mum goes into a tiny beige room, smaller than the one I had in my first year at university. There is little natural light. There are no pictures on the walls, there is no lock on the bathroom. The only lock is the one separating the ward from the outside world. I have nine days left before leaving for holiday. Even though she is under section, I could go and visit her. I should go and visit her. I don't.

Dad struggles on for one more day with a limited emergency care package until Carrie calls Marina. He agrees to let Marina come and care for him full-time. Marina and Carrie tell me to go on holiday and not to worry.

'Your letters have done the trick, Anna,' my sister reassures me. 'Everyone is doing their utmost to get Mum better and to make Dad as comfy as possible. There's nothing more you can do. And if I need you to come back, I will call you,' she promises.

I don't expect a call. Not now that everything finally seems to be put in place. Before I leave, Carrie tells me that Dad is doing really well now that Marina is there.

'I honestly think he could go on for a bit now,' she says. 'He's perked up so much, being at home.'

⌒⌒

I go. And the first week passes like a dream. Mainly because I spend so much of it sleeping. The minute I sit down on a bus, in a taxi, on a train, on a boat, I fall fast asleep. It may be the heat; it may be that I have months of sleep to catch up on. It doesn't matter. It's bliss.

I get regular texts from Carrie. She says Dad's lungs continue to fill up with fluid and that he will need a drain. She remains positive, though. I get texts from Dad too.

On 23 July Dad writes:

It's so great to be.home. Marina came at 05:00 for a change of sheets and pyjamas. Instant attention, unlike hospital! I'm going to lie back and enjoy it for a while. Bless Carried andd you for finding her. I love you, my poppets. We all hope you are having a great time. XXXXDad

Dad has never sent a misspelled or mispunctuated message before in his life. I feel a lurking sense of dread. He is fading, his mind is awash, drifting. It can't be long now.

Fifty-seven

'Death, which others may prefer to forget about, certainly preys on my son's mind.'[57]

It is 7 a.m. on Monday 27 July 2015. I am dozing in a wooden cabin on the island of Koh Tao. It's the beginning of the relaxing part of the holiday. No more boats and buses and trains. Just swimming and sleeping and reading. I'm going to learn how to scuba dive. I'm going to sit out under starry skies and drink exotic cocktails . . .

A bell is ringing.

'Anna – Anna – answer it!'

David is shaking me. *Like he did when Grandma—*

I leap to answer the phone by the bed.

'It's Carrie. I'm sorry. He's gone into the hospice.'

'Oh.' My throat clamps.

'I don't want you to have to come back. I just think there may not be much time left. It's up to you. We're doing fine,' she adds. Her voice is cheerful, as it always is. But there is something measured about it.

'We're doing fine'; not, 'He's doing fine.'

This is it, isn't it? This is real. This is more real than any of the other crises. This is the big one.

I want to ask if Mum knows.

We're going to have to tell her.

She's in a mental hospital. Sectioned. And Dad is dying. And I am here, in paradise. In bloody paradise!

How am I going to tell Mum?

I wish you'd shut up about your fucking mother! Your father. Is. Dying.

Carrie is speaking, but all I'm hearing is: Mum. Mum. Mum.

She won't see him ever again.

He won't see her.

He's dying!

I don't move. I don't speak.

Carrie's voice is as clear as if she were standing in the next room. She is choosing her words very carefully and speaking much more slowly than usual.

As I listen I have to acknowledge that, however much she keeps insisting, she isn't fine. She is completely and utterly exhausted.

'I just think there may not be much time left.'

'How long do you think he's got?' I manage to croak.

Carrie hesitates.

Don't let it be too late. Why did I come all this way? So far from him? Don't let it be too late.

Mum's right – I'm always too bloody late!

'They said last night they thought thirty-six hours at most,' she finally answers.

Measured. Calm. In control. My little sis, suddenly the older and far, far wiser one.

David says something about ferries. He is gesturing to me to get off the phone.

I am going to have to go back. On my own.
I can't.
You'll bloody have to.
It's all happening too quickly.
I can't. I can't.
I can't just leave.
I can't leave my kids on a remote island.
I can't.
A boat. A plane. Another plane.
It's too far. I *can't*.
I can and I will.

'I'll be there. I'll call you back,' I tell Carrie. 'David's going to find out how. I'll be there,' I repeat, resolve growing with every word. 'I'll come.'

∽

We go to wake the kids. They look at us, wide-eyed, suddenly so much younger than their fourteen and sixteen years. They nod as we tell them, their mouths thin and tight with the beginnings of grief. Their lovely grandpa. Their funny, cuddly, lovely grandpa who sang to them and told them stories and jokes. Leaving them.

Martin! Martin? I need you, Martin!
He can't leave us.

Fifty-eight

'We analyze our existence, the meaning of life,
the meaning of everything, continually.'[58]

I am walking along the beach now, waiting for David to come back from the hotel reception. The tropical sand really is white. There really are palm trees. The water is a rippled sheet of light-blue glass. This really could be paradise.

Meanwhile Dad and Mum – and Carrie – are in hell.

I bend and scoop a handful of sand. It falls through my fingers like ashes, one tiny piece of coral remaining in my palm. A bleached white bone.

'I don't want to offend anyone.'

Dad never mentioned Mum playing a part in his funeral. He knew she wouldn't be able to. He has probably never even talked to her about what he wants, what he hopes, what he fears.

'This is my fear: that my body will be confined to the cold, dark earth. This is my wish: that you will scatter my ashes to the stars.'

I pick up another handful of tropical sand, formed from the bones and shells of long-dead beautiful creatures, transformed into this glittering treasure trove of tiny shards and specks of colour.

When Grandma died, Mum put herself in charge of the funeral arrangements. It was a dismal, supermarket conveyor-belt affair in the local crematorium. One in, one out. Efficient, tidy, drab and soulless. 'Thank God that's over,' Mum said afterwards. Her mother's funeral was just another event to get through, like Christmas or a birthday. A year later we asked Mum if we could scatter Grandma's ashes near the river in Maidstone, the town where she was born. Mum was horrified. 'Why do you want to do that?'

Dad is right not to expect Mum to arrange his funeral.

He's not a man to be dealt with as though he were house-hold refuse, to be parcelled up and disposed of.

He is not a man to be locked away in the cold, hard earth.

He will get his last wish – Carrie and I will make sure of it.

We will scatter his ashes to the stars.

Fifty-nine

'My son is extremely worried about dying and any members of his family dying.'[59]

I am on the ferry to Koh Samui, watching the waves rise and fall, willing that with each wave Dad is still breathing. *In and out, in and out.* I concentrate on my own breathing, as though that might help him. Thirty-six hours is a lot of breaths. Has he got that many left?

The one thing Dad wanted more than anything after having his leg amputated was to get back on the river. Now he's preparing for a river crossing of a different kind. Will he be able to hold on to the shores of life a little longer before making this last journey? What will it be like? Will it be dark, as in his stories of Charon ferrying poor souls across the Styx to Hades, King of the Underworld? Or will it be a release into light?

It took thirty-six hours for my daughter to make her journey from the warm darkness of her foetal bed into the bright lights of the hospital, sixteen and a half years ago. Hour upon hour filled with pain, fright, struggle, release, joy and love. Birth and death. Each act as mystical, terrifying and inevitable as the other. You can't hold back the tides.

I think of Dad rowing, of the rhythmic rock and swish of the oars. Of the music of the coxswain's orders. Of the movement of eight men, pulling together. Heave-ho. Legs for ten. Wrists flat and quick away at the catch. *Michael, row the boat ashore.*

Keep breathing, Dad. Keep breathing.

Sixty

'Being with someone you love at the point of their death is a profound experience. Nonetheless, you may find the anticipation emotionally and mentally exhausting. At times you may fervently wish for it to be over. And then you may feel guilty for thinking like this. But it is a normal and understandable response to a very stressful situation.'[60]

It's 28 July 2015. The plane is one of the first flights into Heathrow. I run through the airport. I run to the taxi rank. The driver speeds down the motorway.

Push, push, push.

It's nearly six o'clock. Almost all of the allotted thirty-six hours are up.

Not much time left.

I try not to think of this as a deadline, but the word pops into my head and I almost laugh as it spools off a mind of its own. Deadline. Dead. Line. Flatline. Dead. Dad.

We're hurtling along familiar Kentish lanes now. Orchards. White weatherboard and red tiles. Oast houses. It's so quiet at this time of the morning. No heavy commuter traffic on the road yet. The lanes are empty, green and luminous with early morning light filtered through the tree canopy. So quiet, so beautiful. I used to cycle down a lane like this in late summer to go and pick apples in the orchard near home. I would arrive at six o'clock, the low-branched trees swathed in mist, the grass glistening with dew. The apples would glow in the soft light, the bloom on their skin intensifying the rich reds, golds, russets and greens. I was not a morning person – I was a teenager – but I loved that moment of arrival in the quiet orchard. At that point in my life I still loved home. Home. I haven't thought of it as such for over twenty years. My broken relationship with Mum meant it was a place I didn't want to come back to. And whenever I did I was late. I can't be late today. I'm coming home, Dad. Wait for me.

∽

We pull up outside the hospice in the Weald at 5.55 a.m. My hand is on the door handle before the driver has come to a halt.

I run to the night entrance. I have been told to come here. Carrie said they would let me in, whatever time I arrived.

A nurse comes to the door, calm and smiling. 'Anna? We've been expecting you.'

I can't say it, can't ask: is he still alive? I can't say anything until I see his face.

It is so, so silent here. Quieter than Stanmore. Quieter than the plane last night. Quieter than the summer lanes. Silent and still. Like a waiting room. Dad is in a waiting room, waiting to cross from this world to the next.

Not yet. Please, not yet.

I follow the nurse down a corridor, not daring to look through any doors, terrified of what I might see in this place where death haunts the walls. Dad is in a large room. The curtains are drawn. There are flowers on a table.

He is lying on his back, his head slightly to one side, his mouth open. He looked like this after the amputation, his face a death-mask-in-waiting. His cheeks are more sunken than the last time I saw him. Just over a week ago. No time at all. Looking at the change in him now, it might as well have been an eternity.

His breath is rattling. Wheezing. Slow. Desperate. It sounds painful, but he is not in pain. I can tell this even before the nurse reassures me that this is the case. His face and brow are smooth and his beautiful wild bushy eyebrows twitch as though he is dreaming. A tiny frown passes over his face. I want to kiss him and hold him. *I want to eat you up.* It's what we say to babies. I want to gobble him whole.

I hardly dare touch him. When I do, his skin feels alien. It is clammy and cold. I take his hand. Still I say nothing. I am waiting for him to open his eyes and see me. The nurse draws back the curtains, letting in the grey morning light, and tells me to talk to him to let him know I am here. Then she leaves.

I watch him. He might wake up, mightn't he? He might see me and smile sleepily as he did on some of those morning hospital visits earlier this year. I think of that morning when I had dropped off Tom to catch and ring birds on the Marlborough Downs at dawn. Dad smiled then when I told him what his grandson was up to. I think of him lying in his hospital bed, listening to the dawn chorus. I think of this as I watch him lying here now and I hear a chirrup outside and the soft call of a wood pigeon. Can Dad hear it? Can he hear me? The nurse thinks so. Will he wake up one last time?

I start talking. I talk about Thailand and Laos; I talk about the people and the food and the language and the warmth of the sea. I know he would have loved it all. I find myself telling him about *Martin: the Kingfisher*. I tell him the story and say that I wish I had read it to him when he'd come home from Stanmore. I tell him I think it's his and Mum's story, and how funny is that? A book you were given when you were four is, in a way, a prediction of your adult life. The magic of stories, Dad. The magic of the tales you told me.

Carrie walks in. Unlike me, she is, as always, immaculately made up. Marina would not call us 'two peas in pod' today. Carrie is wearing clean, un-crumpled clothes and a weary smile. A smile that doesn't reach her eyes. I am dirty and am wearing dirty clothes. I try to smile, but my face crumples to match my outfit.

We hug. We are here, together. It is unreal. I went to sleep in Thailand and now I am here, waiting for my dad to die.

'I woke early and thought, "I might not come straight away." I was so tired.' Carrie looks at Dad. 'I don't know what I was thinking.'

That's when I know. That Dad will not wake up. He will not see me one last time. He has not been waiting for me to get back.

If he has been waiting for anything, it is release.

Carrie sits next to me and we lean over Dad together. We stroke the golden hairs on his poor thin arms. The muscles have long since atrophied and his once tanned, strong limbs are embarrassingly white and almost feminine. The skin here is soft and warmer than his hands.

We hug him and cry. We tell him we love him. We sing to him, his favourite songs. We sing the songs we used to sing as children, to pass the time on long car journeys to see Dad's parents in Maidenhead or John and Euphan in Winchester. To make the journey pass quicker. Is that what we're doing now?

We talk and we sing and we laugh and we cry and Dad's breathing becomes more laboured. At one point he pauses and tilts his head back a little. I realise I am holding my breath with him and at once urging him to breathe again, while at the same time waiting for each breath to be his last.

I start to panic. 'Is he – is he dying now?' I ask Carrie.

It seems so stupid not to know.

But we don't. We've never seen anyone die before.

The nurse comes in. 'Would you like me to give him something to make him more comfortable?'

Carrie and I answer as one. 'Yes, please.'

I don't know what Carrie is thinking, but I assume 'making Dad more comfortable' might lead to him opening his eyes. I cling to this idea of him waking, even as I know how hopeless it is. Maybe the drug the nurse is injecting into Dad's paper-pale skin will ease his breathing. He will stop gasping; his breathing will slow. He will open his eyes and smile.

Stupid again! Of course it's not Dad's breathing that the nurse is wanting to ease. It's his passage from here to – not here.

Nothing can keep Dad here now. I see this as his breathing continues its shaking pace of shuddering to a halt and then rasping into gear again in such an alarming way. It is as though he is drowning. It is unbearable to watch and yet I can't drag my eyes away from him.

Now I don't want him to wake. I don't want him to be conscious of what he is going through.

We both start talking at once. We know without any exchange of words or glances that we are nearly there. He is nearly there – not here. And he needs us to help him leave.

We urge him on as sixteen years ago the midwife urged me. Thirty-six hours for Lucy to come into the world, thirty-six hours for my father to leave.

We call him 'Daddy', a name we haven't used for years. He strains and struggles as though in the last stretch of a race. The race of his life.

His breathing becomes harder

He pauses

Tilts his head a little

We will him to breathe

We will him to let go

We will him to stay

We will him to leave

'It's OK, Daddy. You can do it.'

'You're nearly there. Nearly there!'

'You're doing really well. You can go now. Go down the river.'

'Follow the kingfishers.'

We say that last phrase in unison. Even though I have said nothing to Carrie about the book. Even though I have told her nothing of my thoughts on the ferry – of crossing to the other side, of Charon and the Styx. We have not talked of such things for years.

'Go, Dad, go,' we tell him. Even as we want so much for him to stay.

A strange high-pitched moan.

A last gasp.

His eyes roll into the back of his head. For a short, sharp second I am sure he is going to say something.

But no. That's it. No more rasping breaths. No more struggling. No more pain.

No more Dad.

The time of death is 6.55 a.m. Thirty-seven hours after I left Koh Tao.

'He waited for one extra hour,' Carrie says. 'He waited for you.'

Sixty-one

'Emotional pain can and does manifest itself in various ways. It can be so overwhelming that you feel frozen in time, like you are on the outside of life looking in at a world you no longer feel part of.'[61]

In the moments after Dad's death, we are euphoric. The sense of release is everywhere. We see it in the light that floods the room, we hear it in the birdsong from the garden outside, we smell it in the scent from the flowers on the windowsill. Dad's face is smooth and pain-free. We find ourselves laughing over the things he used to say, the things we used to do as a family before all the sadness swept laughter away. It's over. At last. It's over.

Dad is washed and dressed by the nurses and changed into his own cotton pyjamas, lovingly ironed by Mum before she was taken away to her own newly institutionalised life. That airing cupboard: that hallowed space. It broke my heart when I looked into it three weeks ago to fetch Dad a shirt and I realised that no one would ever look after him as well as Mum used to – and that this was one of many reasons why he missed her.

The thought of her immediately sends me plummeting.

'We'll have to go and tell Mum,' I say.

Carrie's face says it all: do we have to? What she says aloud is, 'Marina said she'd take us. I've texted her. She'll be here soon.'

How are we going to tell her?

They had been together for forty-nine years. He was her North, her South, her East, her West. The only one who understood her. The only one besides her parents who could forgive and forget the darker side of her. He adored her and she adored him. If he had lasted one more month they would have reached their Golden Wedding.

She is going to hate us for this.

Bloody kids, bloody kids, bloody, bloody, bloody kids.

Marina comes into the room. She is tearful. 'Such a gentleman,' she says, gazing on Dad. 'It was a privilege to look after him.'

There is so much love in her eyes. I find myself wishing Dad had had a wife like her – a wife who would care for him until the end. I shake the thought away. I astonish myself by how disgusting I can be, having thoughts like that at a time like this.

I don't want to leave Dad. I know he has already gone, but I don't want to walk out, knowing that I will never see him again. I feel something like a toddler tantrum start to build in me. I don't want to have to rush this just because I have to go and see Mum I don't want to see Mum at all why does she always have to come first why can't I stay here with my dad my darling dad why can't I just take my time and not have to rush off to HER!

'We have to go,' Marina says.

I breathe and swallow and pull my shoulders back.

'Pull yourself together.'

∽

As Mum is still officially detained under the Mental Health Act, we have to phone ahead to the hospital in Dartford to say we are coming. They guess the reason immediately.

Marina drives us there. I remember what Martin the social worker told me: that Mum can be held under the Mental Health Act for up to twenty-eight days only. Today is day nineteen. We have only nine days left before she could be sent home.

I can't think about that now. And I don't want to bother Carrie with it.

We are let in through the locked doors and Marina leads the way down colourless corridors to Mum's soulless room. I am steeped in guilt that Marina knows the way while I do not.

'I've been visiting her while your Dad was in Stanmore,' she tells us.

We hadn't asked her to do this. The kindness is too much. It's like a dull punch in the stomach.

There is a cry – a shout from somewhere behind me. I flinch.

The last time I visited someone on a secure mental health wing was in 1991, when one of my dearest school friends had been admitted after a psychotic episode. Mum had not wanted me to go and had become very angry with me when I had insisted. No doubt the reason she was angry was because she knew that the experience would terrify me and she wanted to protect me. I didn't see it like that at the time. I was hot with anger and the impetuousness of youth. I would go and see my friend because my friend needed me, and nothing Mum could say would make any difference.

The experience did terrify me. Not because my friend's behaviour was alarming; she was upset and confused, but still my dear, gentle friend and I could still talk to her, and she could still understand me. It was the others. The raving women, hurling themselves along the corridors at top speed with a lurching, frantic gait, staring, shouting, screaming through glass doors, moaning, wailing, begging to be let out.

I don't see any of that here, though. Not yet, anyway. The cry has come from behind closed doors. Mostly this place is quiet. Not the deep, peaceful quiet of the hospice. It is far colder and more deathly.

Some nurses walk past. They don't smile reassuringly like the hospice nurses. Their faces are unreadable. Pent-up. Closed.

We knock on the door of Mum's room. Marina goes in first.

'Hello, Gillian!' she trills.

A tiny, bent, ancient woman gets up slowly from a plastic-covered armchair. She stares back at us, her mouth half open. She lets out a small, crackled groan.

'Mum?'

It is Mum and not Mum.

Her once carefully dyed hair is now snowy white, wild and woolly. Her chin sprouts a beard of fluffy white to match. Her eyes are wide and staring. Her skin is ghostly pale and papery. Her fingernails are yellow and claw-like. She's wearing thick glasses. She never wears glasses. Where are her contacts?

More to the point, where is the woman who took so much care over her appearance, asking Grandma to alter hems and seams, taking outfits back to Marks and Sparks until she found just the right one? Where is the woman who spent hours over her hair, curling it, setting it, dyeing it, never truly satisfied with the results? Where is the Mum who religiously rubbed Oil of Olay into her skin? Where is the immaculate, upright mother who stood at Dad's side at Round Table functions and Law Society dinners and Cambridge reunion teas, her clothes neat, her nails manicured, her smile perfectly lipsticked and beautiful, beautiful, beautiful. Where has she gone?

It's as though a wicked witch has come and cast a spell on Mum. She has aged twenty years, even since the last time I saw her.

She totters backwards and forwards, making those unsettling whooping noises. We should be used to this by now. We are not.

Carrie and I try to give her a hug. She hangs loosely in our arms while her feet tip and tap.

How had I imagined this scene? I, who am so good at imagining? I, who make a living out of it? Who have been accused by my mother so many times of being 'romantic' and 'a dreamer', 'always thinking of the sublime'? Well, I guess I had imagined something like this: Carrie and me holding our mum in a huddle, weeping with her for the loss of our father, her husband. Consoling one another, reassuring Mum that we will take care of everything. Sharing the pain and the loss.

Instead, as soon as we start to talk, she sits down – and shuts down. Completely.

And it goes like this:

'Mum, we are so sorry. We have to tell you that Dad has died.'

Silence.

'You know Dad was very ill. But he's at peace now.'

Silence.

'We were with him. It was very peaceful. He wasn't in pain.'

Silence. Stony-faced silence.

Not. A. Word.

My sister and I look at one another, at Marina. We start to cry. The nurse who is with us looks sorry for us all.

Then Mum speaks. Her voice is scratchy as though she hasn't used it in months. 'There's a taxi coming,' she says. She speaks in a monotone, automaton-calm.

What does she mean, a taxi?

Carrie seems to understand. 'No, there isn't. Dad has gone. There's no taxi.'

Does Mum think she's going to visit Dad? Has she not grasped what we have told her? It's almost funny – she never wanted to visit him when he was alive, and now he's dead, she wants to get a *taxi*?

'There's a taxi coming to get me,' Mum repeats. 'You'll have to leave. There's a taxi coming now.'

Nothing we can say will make her stop insisting on this. There's a taxi coming. It's for her. She is going to be leaving and so we must go. It's like her demanding to be let out to fill the car with petrol after Dad's party. It is baffling and worrying and wrong and it doesn't make sense.

Eventually we do leave.

As we approach the locked exit, a woman comes running up to us, chuntering, 'I need to get out. I need to get out.' A nurse grabs her and holds her back so that we can go. I look back to see the woman's face pressed against the glass.

Mum is that woman. She is every woman in there.

Lost. Mad.

She may as well have died with Dad.

∽

In the car on the way back to the house, Marina remarks on the difference in our demeanour towards Mum compared with that towards Dad.

'You become smaller – like two little girls, waiting to be told off.'

I think about this later. It's a lifetime of holding our breath, watching Mum and waiting for the next explosion that has done this to us; the uncertainty of her moods, not knowing what it will be that will tip her over the edge this time. It is a lifetime of being Good Girls.

I had been afraid to tell Mum that Dad had died because I had been preparing myself for her rage. It was so long since I had seen her that I had forgotten that she was no longer capable of rage. What I got instead was far worse. If Mum had shouted, screamed, bared her teeth, grabbed me around the wrists, shaken me, pounded me into the ground, I could have taken that. It would have been real. It would have echoed the rage I feel. The gaping, aching hole of anger and fury at the fact that Dad has gone. I would have been able to forgive her this time.

Go on – hit me! I can take it! Spit in my face! I deserve it! Dad is dead dead dead and I want to feel something. I want to feel the pain. More than that; I want to be punished. I want violence. A fight. Blood, sweat and tears.

This cold, calm . . . nothing – this talk about taxis? It's far more horrifying.

Sixty-two

'People with Asperger's want one friend. The problem is that in adult life your one friend has to be your spouse.'[62]

Marina takes Carrie to join her kids, who have gone out with their dad for the day.

'I'm not going to tell them just yet,' she tells me. 'They are having so much fun.'

She is desperate to get back to them. I think of my kids, on the other side of the world. I miss them so much that it's a physical ache, as though I have left part of my own body behind in Thailand. Dad told me that after his leg was amputated, he could still feel it. 'It twitched, especially at night.' I miss my kids like this – like the twitch of a phantom limb. I wonder if this is how Mum feels, knowing that Dad has gone. Does she feel anything at all?

Marina takes me back to our parents' house and into our parents' room, where Mum has forbidden anyone to go for months and months.

'I'm sorry,' she says. 'I didn't think I should touch any of this.' She leaves and says I should call her if I need anything.

What do I need?

I need someone to tell me where to start. I look around the room and find it hard to take in what I'm seeing.

The place is a mess.

The chairs, the dressing table, the floor, the bed, the bedside tables are all covered in crumpled used tissues, unopened letters (mostly bills, mostly red) and dirty clothes. A thick layer of dust sits on the mirror, the surfaces, the bookcase.

Mum used to take immense pride in housework. She scoffed at me for getting a cleaner. I bridled and became defensive, citing my job and how busy I was, but looking back I think that she took my lack of interest in being a housewife as an implied criticism of her love of the role. She would dust and wash and polish every day. Get down on her hands and knees to buff the parquet, climb onto the kitchen surfaces to clean the windows. No job was beyond her and she did everything to perfection. 'If a thing's worth doing, it's worth doing well,' she would say.

That house, like the immaculate mother who ruled it, has vanished. That house, which had 'a place for everything, and everything in its place', is now in total chaos. It is a cruel reflection of the terrifying disorder in Mum's mind.

I pick up the tissues and throw them away. I take the bills downstairs and stack them on the breakfast bar. I flick through them, knowing I am going to have to call all these companies and tell them that Dad is dead and that Mum is under section.

Tell people – it strikes me that this is what I need to do first. I need to call people. I need to call David and John and my cousins and neighbours and friends.

'Your lovely Dad,' says David, when I speak to him, his voice breaking.

'No!' says one cousin. 'But I thought he was doing so well now that he was back home?'

And so many 'sorry's and so much sympathy and so much love.

'And Gillian?' asks a friend. 'How has she taken it?'

How, indeed?

౿

After the phone calls I know I should sleep, but there's no chance of that. I go to Dad's study instead. When we first moved here in 1976, this room was the garage. Mum quickly decided that a single garage was not good enough. 'All the new houses have double garages,' she pointed out. 'And the girls need a playroom.' Somewhere to keep our toys – and mess – out of the way, out of sight, out of mind.

And so the garage was converted into a playroom and a new garage was built next to it. In later years the playroom became the music room where I would spend hour upon hour, playing the piano, the saxophone, practising scales and arpeggios and learning pieces for performances and exams. It was my sanctuary. My place. As long as I was making music, I couldn't be asked to do anything else. And I was out of Mum's way. Music got me through my teens, just as art got Carrie through hers. If ever a row was brewing, I could shut myself away and play and play and play until Mum – and I – had calmed down. It saved our relationship during those stormy adolescent years.

Looking at Dad's desk now, I have no doubt that this room saved my parents' marriage during Dad's retirement. Dad would come in here to 'fart about on the computer', as Mum used to say.

Since his illness, this room has had many changes of use. It has been a makeshift bedroom, a dumping ground for furniture to make way for the hospital equipment, and now, by the looks of it, it is a recycling station – or landfill site – for yet more unopened mail.

I stand and look at the piles and piles of paper on the sofa, table, desk and floor. I feel crushed, as though I am now lying under it.

I think of Carrie and my small niece and nephew who need her so much more than my two now need me. She won't be able to help with any of this. I will have to do it. I will have to pay bills and find the will and go to a solicitor and get a death certificate and plan the funeral and organise the wake and sort through Dad's possessions and give away his clothes. Oh God, his clothes . . .

I will have to do this. Me. Anna. The eldest child.

Be a Good Girl.

You are the eldest.

You should know how to behave.

I should, but I don't. I'm not up to the task. I'm not grown-up enough. I'm not strong enough. I am weak and small and cold and tired.

I go to Dad's desk, which is the only tidy area in the room. Orderly in- and out-trays, files neatly arranged. The last time I sat here, Dad was showing me his will. I pick up a pen. A fountain pen which has poured out pages and pages of Dad's beautiful, regular, Italic hand. This pen: it is only a thing. I run my fingers over the computer keyboard. *Martin! Get off that bloody computer!* It is only a thing. I pick up a Perspex paperweight, which contains a miniature document from Dad's time in the City. I used to covet it. It could be mine now, I guess, if I want it. I'm not sure I do want it. It is only a thing. This house where I lived for most of my childhood, for almost half my life so far – it is only a house. Only bricks and mortar and double-glazed windows. It is only stuff. You can't take it with you when you go.

I turn away from the desk. I suddenly can't bear the tidiness, the order that Dad left before Mum came into the room, bringing chaos in her wake. It seems so pathetic, the way everything is put away so carefully. Who cares now where the paperclips are?

And yet it's so Dad. No wonder Mum adored him. No wonder he was the only one who could keep her safe. A place for everything. Predictability. Neatness. A match made in heaven. Perfect.

Sixty-three

*'It could take days, weeks or even months before they
show any signs of grief . . . Do not expect a response
(crying, sadness, aggression). Do not tell them how
they should respond. Instead, observe their response
and work with them.'*[63]

'What shall we do about Mum?'

Carrie and I bat this question back and forth. It
contains a multitude of worries.

What shall we do if she gets sent home in a week's time?

What shall we do about her health?

Her safety?

Her well-being?

Her loneliness?

Most importantly right now: what shall we do about her
during the funeral?

It has never occurred to me not to include her in the funeral,
but when I ask Carrie how we are going to manage her while
we also give the eulogy, look after our own families and Dad's
friends and orchestrate the whole day, Carrie's husband gently
steps in and says, 'You don't.'

Carrie agrees. 'We can't have her at the funeral. It'll be too much for her and too much for us.'

Really? We don't bring Mum to her husband's funeral? I can't accept this. It feels so, so wrong.

'Anna, remember how she was at Dad's party,' Carrie says.

This brings back memories of other parties where Mum had been aggressive or had meltdowns. There was the one David and I held as a farewell to our neighbours when we moved from the Midlands to Wiltshire. Mum was furious we were moving. It upset a routine she had got used to: go and stay with Anna and then drive on to Norfolk to see Carrie. Why was I being so selfish, taking her grandchildren to the other side of the country? She would not accept that a new job was taking us there. We were doing this to upset her, so she made sure that her behaviour at that party upset me. She drank too much, humiliating me in front of my friends, was rude to my neighbours, snapped and growled and raged at anyone who would listen. Even then I felt the need to explain. She is upset. She doesn't mean to be rude. Don't take it personally. Please.

Maybe Carrie and her husband are right. Maybe we can't risk having Mum there.

But she has to say goodbye, hasn't she? Surely it's morally wrong to deny her that?

'She won't be able to cope,' Carrie persists.

And then David agrees with her. And Marina. And the funeral parlour. And the mental health nurses. And – what tips me over in the end – the reader who is going to conduct the service and who was a great friend of Dad's says the same.

'She'll be overwhelmed,' the nurses say. 'It'll be too much of an ordeal. You're right, though: she does need to say goodbye. Perhaps you could talk to the funeral directors and see what they think about having a private service.'

I've been given permission, again. To listen to my head rather than my heart. Guilt is there, though, all the time, singeing the edges of my relief.

'It's not a problem,' the funeral directors tell us. 'It's more common than you think. We can arrange for your mum to be brought to the chapel and we'll let you have as much time as you need to have a private ceremony. It can be on any day you like – it doesn't have to be on the day of the funeral itself. In fact, it might be better for you and Carrie if it isn't.'

I am not used to people suggesting that Carrie and I put our own needs before Mum's. It is shocking. I have to hear it many times before I allow it to be true.

‿

On 14 August 2015, two days after Mum's seventy-second birthday, I meet my sister and her husband in the tiny chapel that backs on to the car park of the pub where we used to get together with our school friends on Christmas Eve.

Predictably, Mum is already there, waiting. I half expect her to frown and growl, 'You're late!' But Mum is heavily sedated. She looks tiny: frail and frightened, as though she has no idea why she is here. She is not capable of being the rude, aggressive person she was seven years ago at that party in the Midlands. She is not capable of anything much today.

Her eyes stare into the distance behind those thick glasses. She has had her hair blow-dried and, thank God, someone has removed that fluffy beard. She is wearing a simple black linen dress. She looks sweet, fragile, in need of love. I go to hug her, but she is sitting down and doesn't want to get up.

Everyone else is standing. The room is small with a low ceiling and it is very crowded now that Carrie and her husband and I have arrived. There is someone from the funeral parlour and Mum has two nurses with her – does she really need two? She doesn't look as though she could run off even if she wanted to – and Brian, the reader who is going to lead Dad's funeral, is also here.

And Dad. Dad is here too, inside his bamboo coffin. I had never expected to get this close to it. To him. It's too awful, too difficult to acknowledge, that he is lying inside, and that I cannot see him or touch him. But if I feel this, how must Mum feel? Can she feel anything at all through the fug of diazepam and goodness knows what else?

Mum sits. Stares. She doesn't look at the coffin. She looks at some other point, far away.

Brian says a few words and also a prayer. I am not listening. I am watching Mum, holding my breath to see what she will do. Will she cry? Will she say anything? Will she ask if this is the real funeral? Will she get angry at the praying? She has always hated people praying aloud. She has always hated anything 'happy clappy'.

'Would you like to say something?' Brian asks. He looks at me and Carrie, then asks, 'Gillian?'

Mum says, 'No.'

Then she makes to get up.

'I want to go now.'

Carrie and I have brought some flowers from Mum's favourite florist. 'Here you are, Mum.' Carrie holds them out. 'You can put them on the coffin.'

'No!' Mum barks.

She looks so alarmed that Carrie and I rush to lay the flowers down. My stomach clenches with the unsayable. I want to give in, to groan, moan, sob, cry out. I can't. I can't do it in front of all these people. And I can't upset Mum.

I want to leave now too. I need to get out of here, for this to be over. I can't stand the sight of the coffin any longer, the claustrophobia of the chapel, the gentle smiling faces around me.

There is nothing beautiful about this, nothing remotely appropriate. A woman is saying goodbye to the love of her life, her husband of forty-nine years. Yet she is saying, doing, nothing. She wants to leave. She's been here for *ten minutes*. She will never see him again. This was her chance. To say goodbye, to show some grief.

Nothing.

It should not be like this. I wish I hadn't come. I wish I didn't have to see my mother so ravaged by illness, so distanced by drugs, so diminished. I wish she could show grief, even if it were loud and ugly and terrifying to watch. Even if she bared her teeth and shook her fists.

Bloody death, bloody death, bloody, bloody, bloody death.

Mum bustles out of the chapel, the nurses hurrying to keep up. She can't get away fast enough. She gets into the taxi, flanked by the nurses. So she did need two of them after all.

We wave and call, 'Goodbye.' She doesn't look at us as the car pulls away.

The funeral was held on 18 August 2015. It was a day of contrasts: of smiles and tears; of laughter and sobbing; of colour and darkness; of music and silence; of jokes and solemnity; of youth and old age; of life and death. It was appropriate and it was beautiful. It was calming and hopeful and joyous. Completely and utterly befitting the man Dad was. Everyone had been right: it was better that Mum was not there.

Sixty-four

*'When children become adults and recognise later in life
that one of their parents had Asperger's syndrome, they can
finally understand the personality, abilities and motive of
their mother or father.'*[64]

Mum's sentence of twenty-eight days under section is up
on 5 August 2015. From that day on, Carrie and I live
in fear and dread of her being discharged from Dartford and
sent back home.

Thankfully, this doesn't happen straight away. Most probably because of Dad's death. Instead, we are told we have to
come to monthly reviews with her new psychiatrist, Dr E,
and her mental health nurse and a social worker newly
assigned to her. Mum is allowed to come to these meetings.
Sometimes she does, sometimes she doesn't. Even when she
does, she rarely makes it all the way through. She gets up,
sits down, whoops, pants, runs out, runs in.

Carrie and I prepare for these meetings as though going
into battle.

Remembering the advice of my psychiatrist friend, we put
everything in writing, drawing up agendas for the monthly

reviews and writing up minutes of every meeting. We are determined not to let Mum be discharged without a full psychiatric review and an agreement for a twenty-four-hour care package. We know the form now; we have the language at our disposal. We are not going to be railroaded. Our ultimate aim is to find a suitable residential care home for Mum as we have no confidence in her ability to cope with people coming and going at home. And friends and neighbours have made it clear that they no longer wish to be relied upon. Marina is there as back-up. She comes to the meetings with us, providing testimony when needed.

The silver lining during this dark time is that Carrie and I spend a lot of time together. We meet in London on the platform at Charing Cross and take the train to Kent so that we can use the journey to rehearse everything we want to say in the meetings. We also use the time to reminisce, to share our grief, to eat cake and talk and laugh and become closer than ever, not just as sisters but as the best of friends.

'I couldn't do this without you,' we repeatedly tell each other.

These monthly appointments involve both Carrie and me travelling for four hours to get to the unit and four hours to get back to our families. By now Carrie has lost her job at the hotel and I have given up trying to get any new contracts.

From August through to November 2015 the planning of these meetings, the organisation involved in getting to them and the time we spend afterwards reassessing and rehashing information take up as much time as a part-time job. Mum is our career now. We are fortunate to have supportive husbands, friends and other relatives who can chip in when needed. What do people do if they don't have a sibling to share the load? What do they do if they can't get time off work? If they don't have enough money to make these long trips? If they have no one to mind their kids? If we had not had all these privileges, what would have happened to Mum?

Doubtless she would have been sent home, checked on whenever the mental health team had the time or resources and left until she fell again. Or worse.

She would have been stuck in a cycle of neglect, drama, hospitalisation, loneliness and despair. As so many people are on a daily basis.

Even with our combined efforts and all the knowledge we have accrued, it takes just over three months to get the mental health team to agree that Mum should see a psychologist. And that meeting is to change everything.

∽

On 4 November 2015 Carrie and I go to Dartford. This time a psychologist called Dr R joins us, along with Dr E, a mental health nurse and social worker. Mum comes in and immediately goes out again when she sees there is someone new in the room.

I fail to see why Dr R should put Mum off. He is hardly intimidating. He is a small, bespectacled, mousey-looking man; diminutive and unimpressive next to the large, big-hearted, deep-voiced psychiatrist. When he opens his mouth, however, he speaks with the voice of angels.

'I've read all your mother's notes and the many letters that you've written,' he says, looking at me and Carrie in turn. 'I've also read the letters that your mother's carer, Marina, has gathered from neighbours and friends. It's clear to me that your mother can't go home.'

An electric surge of excitement shoots through me. Carrie and I exchange a quick glance. This is what we want to hear! This is what we have been pushing that boulder for, every day for nearly two years! It is hard not to leap up and dance.

'We do need, however, to think carefully about the correct course of action,' Dr R goes on. 'And bearing that in mind—' He pauses and looks at us both in turn again, fixing us with his serious brown eyes to make sure he has our attention. 'I wanted to ask you if you have ever thought that your mother might be on the autistic spectrum?'

Another jolt of electricity. Cogs whirr. Gears shift. Clunk clunk clunk.

The pieces fall into place.

An axe is hurled against the glass box, and we are free.

～

We talk and talk and talk. Dr R asks a lot of questions. We have a lot of answers for him. He scribbles notes. The psychiatrist makes approving noises. Everyone nods in agreement.

Most importantly, Dr R *listens*. Carrie and I are being listened to. We are being heard.

It feels incredible.

No one is telling us to 'just forgive her'. No one is saying, 'She's always been like this.' No one is frowning at us to be quiet, to not say 'nasty things' about our mother, to sweep it all into that mountain under the carpet. No one is brushing us aside.

'Do you have any extreme examples of her anxieties over timing?' Dr R asks at one point.

Another shared sisterly glance. I almost laugh. Any examples? How much *time* have you got?

'I was expecting my son and he was overdue,' I begin, the words tumbling out. 'Mum became very angry, as we were living in France at the time and she thought she would miss the birth – her train ticket back to England was booked and my son was showing no signs of wanting to be born.' I catch my breath. 'The week before Tom was delivered, Mum insisted on going out to lunch, even though I was very large and uncomfortable by then and didn't want to leave the house. She said that I needed to get up and about and move more to get the labour going. So I agreed. Then, once we were in the café, she became furious with me and shouted that I should ask the doctor to induce me so that she could be there for the birth.'

The social worker gasps.

My words hang in the air. I realise everyone is staring at me.

Dr R coughs. 'Yes, well, that is pretty extreme.'

Is it, though? It was pretty normal behaviour as far as the family was concerned. I remember Dad hugging me after that lunch as I cried and said I was sorry about the baby being late. I remember him telling me Mum was just worried about me. That she didn't mean to be angry. Didn't mean to upset me.

And when Carrie was expecting her son it was the same, all over again. Except that time I told Mum to phone me and to leave Carrie alone. She called me multiple times a day in the weeks leading up to my nephew's birth – and then was livid, again, that the baby was late. On the day Carrie went into labour I was shopping with a friend. I had to keep stepping out of shops to take calls from a spitting, vitriolic, frenzied mother while my sister endured an excruciating thirty-six-hour labour with complications that ended in a Caesarean. I had to field the phone calls and listen as Mum ranted that, 'this is much worse for me than it is for her – she might die!'

Extreme. Yes. But our normal.

Dr R wanted to know about Mum's early life. The stories about suicide attempts are repeated. Carrie chips in to give extra details.

'I see that she was a Latin teacher?' Dr R says. 'That's interesting. Teaching is quite an unusual profession for someone on the autistic spectrum to choose. Children's behaviour can be too unpredictable for them. Where did she teach?'

We explain that Mum went back to her old grammar school after university.

'She knew most of the teachers – I don't think even the timetable had changed much from when she was there.'

Dr R nods, scribbles. 'Interesting. And Latin is, of course, a nice, orderly language. And you don't have to speak it,' he comments.

Box after diagnostic box is ticked.

'Have you heard of sensory systemising?' Dr R asks.

We have not.

'It's something a lot of autistic people do – it's also known as "stimming",' he explains. He taps a hand on the arm of his chair. 'The person might tap surfaces like this, or let sand run through their fingers or rub their fingers over their lips or hum. They do it to calm themselves down when they're anxious. The more anxious they feel, the more they "stim".'

Carrie and I are nodding and talking over one another.

'Yes! The tapping – definitely.'

'And the rubbing-the-finger-over-the-lips thing.'

'And – well—' I look embarrassed. 'She used to stand in front of the mirror and shake her fists and say, "Bloody kids" over and over again when we were small.'

Carrie laughs nervously. No one joins in. If anything, their faces soften. They get it. They understand.

'What about routines?' Dr R asks, pressing on.

Again, how much time have you got?

'Does she wear the same clothes every day?'

'She has done since she became very ill, yes.'

'Does she prefer loose-fitting, soft fabrics that aren't scratchy or irritating?'

'Yes! She used to be so smart, but in recent years she's worn elasticated trousers and fleeces and things like that.'

'What about food? Any rituals over that?'

Yes! Yes! The fads. The diets. The ham and lettuce and lettuce and ham . . .

'There is also something we call "motoric systemising",' Dr R says. 'For example, did your mum learn knitting patterns?'

'Oh my goodness – YES!'

Carrie nods excitedly. 'She loved to knit.'

'What about "collectible systemising" – that is making lists and catalogues?'

This is too much. He is describing Mum to a T. 'Yes, she is – was – the Queen of Lists,' I say. I stop, choking back tears. The image of a list I found while clearing up the paperwork springs to mind – an old list of things Mum was going to pack to take on one of the last holidays she took with Dad.

Carrie takes over. 'Yes, and catalogues – she used to say she wished she'd trained as a librarian, do you remember?' She looks at me, and I nod.

As the questions go on, I fight back the sadness. This is good, isn't it? To finally understand? To be understood? To have Mum understood? But there are so many questions about systemising. And I can't help thinking of that mantra: a place for everything. It was the only way she could function. It was the only way she could feel safe. And when the systemising didn't work any more – when order broke down and chaos took over – Mum couldn't function.

'Did she obsess over calendars or timetables?'

'Yes – she remembered everyone's birthdays and never got the time of any event wrong – and woe betide anyone else who did! And historical dates – she could remember EVERYTHING. Made us both feel stupid that we were no good at history.'

'Then there's something we call "environmental system-ising",' Dr R goes on. 'Did she ever insist that nothing is moved from its usual position in the room?'

Carrie sighs. 'All the time. That got worse and worse too – when Dad came out of hospital, she wouldn't let us move the furniture to set up a hospital bed for him.'

Dr R is scribbling hard now. No one else is saying anything.

'So, your mum liked to follow rules, I'm guessing?' Dr R continues. 'Latin grammar being a perfect example of this.'

'Yes – and cricket – she loved cricket,' Carrie says.

'She couldn't understand why I didn't love it as much as her,' I say. 'In fact, she couldn't understand why I didn't love ALL the same things as her. For example, she hated reading fiction, which is one of my greatest passions. "I much prefer facts," she would say. As for me having a career as a children's writer, she'd say, "Why don't you try and write something a bit more serious?"'

Dr R nods. 'People on the autistic spectrum are said to lack a "theory of mind",' he says. 'That means that they have trouble working out the thoughts and intentions of other people. They also find it hard to imagine a scenario that they haven't experienced yet.'

'She always said she had no imagination,' Carrie says. 'So it's literally true . . .'

Always thinking of the sublime, Anna. No wonder she didn't get me.

Dr R finishes the session by recommending us some litera-ture to read. He says he will press for a formal diagnosis if

we would like, but that we should understand that Mum
would need to consent.

'The diagnosis will take at least a day. And I should warn
you that, although it is clear to me that your mother is a very
intelligent woman and that she probably has what some people
call Asperger's syndrome – or high-functioning ASD – autistic
syndrome disorder – and so would definitely understand the
questions asked, my concern is that she's not well enough to
go through with the diagnosis. Not yet, at any rate. She is
highly anxious – something that is a symptom of undiagnosed
and unmanaged autism, I'm afraid. Until we can control her
anxiety, I'm doubtful that a formal diagnosis would make
much difference to your mum's quality of life.'

The conversation moves on to next steps.

'When will Mum be ready to move into a home?' we ask.

The psychiatrist speaks up. 'We would recommend that
you find your mother a residential home as soon as possible
– within the next couple of weeks.'

We walk out of the meeting, dazed. We have answers to so
many questions that have plagued us for most of our adult
lives. We also have yet another daunting duty set before us:
to find Mum a home as quickly as possible. The financial
implications of this alone are overwhelming. The idea that
we'll have to tell Mum that this is what we are planning seems
an impossible task.

But we do have answers. Mum has ticked so many boxes,
and so many more occur to us as we talk about it on the train
back to London. Her systemising, her obsessing, her repetitive actions. We can begin to understand – and to forgive
– Mum's behaviour in the past, to see what makes her tick

and what has been her undoing. We have a diagnosis that explains her anxiety and depression. We have the ultimate golden key, which unlocks the mystery that was our mum.

There is an underlying sadness, though, in all of this. Because the answers come too late. Mum has lost her husband and now she has lost her independence. She has missed out on a diagnosis that could have been life-changing for her had she had it sixty years before. She is stuck now, caught in an ever-increasing cycle of over-medicalisation from which she is too old to be released. She will never be well enough to undergo the full formal diagnosis. The best we can hope for is that we will find her the right care for the next stage of her life.

Sixty-five

'Diagnosis is only of value when it is not just a label but a passport into accessing all the necessary support services that each individual may need.'[65]

Carrie and I read books about autism, we watch documentaries on it, we read blogs and forums and newspaper articles and we phone each other and talk it over and over. Autism and information about autism are suddenly everywhere. We read and watch and talk and read and watch and talk.

We learn a lot in the short time we have to find Mum a home. We learn that people on the autistic spectrum often prefer to be with others, even though they might ignore them while they are engaged in a solitary activity. We learn that they prefer to do things the same way over and over again. We learn that they can't easily create a picture in their mind of something they are trying to imagine. We learn that they often notice, and are bothered by, small sounds that other people do not notice. We learn that they frequently come across as abrasive or impolite when they don't mean to be. We learn that they find small talk difficult. And we see that all these things are traits our mother has always had.

We also learn that anxiety and depression are huge factors
for people with Asperger's syndrome, and with that double-
edged sword comes a whole raft of other problems, including
physical symptoms, predominantly gastrointestinal pain.

We are excited to discover that Mum can now be understood. We are furious that no one has thought to go down
this route before. How can she have slipped through the net
so many times? All those doctor's appointments for high
anxiety. All those appointments about stomach upsets and
constipation and cramps. And that last obsession, about
prolapse. Why did no one think to join up the dots?

One day, as I am driving, I catch, by chance, a feature on
Woman's Hour on Radio 4, which explores the reasons that
so many women and girls miss out on receiving a diagnosis
of autism. One reason given is that clinicians often do not
see beyond the mental illness they are presented with: eating
disorders, depression, anxiety – all these things and more can
be secondary to autism and possibly even controllable if the
autism is discovered earlier in the patient's life. So it was with
Mum: those GPs who saw her for stomach pain and prolapse
– even postnatal depression – they didn't have the information to be able to probe further to see what lay behind these
more overt symptoms.

And if they had? Would it have made a difference? It's
well documented that some people with autism – particularly
high-functioning, intelligent people, such as Mum – do not
agree with their own diagnosis. They are even sometimes
angry when told that they are on the spectrum. Carrie and I
fear that Mum would have been one such patient. She insisted,
right up until she was sectioned, that her problems were

physical, not mental. And that's perhaps because, from her perspective, they were.

∽

Shortly after the meeting with Dr R, Carrie and I find a home for Mum. It is not far from our home town, so the friends and neighbours who have said they would like to be able to visit her can access it easily. It will still be an eight-hour round trip for me and Carrie, but after many a long, heart-rending phone call, we have decided that it's better for Mum to remain in Kent than to force her to make a long journey to either Wiltshire or Norfolk and move into a home near one of us. The home is sparklingly clean, modern, light and is run by a team of gentle, smiling, patient women to whom we immediately warm. One of them, who turns out to be assigned to Mum as her key-worker, has a son who is on the autistic spectrum. We are able to talk to her about Mum's needs, her fears, her anxieties, and this woman understands. We feel as happy as it is possible to feel about moving Mum from a mental health wing to a small, impersonal room in a residential care home, knowing that she will most likely never go back to her marital home ever again.

We have no complaints. It is definitely the right place for Mum. We struggle to reconcile ourselves to her ongoing medical care, though. She is now on such a comprehensive menu of drugs – for anxiety, depression, sleeplessness, psychosis – that we worry her body can't cope with the mixture. She is incapable of a proper conversation now and seems to want only to sit in a chair or sleep. We press for more assessments, more discussions about the drugs she's on. We don't get any answers. It feels as though, now that Mum is in a home, she is no longer anyone's priority. When we do speak to doctors, the implication in their voice is, 'She's safe. What more do you want?'

What we want is for Mum to have some quality of life. We want her to be able to appreciate the beautiful gardens outside her window, for her to agree to go for short walks with her carers and with friends and with us. We want the drug-fog to lift and for Mum to able to talk to us, about how she is, about what she wants. And about Dad.

Because she won't talk about him. She won't let us reminisce or talk about how sad we are, or tell us how she feels. It's as though he never existed. And it's heartbreaking.

We do finally manage to arrange a meeting with a psychologist who specialises in autism. He comes to the home and tries to talk to Mum. The minute he sits down, she wants him to leave.

'I can't force her to talk to me,' he tells us. He looks and sounds irritated with us when we push him on this. 'Listen, what exactly is it that you hope to achieve by pressing for a formal diagnosis?' he says.

I am put out by his tone. 'What we "hope to achieve" is a better quality of life for our mother. She sits in her room all the time. She won't go out with us or friends. She won't join in with any of the activities her carers suggest. She's not getting any fresh air or exercise. It can't be good for her!'

'But that's just your opinion,' the doctor says. 'For her, the outside world represents total chaos. It's bright and noisy, the wind against her skin is like a violent attack, the idea of going for a coffee anywhere is about as close to hell for her as you or I could imagine.'

Carrie and I feel like two small children again. Told off for something we've done wrong.

But we can't do anything right either. We love her. We want the best for her. We want to be heard. It's all we've ever wanted. Now we're being told that it doesn't matter what we want: Mum sees the world entirely differently from the way we see it.

It makes you wonder – were we living in completely separate houses the whole time?

Sixty-six

'It's sad that for many females, we've perfected our masks so well, that by the time we're eventually diagnosed, a lot of people don't even believe us.'[66]

'**B***ut that's just your opinion.'*
Maybe. Maybe we have been guilty of not seeing things from Mum's point of view. Maybe this has been the main flaw in our relationship with her all along.

Except that it wasn't always obvious that Mum had autistic traits. Before she was psychotic she was just Mum. Other than the outbursts and the meltdowns, she was perfectly capable of functioning well. And she could be sparkling. Even funny on a good day. In any case, didn't everyone have the odd tantrum now and again?

That's just the way she is.
You'll just have to forgive her.
She's always been like this.
We grew up thinking *we* were the problem, if anything.

It's easy to put a puzzle together from the pieces if you have the image on the lid of the box. If you are given a completely different image, you have a fairly slim chance of getting it right. Mum wasn't always the way she is now: closed down, silent, fearful, alone, so it's hard to accept that this *is* how she is to be from now on.

Friends call us, baffled.

'She asks us to leave her the moment we arrive,' they say. 'Should we stop visiting altogether?'

'She doesn't seem very stimulated in the home,' they say. 'She ought to have people to talk to, someone to play bridge with. It's not right.'

It's not right. It's not fair. It's exasperating and heart-breaking. But what can we do? We try to get Mum to engage with the world, and she says, 'No. Leave me be.'

We decide to tell friends and family about the diagnosis in the hope that it will help them understand.

It doesn't. Many of them are sceptical, disbelieving even. Some of them say outright that they 'don't see the point of these labels' in much the same way that Mum used to.

'Your mother was so bright,' 'so sociable', 'we got on so well,' they say. As if those traits cannot sit alongside the obsessions and the anxieties and the repetitive patterns of behaviour.

We explain what we've learnt about women with autism: that the high-functioning ones are good at mimicking in a way that men are generally not. That they learn social cues, that any time they have to leave the house it's like going on stage: they have lines they have memorised and body language they've learnt and they observe others around them carefully to make sure they're fitting in.

'It's exhausting,' says a friend my age who has recently been diagnosed. 'Every social occasion requires me to concentrate really hard. It's particularly tiring going out with groups of women. There is so much emotional bonding that goes on and I can't see the point of it. And they don't always say what they mean.'

I tell my friend what Mum's friends are saying. 'It's like they don't believe she's autistic. One person even said, "But isn't autism something to do with being good at maths? Your mum's a linguist."'

My friend rolls her eyes. 'People have this image of autistic people – that we are completely closed down, mute, only fit for a job at Google or something. Why can't the general public understand that we're humans first and autistic second? It's just a different way of viewing the world. We need a different kind of access, that's all. Just like if you can't walk and you need a wheelchair and so you need ramps and things – we may need things explained to us in a different way, or we may not have the same social needs as neurotypical people.'

It's no use me talking like this to the nay-sayers, though. Many of them are from a different generation and they just don't like the idea that their bright, beautiful, intelligent friend has the same diagnosis as the character in *The Curious Incident of the Dog in the Night-Time* or Dustin Hoffman's character in *Rain Man* or Sheldon in *The Big Bang Theory*. They would rather believe that she has dementia.

And so we stop trying to explain.

Sixty-seven

'According to a report by healthcare specialists Laing & Buisson in 2018, carehome costs can range from: £27,000 to £39,000 per year for a residential carehome, or £35,000 to £55,000 per year if nursing is required.'[67]

The comments from friends stoke our guilt, not that we need their negative comments. Carrie and I feel guilty enough as it is. We feel guilty that Mum is unhappy. We feel guilty that we live so far away from her and can visit only once a month. We feel guilty for 'putting her' in a home. We feel guilty that the diagnosis has come so late and is of so little value. We feel guilty that we are spending so much of the money Dad saved on keeping Mum safe. We feel guilty that we have had to put our childhood home on the market to be able to plan for Mum's future. The home is not cheap. The good ones rarely are. We are spending close to £1,000 a month on basic healthcare for Mum, and this is before any 'extras' are added to the bill. The savings Dad put aside will not last forever. Selling the house is the only way to go.

We've spent months emptying it. Every visit to Mum has dovetailed with a trip to the house to sort through more belongings and clothes and books and paperwork. Every trip has brought memories and tears and sleepless nights over what we're doing.

Night after night I have nightmares that Mum is well again, smiling, happy, ready to go home.

She can't. The house is empty now and soon it will be sold.

What if we've made a huge mistake? What if she wants to come back, says she'll accept care in her own home after all? What if the drugs do suddenly work and she's back to her old, feisty, energetic, angry self, shouting at us for sending her packing, for getting rid of all her things?

∽

She doesn't get better, though. If anything, she gets worse. Every visit brings more pain – for her and for us. She talks little, spends most of the day lying on her bed, staring at the wall. She sends visitors away and does not want me or Carrie to stay beyond twenty minutes. She doesn't want to talk to us, doesn't even enjoy it when we bring her grandchildren to see her.

∽

Almost two years have passed since Dad died. I'm sitting in the house and it is completely empty now. Potential buyers have come and gone over the past months, getting our hopes up, making us feel we're closer to closing this painful chapter of our lives.

Now we've found a young family ready to move in and this is my last visit to the place before we complete on the sale. I should feel happy – or at least relieved. Instead I feel as empty as these rooms.

I'm sitting on the window ledge in the living room. The only other time I've seen this house empty was forty-one years ago. I was six years old and we were the young family, ready to move in. I chased my little sister around and around on that parquet flooring, laughter bubbling through me at the thrill of being in 'our new house'. It was a new beginning, a time of exciting new possibilities and adventures – even aged six I knew that. I would be able to walk to school; my best friend lived down the road; there was a boys' school next door where a lot of my friends' brothers went. We would be able to swim and play tennis there in the holidays. I was fizzing with happiness.

Today I'm weighed down with sadness. My parents put their hearts and souls into this house. They made it a home. I didn't always appreciate it or even want to be there. And now it's moving on, passing into the hands of another family who will put their own energy, hopes and dreams into these bricks and mortar. They will no doubt remodel it, as Mum and Dad did. They will knock down walls that Mum and Dad put up, they will pull out the kitchen and bathrooms of which Mum was so proud; they will modernise it, possibly beyond all recognition. And we will take the money and pay for Mum to sit in a tiny room and stare at the wall.

It's too much.

Yet, as I sit on this window ledge and look out at the garden, watching the watery January sunlight filter in through the faded floral curtains, I feel the house telling me not to mourn. *This is another new chapter*, it seems to say. I am feeling this a lot lately. Blank pages. New beginnings. Ever the writer, searching for narrative.

As I leave, setting the alarm for the last time, locking the door and walking out into the driveway, I know this is right. I must put away childish things. I have my own home in a different town, in a different time. Dad would not want me to try to hold on to the past. There is a time to weep and a time to laugh. A time to mourn and a time to dance. A time to heal.

And Mum's time is nearly up, though I don't know it yet.

Sixty-eight

Friday 28 January 2018. It is a bright, sharp morning. A day which hints that spring might be closer than you think. The sun is golden. If you stand in a patch of its light and tilt your head back, you can feel its warmth. Mum used to like doing that. She would close her eyes and smile and stretch like a cat. Luxuriating. Basking.

I wake and look out of the window and decide to do a bit of basking myself. I have no classes to teach and I have delivered all my chapters to my editor for the book I'm currently working on. I'm on top of things for the first time in months. In fact, I've been feeling on top of the world all week.

I've said goodbye to the woman who has been helping me through my grief and helping me come to terms with my guilt over Mum. 'I don't think I need to see you any more,' I told her the last time I saw her. I told her I felt lighter, freer than I had for years. I am confident now that Mum is safe in the home. I know we've done our best for her. I'm going to visit her soon and I'm looking forward to the visit instead of dreading it. The last time I saw her I took the kids with me. Mum had actually smiled and had even hugged us. I had kissed her and told her I loved her and she had thanked me for visiting. It had been a very different encounter from previous ones.

I really am happy today. I'm no longer striving, worrying away at things I can't solve.

I look out at the sun, streaming through the bare branches of the beech tree outside my study window, and decide to give myself permission to take the day off.

I go to meet a friend. He's giving himself the day off too.

We laugh as we crunch over the frosty grass towards the lake where we've been swimming through the winter.

'It's the first day for a while that it's actually felt inviting,' he says, as we approach the chilly water. It is silver and millpond-still.

The sun seems to lift a little in the sky as he says this, as though smiling on us, and in that moment a flash of sapphire catches my eye.

'Kingfisher!'

We haven't seen one for months. We stop and hold our breath, whispering wonder at the small bright jewel as he skims the surface, laser-sharp, and lands on the far bank.

We change and run to the water before we can stop to think how cold it will be. Plunge in. Squeal. Whoop. Swim ten metres, then haul ourselves out, panting and jumping about like a pair of excitable Labradors.

After coffee, gulped down as hot as we can bear to chase the bone-chill away, we say our goodbyes and agree that it has been a beautiful morning. A golden moment. One of the best.

⌒

Back home I hear the landline is ringing as I approach the door. I fumble with my key, run to the phone. It's Carrie. We haven't had a proper chat in weeks. Christmas, illnesses, a busy start to the term – we haven't had the time. We've been getting on with things. Learning to live our lives again.

We spend a good three-quarters of an hour catching up. She's happy. She feels lighter and better than she has in ages.

'Same here!' I tell her.

We make plans to see each other. We wish each other a good weekend. I'm beaming as I go upstairs to run a scalding bath.

I lower myself carefully into the steamy water just as my mobile rings. I never bring it to the bathroom with me, but today I have. I lean forward and see my sister's face and name on the screen. Something makes me reach to answer immediately without pause.

'I'm afraid I've got some rather shocking news.'

Her voice is unsteady. Sharp blue light jolts through me. I know what she's going to say – and at the same time I don't.

'It's Mum. She's died.'

'No. What? No.'

'Just like that. Gone. Fallen awkwardly on to the end of her bed. Probably a heart attack.'

My sister's voice is far away.

I'm out of the bath, curled under a towel on the mat. Rocking. Crying. 'No. No. NO. But I've had such a beautiful day.'

Later that evening, after phone calls have been made, grand-children told, hugs given and received, my sister calls again.

'I think we let her go. I think somehow she knew – that we were happy at last. That we felt free. She has freed us.'

Yes. She has. She has freed us and she herself has found freedom. She turned her face to the sun one last time, just as the kingfisher zipped across the water. She went quietly, quickly, without a fuss. She crept off like a cat and vanished.

Sixty-nine

'As a society we need to recognise the value of having people with Asperger's syndrome in our multi-cultural and diverse community . . . perhaps Asperger's syndrome is the next stage of human evolution.'[68]

The promise of spring stays with us right up until Mum's funeral. On the day itself I wake early. The faint dawn light hovers at the edges of the dark hotel curtains. My daughter sleeps soundly in the twin bed next to mine. I dress and creep out on to the silent landing.

I walk to the river, where we scattered Dad's ashes. I cry as I tell him Mum will soon be joining him. I say sorry – again – for the way things have turned out. Cold yellow light filters through the bare branches. The water is black and uninviting.

I walk back along the river, looking out over the town's playground where I, and then later Lucy and Tom, once played on the swings and climbing frames. I walk past the swimming pool where, in a former life, I spent hot summer days and where my children have played tag and learnt to swim underwater. I walk on, through the castle grounds, feeling the sun grow warmer, listening to the birds. I see two goldfinches. One for Dad and one for Mum.

I walk up to the gatehouse and put my hand on the ancient sandstone wall. I feel the weight of ages past beneath my skin. I look out across the castle lawn and think of what the town has seen, from the Norman conquest and on, on through the more recent world wars up until the much discussed present town 'improvements'. I think of my grandmother, her adult life spent here, watching the town change, watching shops come and go, the landscape around the town adapting and evolving as its status as a commuter-belt community altered the fabric of the place. She was my mother's rock, breast-feeding her under the kitchen table while bombs were off-loaded by German planes heading back home; bringing her up on post-war rations, struggling to understand her as it became apparent that she was 'different'; not wanting to leave her, not even when she herself was dying. She was my rock too. I miss her still.

I walk back to the hotel and get ready for the day ahead.

The funeral goes as well as a funeral can ever be said to go. People come from far and wide; from Mum's distant and more recent past. The service goes smoothly. The readings and hymns are just right. I hold it together. I get through the words I have to say. It isn't the same as Dad's, but then Mum was a very different person and our relationship with her was different too. We try to tell the truth, my sister, my uncle and I. We speak of Mum's late diagnosis, of how Asperger's and autism were not things people had heard of or understood while Mum was growing up. People come up to us afterwards and thank us for explaining. It is a good farewell, but it isn't a celebration in the way Dad's funeral was. I struggle to feel the peace I felt after Dad died. It eludes me.

We drink tea and eat sandwiches in the newly built wing of the local school, looking out over the cricket pitch. The sun sets over the pristine green lawns. Mum would like this, I tell myself.

∽

And then it's over and we're on the train back home to Wiltshire – to my adult home, over a hundred miles away from my Kentish roots. No childhood house to deal with this time. No parental possessions to make decisions about, other than the wedding ring that the undertaker handed to my sister before they drove the coffin away. Nothing left to do or say. Just the sense of an ending lingering in the air.

∽

Two days later I am running along the riverbank near where I live. I am crying, feeling empty and lost.

I just want to know that you're at peace, Mum. I want to know that you are where you wanted to be.

I've barely finished forming the thought when two herons come flying low across the water towards me. In all my time running and swimming here, I have never seen two herons flying together. One rises up and lands in the tree above me. The other lands right by me and looks me straight in the eye. One for Dad and one for Mum. My feelings of emptiness vanish and are replaced at once by a calm so deep, so strong.

I know. She is. She is at peace. And so is Dad.

∽

Six days later the snow comes. Thick and fast and deep. It cuts us off from the neighbouring towns and villages. It snows for hours and hours so that I can't even go out into the garden. The quiet surrounding the house is profound. It is a beautiful white purdah. An imposed period of quiet, secluded mourning of which our Victorian ancestors would have approved. We light fires and hunker down. I do nothing for two days other than sleep, eat and read.

And then the snow goes. As quickly as it had come. And I think: what a blessing, after the shock and the pain and the rushing around that comes with death, to be given permission to stop. Now I, too, can go on and find peace.

Seventy

'Just imagine how many judgements we could avoid if there was a better understanding of the disorder.'[69]

Dear Mum,

You always said I wrote things better than I could ever express them aloud. Now that the glass box has been smashed, the witch's curse removed, this is what I've tried to do: to give sense and meaning. To find your story. Mine too.

The summer after you died was a gift. It lightened my spirit and had me running to my laptop to write and write and write. The words poured forth like the sunlight streaming into the house. I had not written like it for years, but then we had not seen a summer like it for years either. Dry weather. Light, cloudless mornings. I've never been a morning person – something which infuriated you – but that summer I was up with the lark. And my new puppy, come to join us after my beloved old dog died just six months before you did. I used the time to walk and write while the rest of the family dozed.

Evenings stretched on as the sun lit up the sky until the last speck of light sank below the trees. Swifts and swallows and dragonflies and kingfishers and herons and bats and owls and hawkmoths danced for joy in the heat and the light. My new puppy joined them, bounding out with me on early morning walks, showing me how to live and laugh again. Not that you would have cared about the wildlife. Or the puppy.

The heat and the summer breeze dried a line of laundry in minutes. Now that you would have loved. Particularly the lines of laundry, which I hung neatly in your honour. The heat in the middle of the day would have got you down. But a patch of shade, a glass of cold lemonade and a stack of books – you could have pretended you were back on a Cambridge lawn in May week. Except that you couldn't pretend, could you? And maybe now I see that as a strength. For I live too much in my head.

'What's the matter with you?' you would ask, as I sat at the kitchen table, scowling at my thoughts and dreams. 'Anna is always dreaming. Always thinking of the sublime,' you said. It was meant as an insult. Better perhaps to take life at face value, to see it for what it is: fleeting, ugly, beautiful, violent.

I hear a woman on the radio talk of what it is to wake up on a morning when the world is at war, to look on the beauty of the dawn and to know it might be the last time she is able to see it. I am trying now to do this, to drink it all in, knowing that I won't be here forever. I am trying to stop thinking, 'And then, and then, and then'. I have spent so much of the last twenty years looking forward: to the day you and I would see eye to eye; to the day my kids would grow and settle; to the day I would have more time; to the day I would write the book of which I could be the most proud; to the day I would be happy. There are no days like this, as you knew. There are only the days in which we sit and walk and breathe and sleep. And we must live them all, one breath at a time.

Maybe this is why I swim so much nowadays: so that I can focus on the in and the out, my lungs filling as I emerge from the dark-green silence, my body stilling as I dip down again. I swam every day that summer. In rivers, in lakes, in the sea. I loved the river best of all. You would certainly not have approved, citing Weil's disease and worse. Wild swimming was your idea of foolishness and danger. But it is my place – my element, water. When I am in a river, or a lake, or the sea, I am in my element. It was Dad's too.

That's why we laid Dad to rest in the river. We chose a spot where you and he had paddled together. So when your time came, we laid you down in the same place. Because although you wouldn't have liked to discuss it, we knew that wherever you ended up, it had to be with Dad.

I miss you. I miss Dad. I'm sad that you'll never see your grandchildren grow up, that you'll never come to visit us again. That you'll never read this and see how much we've come to understand you. As the wonderful children's writer Eva Ibbotson said, 'You cannot stop the birds of sorrow from flying over your head, but you can stop them nesting in your hair.'

There's no doubt that they have changed me, those birds. For a while I've felt so distracted by them that I lost sight of the person I'd always been. I've felt cast adrift. Without moorings. Without direction or purpose. Unsure of what to do next with life. As you must have felt when Carrie and I left home and your father died and your mother became infirm.

Perhaps as a consequence I have held on to the past, clinging to a raft that will ferry me back to a place I felt safe. And I've worried over a future which is a place that looks anything but.

Is this how you felt Mum? We never really talked about it. Perhaps it's how you always felt: out of kilter. Out of place. But I know now that there is a place for people like you in this world. We just have to learn how to accommodate you, as my friend said: we have to learn how to give you the access and understanding that you and others like you need. Because as you used to say, there is 'a place for everything, and everything in its place' – and a place for every human too.

Your loving daughter,

Anna

Endnotes

1 www.researchgate.net/publication/264422542_The_Successful_
use_of_Pregabalin_in_the_Management_of_Autism_Anxiety_
and_Challenging_Behaviour

2 B. Boyd, *Appreciating Asperger Syndrome*, Jessica Kingsley
Publishers, London and Philadelphia, 2009.

3 T. Attwood, *The Complete Guide to Asperger's Syndrome*,
Jessica Kingsley Publishers, London and Philadelphia, 2007.

4 N. Higashida, *The Reason I Jump: One Boy's Voice from the
Silence of Autism*, Kindle edn, Hodder & Stoughton, London,
2013, p. 2.

5 www.theneurotypical.com/rage-cycle-in-hfa.html

6 www.theguardian.com/lifeandstyle/2017/apr/15/women-autistic-
mothers-undiagnosed-children

7 T. Attwood, *The Complete Guide to Asperger's Syndrome*,
Jessica Kingsley Publishers, London and Philadelphia,
2007.

8 Ibid.

9 Ibid.

10 www.mind.org.uk/information-support/guides-to-support-and-
services/crisis-services/accident-emergency-ae/#.XNQbT9NKhBw

11 S. Baron-Cohen, *Autism and Asperger Syndrome*, Oxford
University Press, 2008, p.40

12 T. Attwood, *The Complete Guide to Asperger's Syndrome*,
Jessica Kingsley Publishers, London and Philadelphia, 2007,
p. 58.

13 S. Baron-Cohen, *Autism and Asperger Syndrome*, Oxford University Press, 2008, p.115

14 Ibid.

15 C. Lawrence & M. Winter, *Asperger Syndrome: What Teachers Need to Know*, 2nd edn, Jessica Kingsley Publishers, London and Philadelphia, 2011, p. 63.

16 T. Attwood, *The Complete Guide to Asperger's Syndrome*, Jessica Kingsley Publishers, London and Philadelphia, 2007.

17 Ibid.

18 www.mind.org.uk/media/23671047/nature-and-mental-health-2018.pdf

19 www.autism.org.uk/about/behaviour/challenging-behaviour.aspx

20 community.autism.org.uk/f/adults-on-the-autistic-spectrum/7871/as-and-birthdays?Redirected=true; posted by forum user 'AndyC', 2017.

21 S. Baron-Cohen, *Autism and Asperger Syndrome*, Oxford University Press, 2008, p.115

22 autismawarenesscentre.com/christmas-with-autism-hold-the-expectations/

23 aspiewriter.wordpress.com/2013/03/15/sunshine-and-the-aspie-when-the-weather-affects-our-neurology/

24 adaa.org/learn-from-us/from-the-experts/blog-posts/consumer/anxiety-autism-spectrum-disorder

25 raisingchildren.net.au/autism/communicating-relationships/communicating/paying-attention-asd

26 network.autism.org.uk/good-practice/evidence-base/reflections-stress-and-autism

27 T. Attwood, *The Complete Guide to Asperger's Syndrome*, Jessica Kingsley Publishers, London and Philadelphia, 2007, p. 36.

28 www.carersuk.org/help-and-advice/health/looking-after-your-health/guilt-and-resentment

29 A. Rowe, *The Girl with the Curly Hair: Asperger's and Me*, Kindle edn, Lonely Mind Books, London, 2013.

30 www.autism.org.uk/about/communication/social-isolation.aspx

31 A. Rowe, *The Girl with the Curly Hair: Asperger's and Me*, Kindle edn, Lonely Mind Books, London, 2013.

32 From the Mental Capacity Act 2005, Section 2

33 A. Rowe, *The Girl with the Curly Hair: Asperger's and Me*, Kindle edn, Lonely Mind Books, London, 2013.

34 S. Craft, *Everyday Aspergers: A Journey on the Autism Spectrum*, Kindle edn, Your Stories Matter, Lancaster, 2018.

35 www.england.nhs.uk/wp-content/uploads/2017/02/adult-pocket-guide.pdf

36 S. Craft, *Everyday Aspergers: A Journey on the Autism Spectrum*, Kindle edn, Your Stories Matter, Lancaster, 2018.

37 A. Rowe, *The Girl with the Curly Hair: Asperger's and Me*, Kindle edn, Lonely Mind Books, London, 2013.

38 autismallianceofmichigan.org/effective-crisis-planning-management/

39 www.carersuk.org/help-and-advice/health/looking-after-your-health/stress-and-depression

40 S. Craft, *Everyday Aspergers: A Journey on the Autism Spectrum*, Kindle edn, Your Stories Matter, Lancaster, 2018.

41 A. Rowe, *The Girl with the Curly Hair: Asperger's and Me*, Kindle edn, Lonely Mind Books, London, 2013.

42 www.nhs.uk/conditions/end-of-life-care/lasting-power-of-attorney/

43 pathfindersforautism.org/articles/home/parent-tips-death-and-grieving/

44 Charlotte B. Mongomery et al., 'Do Adults with High-functioning Autism or AS Differ in Empathy and Emotion Recognition?', *Journal of Autism and Developmental Disorders*, vol. 46, pp. 1931–1940, 1 June 2016.

45 mic.com/articles/61025/when-lifelong-couples-die-together-it-s-not-just-adorable-it-s-science#.ZrJfTBK7u

46 carers.org/getting-a-break/paying-for-respite

47 A. Rowe, *The Girl with the Curly Hair: Asperger's and Me*, Kindle edn, Lonely Mind Books, London, 2013.

48 be.macmillan.org.uk/Downloads/CancerInformation/InfoForCarers/MAC11631LostforwordsE7.pdf

49 www.carergateway.gov.au
50 S. Craft, *Everyday Aspergers: A Journey on the Autism Spectrum*, Kindle edn, Your Stories Matter, Lancaster, 2018.
51 adaa.org/learn-from-us/from-the-experts/blog-posts/consumer/anxiety-autism-spectrum-disorder
52 S. Baron-Cohen, *Autism and Asperger Syndrome*, Oxford University Press, 2008, p.40
53 www.rethink.org/diagnosis-treatment/treatment-and-support/going-into-hospital/when
54 www.england.nhs.uk/wp-content/uploads/2013/08/dis-old-people.pdf
55 www.rethink.org/carers-family-friends/what-you-need-to-know/nearest-relative
56 themighty.com/2016/11/coping-with-grief-as-an-autistic-adult/
57 www.theoldie.co.uk/article/o-death-where-is-thy-sting
58 S. Craft, *Everyday Aspergers: A Journey on the Autism Spectrum*, Kindle edn, Your Stories Matter, Lancaster, 2018.
59 www.ambitiousaboutautism.org.uk
60 www.dyingmatters.org/page/being-someone-when-they-die
61 themighty.com/2016/11/coping-with-grief-as-an-autistic-adult/
62 blog.penelopetrunk.com/2013/10/12/3-things-you-need-to-know-about-people-with-aspergers/comment-page-2/
63 www.autismwestmidlands.org.uk/wp-content/uploads/2017/11/Autism_and_bereavement.pdf
64 T. Attwood, *The Complete Guide to Asperger's Syndrome*, Jessica Kingsley Publishers, London and Philadelphia, 2007.
65 S. Baron-Cohen, *Autism and Asperger Syndrome*, Oxford University Press, 2008, p. 37
66 A. Rowe, *The Girl with the Curly Hair: Asperger's and Me*, Kindle edn, Lonely Mind Books, London, 2013.
67 www.moneyadviceservice.org.uk/en/articles/care-home-or-home-care
68 T. Attwood, *The Complete Guide to Asperger's Syndrome*, Jessica Kingsley Publishers, London and Philadelphia, 2007.
69 www.depressionalliance.org/aspergers-in-adults/

Acknowledgements

Thanks first of all to my family. Without you there would be no book, but more importantly without you I could never have coped during the dark and difficult times.

To my husband David and my children Lucy and Tom, for letting me scream and howl and sob and shout and for still loving me in spite of it all. To my sister Carrie, for standing alongside me through the years of caring for Mum and Dad, for being my best friend, for the laughs, for the tears, for those wine-fuelled nights in that awful hotel while we cleared out our childhood home, and for so much more.

To Uncle John and my cousins Simon and Gemma, for your love and advice and phone calls and for sharing happy memories in the time since these events have passed.

To Uncle Tim and Aunt Shelia: we miss you. To Nick and Liz, for your love and support. To Marina Allen, for being an angel of mercy, and to Richard Powley from Age UK, for decoding the medical terminology.

And to my parents' friends who stepped in when we could not, who visited Dad in hospital and who persisted in looking in on Mum even when she was not an easy person to visit. Thanks also to the incredible staff at Stanmore: Professor Briggs, the OT staff and the wonderfully kind nurses who called Dad 'Uncle' and made him feel loved on his last birthday. And to the mental health professionals and social workers who helped us and Mum, especially

Sam, Susan, Dr E and Dr R, and the wonderful carers at Hazeldene House, where Mum spent her last two years, especially Michaela – your warmth and patience were a godsend.

This book started as a blog. A year after Dad's death and a year after Mum's diagnosis, I suddenly found the words pouring out of me. I didn't know or care about who might read them. I just had to write. It was a relief to know I still could, after two years of feeling blocked by panic and grief. Many people did read the blog, and many urged me to turn it into a book.

So thanks go to the following, for believing in me, for swimming with me, walking with me, running with me, listening to me, encouraging me, inspiring me, writing with me and taking care of me while I wrote: Lou Abercrombie, Rachel Awan, Catherine Bailhache, David Braithwaite, Stephen Browne, Catherine Bruton, Kate Bullows, Elen Caldecott, Lucy Coats, Emma Crowther, Hilary Delamere, John Doherty, Kate Durban, Bernadine Evaristo, Jo Fallon, Natasha Farrant, Sue Fletcher, Catherine Funnell, Cat Godwin, Julia Green, Ceetah and Tom Grieves, Annie Harman, Clare Hawken, Rachel Heath, Fleur Hitchcock, Jem Hobbs, Helen Homard, Cathy Hopkins, Ceri Idris-Evans, Rachel Kellehar, Liz Kessler, Jane Kibblewhite, Katrina and Toby Levon, Annie Pawley (in loving memory), Caroline Peppercorn, David Presswell, Sara Mason, Tamsin May, Toby Mitchell, Gaby Morgan, Tess Morrish, Sue Mongredien, Jo Nadin, Rhiannon Nally, Louise Neill, Michelle Robinson, Helen Roper, Karen Saunders, Melanie Shufflebotham, Amanda Smith, Boris Starling, Claire Stroud, Laura Tonge, Kelley Townley, Clare and Nick Turpin, Sarah Vidler, Steve Voake, Rachel Ward, Victoria Westwood, David Wolstencroft, Fraz Woodward.

Last, but most definitely not least, to my editor Kate Fox at HQ, from whom I have learnt so much about writing non-fiction and about narrative structure, to my excellent copy-editor Donna Hillyer and equally brilliant desk editor Nira Begum, for their incredible attention to detail, and to my agent Cathryn Summerhayes at Curtis Brown: thank you.